WHAT EXPERTS SAY ABOUT THIS BOOK

"Minoti Rajput's book, Beyond a Parent's Love, *captures the complex essence of family struggle devoted to a special needs member."* – THOMAS F. KENDZIORSKI, JD, EXECUTIVE DIRECTOR, ARC OF OAKLAND COUNTY, MICHIGAN

"A powerful read ... whether you're a family with a special needs child, or a practitioner who works with the families, Minoti provides essential guidance and perspective on how to navigate both the emotional and financial challenges." – MICHAEL KITCES, CFP®, CLU®, ChFC®, AUTHOR, EDUCATOR, COMMENTATOR, SPEAKER, BLOGGER, CO-FOUNDER OF XY PLANNING NETWORK, PARTNER PINNACLE ADVISORY GROUP

"Minoti weaves real-life storytelling with practical tips on how to prepare for a special child's future. Often overlooked, the stories behind the family help the reader to understand the necessity for advanced planning and the steps needed to get there. This book is great for parents just starting the path of special needs parenting, social workers and of course financial planners looking to provide services to families with an individual with special needs." – RABBI TZVI SCHECTMAN, DIRECTOR SPECIAL PROJECTS, FRIENDSHIP CIRCLE, WEST BLOOMFIELD, MICHIGAN

"Minoti graciously shares her journey as a dedicated and caring professional wealth adviser. Her stories are poignant and provide wisdom and practical insights drawn from her many years of experience. Beyond a Parent's Love further distinguishes Minoti as a truly compassionate expert in the field of special needs planning." – SANFORD MALL, JD, CELA, CAP, ELDER LAW AND SPECIAL NEEDS AND ESTATE PLANNING ATTORNEY, FOUNDER AND SENIOR PARTNER OF MALL MALISOW & COONEY P.C.

"Beautifully written stories about the challenges families face raising a child with special needs. Minoti has found a way to educate her audience about the unique, critical process of financial planning in the context of passionate, heartwarming storytelling. The reader immediately connects with the brave families she presents over her long career of giving hope to those parents struggling with the uncertainty of the future. This is a must read for any family raising a child with special needs, almost immediately after diagnosis. The next question becomes, 'What will happen when I am no longer here to care for my child?'" – COLLEEN ALLEN, PhD, PRESIDENT AND CEO, AUTISM ALLIANCE OF MICHIGAN

"Minoti's book about her journey gives insight into how she achieved the unique combination of expertise and compassion so crucial in guiding families through the process of long term planning for their special needs loved ones. This book is such a valuable read for both families and professionals." – MARTIN LEVINSON, MD, FELLOW OF THE AMERICAN ACADEMY OF PEDIATRICS, BOARD OF DIRECTORS, WILLIAM SYNDROME ASSOCIATION

"Minoti's book brings people with disabilities and their families to the forefront while providing a unique view of how financial planning tools can be used to help families make decisions for the current and future financial needs of their loved ones with disabilities. Minoti's case studies provide invaluable context and perspective to special needs families and their financial, legal, family office and other advisors. Beyond a Parent's Love *is a unique look at the intersection between special needs planning and financial planning for families with family businesses and other complex financial situations. When a loved one has a disability, the entire family is affected, and if the family has a business, the business is affected. This book provides practical case studies on how families can maximize care and resources for their loved ones with special needs, in the context of each family's priorities and goals. Her compassionate and nuanced descriptions provide a realistic roadmap for families dealing with mental illness, developmental disabilities and acquired disabilities."*
— Lauretta Murphy, JD, Member of the Special Needs Alliance and chair of the Trust and Estate Practice Group at Miller Johnson law firm, Grand Rapids, Michigan

 MISSION POINT PRESS

Published by Mission Point Press
2554 Chandler Rd.
Traverse City, MI 49686
(231) 421-9513
www.MissionPointPress.com

ISBN: 978-1-943995-82-0
Library of Congress Control Number: 2018947225

Printed in the United States of America.

BEYOND
A PARENT'S LOVE

Lessons Learned in Life-Planning
for Special Needs Children

Minoti Rajput

Mission Point Press

To children with disabilities, for teaching me the meaning of unconditional love. You are often unheard as strong individuals. Giving a voice to your unspoken needs and desires has been my life's passion. My greatest hope is that you lead the lives you dream of.

CONTENTS

1. MY JOURNEY WITH SPECIAL NEEDS FAMILIES   1

2. WHEN THE UNPREDICTABLE BECOMES REAL   9

3. STANDING TOGETHER, STANDING PROUD   19

4. WHEN MENTAL ILLNESS CRUSHES YOUR DREAMS   29

5. WHERE WILL OUR CHILDREN LIVE?   42

6. NO TRUE PERFECTION IN THIS WORLD   55

7. OUR BEAUTIFUL DAUGHTER, AUTISTIC AND BIPOLAR   78

8. DADDY, PLEASE DON'T GO   93

9. HE MAY NEVER WALK AGAIN   111

10. FINDING SUPPORT WHEN HOPE SEEMS LOST   131

11. PLEASE GOD, HELP HIM REMAIN STABLE   148

12. SURPRISE INHERITANCE, COMPLEX OPTIONS   164

13. PLANNING WITH DETERMINATION AND LOVE   175

CONTENTS

14. INSPIRING ADVOCATES, FIVE PROFILES
   ON COMMITTED LEADERS 191

   LINDA BROWN 193

   THE COLLETTES 205

   DR. SUSAN YOUNGS 217

   JANICE FIALKA 227

   JEFFREY AND MICHELLE PROULX 245

15. NUTS AND BOLTS OF SPECIAL NEEDS PLANNING 260

   ACKNOWLEDGMENTS 273

   INDEX 275

   ABOUT THE AUTHOR 279

BEYOND A PARENT'S LOVE

1

My Journey with Special Needs Families

I believe events take place in our lives that change and mold us beyond our expectations. My life changed in 1989 when, as a financial planner, I met three different families, each with an adult child with a disability. Their influence on me was profound. They forced me to think about each child's life after the parents passed. Their challenges were incomprehensible to me, compelled me to help and shaped my career from then on.

I began as a wealth adviser and financial planner in 1980 at age twenty-eight. My husband and I arrived in the United States months before from India, our native country.

The financial planning industry was evolving, and few women were in the field. Determination and hard work helped me establish a successful practice in comprehensive planning. I focused on building a clientele of young couples and professionals starting their careers and gradually began working with physicians, automotive engineers, and small-business owners. I helped in their total financial-planning needs.

Ten years later, I felt the need for something more. I sought a challenging role, something more complex and emotionally and intellectually rewarding. The three families I met with special needs children had regular planning needs but were concerned about care for their adult children with disabilities once the parents passed.

One couple in their late fifties had a cognitively impaired daughter in her early thirties. Another was a retired school principal, a widow, with a son diagnosed with paranoid schizophrenia. The third couple in their mid-sixties had their own health challenges and a forty-year-old daughter with physical and mental challenges. In each case, the parents worried about the future of their child but did not have solutions.

These families made me think more about those with disabilities close to me. My older sister's daughter was diagnosed with autism at age three in 1977. My niece was often on my mind, and I became more aware of the special planning necessary to protect the future of the adult children with disabilities. This was a turning point in my life. I made the connection that helping families in panning for their children with special needs would be the future of my practice and my life's work.

Little information was available then to help these families plan for the future of their children. I sought expertise and found scarce research, books, or articles on the laws and government benefits available for adult children with disabilities. I was fortunate to find Phyllis Kramer, a financial adviser in Boston, who practiced in the special needs area and agreed to share her expertise and help me get started.

I spent months learning the complex components of planning, including estate planning laws, the government benefits available to adult children with disabilities and financial planning necessary to protect those with disabilities. I knew providence led me to begin specializing in planning for children with special needs and I was eager to research and learn all I could.

I realized very early on that I needed to learn and understand aspects of different types of developmental and physical disabilities as well as mental illness. It was important to understand what the families went through in caring for a child with a disability as well as to determine the level of planning necessary. The developmental disabilities included the autism spectrum,

Down syndrome, Williams syndrome, Angelman syndrome and others resulting in cognitive impairment. Some included physical impairment such as blindness, deafness and cerebral palsy. Mental illness included schizophrenia, manic depression, and schizoaffective disorders and others.

Arranging financial and estate plans for parents that last beyond their lives is challenging. These families need all the planning strategies others need. Special needs planning adds a layer providing much needed security for a loved one who can never be financially independent.

Learning about the Individuals with Disabilities Education Act (IDEA) and the American Disabilities Act (ADA) is important in understanding the rights of those with disabilities. Government benefits available to a person with a disability such as Supplemental Security Income (SSI), Social Security Disability Income (SSDI), Medicare, and Medicaid are complex and extremely important to learn to provide special-needs planning.

Disabilities spare no socio-economic groups. Families of children with special needs are successful business owners, executives, physicians, assembly line workers, teachers, and farmers. No two families are alike in their values, culture, or financial status, nor are the children with disabilities. Learning about these families is an important criterion. I learned that the art of fact finding had to be mastered with a balance of sensitivity and objectivity.

The firm I started has since counseled over fifteen hundred families nationwide with special-needs children in the past nearly thirty years. I have met hundreds of families with children with disabilities through educational workshops I led. Every family is motivated to create a plan that is best suited based on their financial ability.

The range of disabilities of the children varies dramatically. I met several families with a nonverbal and incontinent adult child; I knew others with cognitively impaired children who were high functioning and occasionally a savant, musically gifted or mathematically brilliant, but unable to care for themselves. Many children struggled with mental illness. Some were intellectually bright and college graduates but unable to function normally. I learned much about these families and learned much from them. I observed the incredible love, patience, and frustration that families experience. Their ability to overcome the initial surprise of having a child with special needs was just the beginning.

Raising a child with a disability is a long journey. Parents must juggle responsibilities if they have other children. They must find time for doctor's appointments for their special needs child, educational challenges, physical as well as speech therapies and arranging care when they have other commitments. Their special needs children have lifetime struggles including finding work after completing school and future living arrangements. Parents also must navigate the cost of raising a child with a disability, and their own financial and career demands.

Parents experience emotions that are hard to describe. The feelings of despair, loneliness, guilt, and helplessness linger forever. They juggle multiple roles as an advocate, protector, care giver and being a loving parent. It can be overwhelming and too much to handle. Some families fall apart under the pressure, and marriages fail, yet I watched families live through this and survive. I learned this is especially true when family members know they have a plan for their children that can be updated continually.

Siblings of a child with disabilities face many challenges. Feelings of neglect, jealousy, embarrassment, and shame are more prevalent in the younger years. I watched siblings also turn out to be great advocates and loving as well as protective of their brother or sister with disabilities.

I also knew that these families did not need pity but understanding. They did not want me to feel sorry for them but appreciated my empathy. Most of the families I have counseled have dreams and aspirations for their children with special needs. My role is to help them realize their dreams of a stable life, not always college or marriage. The dreams include helping their child finish high school, become employed, find a place to live with support outside the family home, and not be a burden on their siblings.

Much has changed since I first began my special-needs focus. Media and technology have made it possible to create awareness about those with disabilities. Today, the internet supplies easy access to information about disabilities, medical treatments, educational programs in schools, advocacy organizations, and family support groups. Schools have more sophisticated resources and education options and parents are more prepared to work with available programs and planning to help prepare their special needs children for lifetime needs.

Most families in my initial years of special needs practice were grateful for help and resources in planning but their special needs child typically remained in the background and uninvolved in their own future planning In the last decade, I have seen a steady shift in parents involving their child in understanding their rights and options in education. That includes advanced training beyond high school and college classes. The children are also involved in decisions on their employment and residential options.

The number of people diagnosed with disabilities is at a record high partly due to early diagnosis and greater awareness. About thirteen percent of students in public schools need special-education services, according to the 2014 National Center for Education Statistics. That includes those with learning disabilities. Nationwide, the number of students ages six to twenty-one classified on the autism spectrum rose one hundred sixty-five percent between 2005 to 2015. Students with "other health impairments" increased by about fifty-one percent during the same ten-year span.

There is a growing crisis in services for special needs families from continued budget cuts in federal funding for state Medicaid programs. Families are already experiencing shortages in residential options and staffing for homes. The budget cuts further impact home-community based services such as case management, home health aides, personal care services and respite care. Services such as job searches, job development and placement, skill assessment and job training are equally at risk.

The shortage in available programs and resources at the state and federal level will require parents to be vigilant and forceful in seeking new solutions and resources to protect their child's future. Meanwhile promising breakthroughs in medicine and knowledge on how to educate, train and help those with special needs brings new hope and opportunity.

Schools need more special-education teachers, aids, and special programs, all of which create financial pressure. Children with disabilities are also living longer from early diagnosis and medical advancements requiring ongoing monitoring of their plans. Parents face the challenge of planning and protecting their retirement and long-term care needs while ensuring their children with disabilities are protected.

My practice has also evolved. Many parents I planned with years ago have passed away. Their financial and estate plans are managed by siblings or others close to special needs adults. In my years of practice I learned to extend my help beyond that of financial planning and was honored to serve as helpmate, teacher, counselor and advocate.

As I look back to the path I have traveled in this journey of special needs planning, several families stand out that have touched me to the core. They humbled me as extraordinary human beings. Their ability to love their child with special needs and their other children, their commitment to their families and the community, and their determination to make a difference in their child's life or other children with disabilities, are all exemplary. Their stories need to be told and shared. There is a lot to learn from these families and from their life experiences.

It is my hope that this book also encourages financial planners to specialize in special needs planning, to be advisors making a difference. These families' stories can help other professionals such as special education teachers, psychologists, therapists, social workers, and others working with special needs children and adults understand the dynamics of these families. Most important, other families of children with disabilities with similar struggles will be able to relate and know that they are not alone.

The families I met during my journey were seeking financial and special needs planning. All the families described in this book have completed their plans, and my firm continues to monitor them. Basic special-needs planning information is provided in the following chapters, but the stories are more about what every family goes through in raising their child and how they deal with other challenges in life. Every family situation and their struggles are unique. Many have found solutions that have worked well for their child and their family. Others are hopeful for a positive outcome. The complexities of their challenges, their way of coping with them, and the solutions they have found need to be recognized.

Perhaps there is a family in this book that is just like yours. Each family described is based on actual people and situations I have had the honor of working with, although some names and minor circumstances have been changed at their request. Professional opinions also differ on the correct terminology describing those with disabilities as research evolves. I am using the overall term "special needs" for now.

Perhaps each child's disability and struggles are similar to yours, and perhaps you are seeking a similar solution. It is my hope that this book provides you with the inspiration to find your solution and know that you are in a similar journey with many others. You are not alone.

— *Minoti Rajput*

2

When the Unpredictable Becomes Real

It is impossible to predict the severe changes a family will encounter as its members age. Illness and death can profoundly affect those caring for special needs children, including unexpected health issues of parents and designated family caregivers. Considerable planning and adjustments for all contingencies are essential over time.

Jeremy Peterson knew his younger brother Michael was not considered normal. He was born with a flattened head, slanted eyes, and small chin. Jeremy was ten when Michael was born, and he remembers feeling embarrassed about having a brother that was different. From an early age he felt awkward about bringing friends home. Years later he remembered his mother crying silently and having anxiety about Michael's disability, although it was rarely discussed. Yet nothing prepared him or his family for the series of unexpected health, emotional, and financial events that required courage and hard decisions.

The love and concern Wade and Ruth Peterson felt for Michael, their fourth child, born with Down syndrome, was clear from the moment I met them in 1994. They were sitting anxiously at a workshop on special needs planning that I led near their home in Macomb County, Michigan.

The overwhelming question the Petersons faced was who

would care for Michael after they passed. Michael was vulnerable and incapable of taking care of himself. Wade and Ruth had cared for him and protected him since he was born. They knew it was time to assess their finances and prepare for the inevitability of his life-long needs.

Financial and legal planning is done assuming worst-case scenarios. Plans based on existing circumstances, caregivers, trustees, and family members can change dramatically over time. The Peterson family's planning was among my earliest experiences of life-changing worst-case moments, including health issues and death.

Wade and Ruth agreed from our first meeting it was imperative to create their own trust as well as a special-needs trust for Michael, and to provide funds for his future. They expressed visible relief that Michael could be cared for with a lifelong plan. However, it took months and then years to complete their plan.

The reasons for their inaction were complex and rooted in their deep love and fear for Michael. Signing the documents affirmed the hard truth that Michael was different from others, and although it anguished them, he was certainly different from their other three children.

Jeremy's memory of his parent's worries about Michael's future is vague. Wade and Ruth did not discuss their concerns as a family. They were struggling with their own fears and concerns over Michael as a person with Down syndrome and felt alone with the stigma of his genetic disorder.

In the early 1960s and 1970s, it was not uncommon for families with special needs children to feel alienated and unaware of how to get help.

"My parents did not want to burden us with their fears and concerns about Michael," Jeremy said.

"They felt it was their responsibility. They did not realize how much sharing could have helped."

It was clear Wade and Ruth needed guidance when they attended my workshop.

Ruth fidgeted and said little, although I learned later that while Wade managed the family finances, Ruth worried more about Michael's future. It was she who nudged Wade to attend the workshop on special-needs planning. Wade asked several questions and took notes. The couple later asked for a deeper consultation on their planning needs.

Michael was twenty-three, in good health, happy and in the moment. He was by his parents' sides when not in school. He had little life experience outside the family home, few hobbies, and no work training. He could take care of his personal hygiene but needed help with all basic life skills. He had obsessive-compulsive disorder in addition to his developmental and intellectual delays and was uncomfortable with change.

Wade, then seventy-three, underwent triple-bypass heart surgery, and Ruth, sixty, knew it was time to prepare for Michael's future. Most of their plans for Michael centered with their oldest daughter, Lisa, who was married and had two boys. Lisa was close to Michael and cared deeply for her susceptible baby brother. Their parents knew that although Jeremy resented Michael growing up, he could step in and help. Another daughter, Megan, lived out of state and stayed distant from her brother's care.

Wade was a retired design engineer from Chrysler. The family was comfortable but not wealthy and used Wade's pension and social security for most expenses, rarely using money from other investments. I recommended the trusts for both parents and a special-needs trust for Michael. And I explained that permanent life insurance placed on the parents for Michael's trust would create an asset and give him needed financial security. Their own assets could be depleted from unanticipated or prolonged health-related expenses. Life insurance would still be available and free from income tax.

We created a written detailed plan analyzing their financial and family situation with recommendations for Michael's future. Ruth decided to purchase a $150,000 life insurance policy for Michael's trust. They also planned to leave Michael forty percent of their investments and their paid home. The remaining sixty percent of the estate was designated to their other three children. After our private meeting' I set up a session with an estate-planning attorney specializing in special-needs planning to complete their legal documents. Unfortunately, each time the Petersons canceled or postponed the sessions.

Six months passed until one day I received a chilling phone call from Ruth. She sounded disturbed and shaken. The husband of her oldest daughter, Lisa, had died of cancer at thirty-eight. Lisa was thirty-five; her boys were four and three. The family was in shock and despondent. They asked me if I could help with Lisa's financial and estate planning.

Planning for the parents and Michael was set aside. Planning for Lisa and her children's future became a priority. For the next three months, we focused on Lisa. I was struck by her calm, caring manner. She was mature, thoughtful, and practical. Lisa was grieving for her husband, concerned about her sons, yet worried about Michael. She was committed and sure she could take care of Michael full time once her parents passed.

Lisa's planning included setting up education funds for her children, organizing her estate planning, and purchasing term life insurance. She was eligible for social security for them, a relief. I waited to hear from her parents regarding their planning and continued to touch base with them every few months.

Nothing happened to move the Peterson family legal planning forward. Finally in 1999, four years after Ruth purchased life insurance for Wade's trust, I knew I needed to take action to finalize the trust. I was becoming frustrated and could not understand why they were holding back. Wade was aging, had heart problems, and the untimely death of Lisa's husband seemed pressing reasons to complete their planning and ensure Michael was not at risk. What was holding them back? I was determined, finally called, and announced I was driving to their house and taking them to the attorney to complete their legal documents. I was not going to let them stall any longer.

Ruth was shaken by my confrontation and broke down. Through tears and soft sobs, Ruth had a serious, long conversation with me. She wanted desperately to finish the planning. Yet she was fearful of adding the extra burden on Lisa, now widowed and responsible for raising two young children. Was it fair to leave such a huge responsibility to her? Were they being selfish? What were their options? There was one more thing. She admitted that the idea of legally stating Michael was special needs was breaking their hearts and holding them back. I counseled and encouraged them as best as I could; it was not easy but they finally agreed. The trust planning was finalized five years after our first meeting.

The Peterson's unforeseen health challenges continued, and I soon learned of another tragedy. Ruth was diagnosed with breast cancer and was undergoing chemotherapy and radiation. She was not optimistic for recovery and worried about Michael. He finished his special education schooling at twenty-six but had not enrolled in job coaching or skill-building programs. He stayed close by his parents' sides, accompanying his mother to all treatments with no awareness of the threat her cancer caused.

Although Ruth was sicker, Wade passed away first in 2001 at eighty years of age. Despite her illness, Ruth had to deal with settling Wade's estate. It was also time to meet with Ruth and Lisa together and review Lisa's responsibility as a successor trustee after Ruth's demise. I also suggested younger brother Jeremy attend to ensure as many family members were involved in planning as possible. Jeremy was married with a son by then.

Ruth was anxious, physically and mentally tired, and grieving for her husband's loss. And she was worried, especially for how Lisa could care for Michael and her two young boys. She was deeply troubled for Michael's future. Jeremy, who had remained less involved until now, was anguished by his mother's despair and assured her he would step in.

Jeremy was close to his older sister Lisa and looked up to her. His mother's impending death, so soon after his father and Lisa's husband's death, alarmed and made him feel vulnerable. He wanted his mother and sister to feel secure. He knew he must help Lisa with Michael's care and not leave her alone.

Ruth passed away nine months later from cancer complications, another blow to the family already reeling with grief. Michael lost both parents in nine months and had to move from the only home he had known. He never expressed sadness but was clearly rattled by the change.

Lisa welcomed him. She arranged a room for Michael in her home and made sure he felt loved and needed. The adjustment was difficult for them both. Michael had no daily activities to keep him busy. Lisa had many responsibilities raising her sons and a part-time job as a student aid. She had to learn from scratch how Social Security Disability Insurance (SSDI), Medicare, and Medicaid worked for Michael. She reached out to the local Community Mental Health for help in basic job training for Michael. It took time to learn how the system worked, how to proceed, set up appointments, and decide best options. The task was onerous and took three months before Michael was lined up for job coaching, transportation, socialization, and other needs.

Lisa was conscientious, caring, and eventually obtained a rhythm with her sons and Michael. The financial planning for the Peterson family worked exactly as intended. Insurance funds were placed in Michael's trust within less than two weeks of his mother's death. The rest of the investments were distributed among the heirs with Michael's deposited in his special-needs trust. Siblings Lisa and Jeremy agreed to leave their parents' home in Michael's trust. Lisa determined Michael's needs and income from his special-needs trust to supplement his government benefits. I checked in periodically; Lisa shared challenges and adjustments, yet was relieved the family was doing as well as possible, and her financial plans were succeeding.

Then came another tragic change.

I was unprepared when Jeremy called one day with shocking news. Lisa had died from breast cancer at forty-eight. Her sons were sixteen and seventeen. She was quiet about her illness and did not share even with Jeremy, Megan, or family members. Jeremy and Megan were now the only survivors of the family. They had two minor boys and an adult brother with Down syndrome to take care of. Megan lived out of state and could not help.

Until then Jeremy and I had little interaction. I knew he and Michael were not close growing up and he stayed in the background as I worked with his parents and Lisa. The series of unexpected events suddenly put Jeremy in charge of three additional family members. We had to meet to discuss Lisa's estate as well as Michael's planning. Considering the huge responsibility he was undertaking, I found him calm, patient, considerate, and ready to do what he must. He admitted that he was deeply hurt and disturbed by Lisa's not sharing about her illness and preparing him better.

"Lisa was quiet and did not communicate just like my parents. The price we all paid is high" Jeremy said.

Jeremy said he was ready to welcome Michael and his nephews Mitch and Paul into his home. He lived with his wife Kathy and son Robert in a different county and knew his decision to move them in his home would be life-altering for all.

The challenges were immense. Michael's government benefits, including his employment and social activities, were tied up in the county where he lived with Lisa. There were questions on available work and transportation for Michael. Yet Jeremy moved forward, never wavering. He believed families should stick together, and Michael was not going to a group home. His parents were gone, but Michael could rely on his brother.

Kathy didn't question his decision; she understood and supported Jeremy's need to welcome his family. Jeremy and Kathy had also never questioned why Lisa was the first choice to be Michael's guardian and successor trustee. In fact, Jeremy said that he was relieved to be second in line for Michael's care. Lisa was the boss, the older sister, and loved her baby brother. Despite Lisa's challenges, she had felt good about caring for Michael in her home.

Every day of the first several weeks was challenging and stressful. Kathy was initially overwhelmed but determined to work through it. She had a full-time job, needed to cook for six people and soon learned the teenage boys had needs around school and sports. Mitch and Paul were also grieving over the loss of their mother, changing schools, and trying to make new friends. It was hard for everyone.

Michael stayed in the moment as always, talking about his sister and parents but never expressing grief. Jeremy and Kathy had full-time jobs, and Michael could not be left alone. Jeremy worked for weeks on needed help with the county Community Mental Health to reestablish a new pattern and routine in Michael's life. Jeremy admitted that without Kathy's unconditional love and duty to the family, this mission to keep the family together would not have been possible.

It has been nine years. Today the family has settled into a new normal. Michael works at a sheltered workshop through Community Mental Health. He loves bowling and dancing – hobbies he started when younger and are supported by Jeremy and Kathy. He also loves traveling to the family cottage in Clare, Michigan. And he enjoys being a passenger on dirt bikes while sitting behind Jeremy's lifelong friend, Peter. Jeremy remembers that Peter was among the true friends who interacted and accepted Michael early on. Mitch and Paul finished high school, are employed, and have moved back to their own home.

Jeremy's wish is for Michael to always live with family. He also realizes the need to help Michael plan an independent living arrangement. Michael is forty-seven and could live to be sixty, the average life expectancy of those with Down syndrome. Michael can always live with Jeremy, but he worries that Michael could outlive him. He has agreed to reach out to a professional advocacy organization and the local Community Mental Health for guidance to plan for Michael's transition.

Jeremy wishes his parents had shared information about their planning for Michael and coached their other three children on their future responsibilities. They would not have felt so lost during their most difficult periods if they had information documented on Michael's care.

Yet his support never wavers.

Jeremy and Kathy notice signs that Michael is aging. Michael has diabetes and thyroid issues. They don't know what the future will bring, but for now, Michael is happy. He lives with a loving family and in a comfortable home. His parent's planning assured his financial foundation, enabling his siblings to help.

INSIGHTS FROM THE PETERSON FAMILY STORY

Start financial planning for special needs children early and adjust, prepare for the worst and communicate. Wade and Ruth might have begun their financial and legal planning years earlier instead of waiting until they were sick and older. The Petersons were pushed to complete their planning under pressure and did not anticipate Lisa's untimely death in their planning. Special needs planning should be coordinated with other family members, all of whom need to know long-term plans.

Learn early about the range of government benefits and training programs available. Take advantage of career training and engaging in social events and interests. Special needs children grow from learning essential life skills. Michael could have benefited from being better prepared by participating in social programs and job coaching early on. Michael's independence could have later helped his sibling caregivers Lisa and Jeremy.

Document the details. All details of caring and planning for a person with special needs should be documented in a **Letter of Intent** document prepared by parents and those who are close to the person with disability. This is essential for guiding the future trustees/guardians and caregivers. Wade and Ruth might have created a Letter of Intent with all of Michael's health needs, emotions, his government benefits, likes and dislikes to help his future caregivers.

Prepare for the worst over life and death, including parents and all caregivers. Consider scenarios for various alternatives for care should the special needs child outlive guardians, trustees and other close family members who are caregivers. Although Michael is happy with Jeremy's family, the family should be prepared for the worst and consider alternatives in case Michael outlives Jeremy.

3

---

*Standing Together,
Standing Proud*

Caring for multiple children with special needs requires complex legal and financial planning as well as a strong support system. The children with disabilities need different levels of care, and families must find and navigate a tight network of advisers and advocates. They also must consider who will provide care after parents pass.

The family clan motto gracing David and Jane Mandy's eventual burial plot mirrors their life's conviction.

BYDAND. Scottish for "Stand Fast. Stand Firm. Stand Together." David and Jane have been living those ideals for the last fifty years. They are unwavering in their love and commitment for their three children. All three are cognitively impaired and will need care and supervision for the rest of their lives.

Their deep concern for their children keeps them awake at night. They remain steadfast and strong in their beliefs.

"You have to fight for your child. You have to listen to your child," David said. "It is important to understand that the word impossible only describes a degree of difficulty."

In my twenty-eight years of working with families of children with disabilities, David and Jane Mandy stand out as an exceptional couple and will always have a special place in my heart. I met David, a pediatrician, at a special needs workshop in Macomb County, Michigan in 1992. He handed me a questionnaire at the end requesting a consultation. I noticed immediately he listed three children as dependents with disabilities. Holly was then seventeen, Joshua was twelve and Drew was ten.

I wondered how they coped. Most families struggle with one child with a disability and they had three. Over the years I developed great respect for David and Jane and learned how they refused to accept limited options, focusing on dedication, endless love and potential for their family.

None of their three children had obvious signs of cognitive impairment at birth. Holly was growing and developing well at fifteen months when David noticed her head nodding one evening as she played by his feet. Jane said she had noticed as well. David was alarmed and took her to Dr. Michael Nigro, a pediatric neurologist. He confirmed Holly had infantile spasm seizure and mild cognitive impairment. While her seizures were soon controlled, David and Jane's lives changed forever.

David was a young resident doctor and already working long hours. The months after Holly's diagnosis in the mid-1970s were a blur of confusion and search for care. As a pediatrician, David was very aware of what Holly's diagnoses meant and how it could impact their family. He said they just rolled up their sleeves and got to work.

Four years later Jane became pregnant again, and she had sophisticated genetic counseling and all appropriate medical testing. Their unborn baby son tested normal. Joshua was born with no issues and to David and Jane's relief developed well until about age three. They realized that despite his growing and strong vocabulary, Joshua struggled with learning the alphabet. This was not normal; David and Jane were concerned. They returned to Dr. Nigro, the neurologist. He recommended they consult a psychologist.

Joshua was diagnosed as mentally challenged with a low IQ.

David remembers the day vividly. He was completely crushed and broke down in sobs. He felt devastated. Jane was stoic and accepted the diagnoses calmly. As they drove home Jane's control came crashing down. She could not hold back her gushing tears. David assured her that together, somehow, they would persevere.

Their son Drew was born three years after Joshua in 1982. Testing again raised no issues, but Drew developed seizures shortly before turning two. Other complications followed. Drew was diagnosed with severe mental disability with greater challenges than Holly and Joshua. Drew needed round-the-clock attention due to his frequent seizures and had severe developmental delays.

David and Jane's faith and determination to hold their families together got them through the early years of discovery and confusion. They accepted the reality with grace and never wavered from their faith or trust in God. Each of their children had specific needs and challenges. Their days and nights were long and exhausting. It tested their patience and ability to cope with the stress. The Mandys formed a tight unit and continually researched and sought care and support. They became their children's constant protectors, fought for their rights, always seeking to enhance their lives.

The Mandys often felt lonely but were blessed to have very special people in their lives who contributed to their children's growth. They found great comfort with their preacher, who gave them needed solace. And they turned to the schools. Dr. Larry Salaty, director of special education in their school district, helped create an enriching educational program for Holly. He also started a Parent Advisory Council (PAC) that David and Jane remained part of for years to come.

Although Holly struggled in many areas of academic and life skills, David and Jane cherished every moment of Holly's accomplishments and worked with her continually in her personal growth.

Holly struggled for years to learn to read. Finally in middle school her teacher, Ruth Battles, helped her learn and opened doors for her progress. Holly's running ability also led to a great athletic career. She was a sprinter in track at school and in Special Olympics. Another teacher saw her potential as a distance runner and encouraged her to compete, making Special Olympics even more meaningful for her. Holly's talent as a distance runner won her many accolades and wins. In an especially proud moment, she was named one of seven to obtain a varsity letter and was fifth in a race. Her parents were thrilled.

Joshua struggled in school as well. He had difficulty in reading and math but showed strength in many sports activities and was a Boy Scout. His sense of humor and charm always delighted his parents.

Drew was Dave and Jane's greatest challenge. Despite several medications, his seizures were uncontrollable and he needed attention round the clock. His disability was the most severe and his care exhausting.

David and Jane accepted the reality that their children needed lifelong financial and emotional protection. They began planning for their children's financial future shortly after our first meeting. Their planning needed to focus on a comprehensive approach that entailed financial security for the surviving family in the event either David or Jane died. Most importantly, they needed planning for their three children through special needs trusts.

We completed a detailed risk management analysis; David was the sole breadwinner, and his death would create severe financial hardship for Jane and the children. Jane's death would leave David helpless and caring for three children. We recommended sufficient term life insurance for both parents until they accumulated assets over the years. Until that time, David had not been able to start a retirement plan for them, and an appropriate plan for a retirement savings program was recommended.

Qualifying for government benefits such as Social Security and Medicaid was a key component to planning for their three children. The Mandys created revocable living trusts for themselves as well as separate stand-alone revocable special needs trust for each of their three children. The special needs trusts have the language to protect eligibility for government benefits. Revocable trusts provide flexibility to make changes if and when they are necessary.

The government benefits alone, however, were not likely to be sufficient to provide for the quality of life David and Jane wanted for their children. The special needs trusts also needed assurance of funding at David and Jane's death.

David and Jane purchased a joint survivor permanent life insurance and made the three special needs trusts beneficiaries of the life insurance. The tax-free nature of the insurance policy's death proceeds is particularly important. We agreed to monitor the plans carefully and regularly as their lives changed as well as the laws changed.

Despite having cognitive impairment and somewhat limited academic skills, Holly and Joshua are very high functioning in other areas and are active and social. Holly was hired at Mount Clemens General Hospital after she completed high school, tasked with picking up and dropping off testing equipment and instruments. She has continued working there many years.

Joshua, too, has held steady jobs. He worked as a custodian at a church for many years and is currently employed at a fencing company packaging, banding, foaming, and putting fences on trucks. His easy going and friendly personality wins people over easily. He speaks well and is friendly and well-liked at work. Joshua struggles with reading but is an Eagle's Boy Scout and excels at cross-country skiing. He saves as much as he can and is a proud owner of a truck he bought with his own savings.

Drew is severely limited. He is dependent on his parents for all daily needs. He is nonverbal, expresses himself with signs or gestures, and wears diapers. He has a sweet disposition, can walk unaided, and attends a day program for recreation and socialization.

One of the most wonderful and special events for the Mandy family was Holly's wedding to her true love, Peter, in 2007. Holly met Peter at work, and they began dating soon after. Their romance blossomed, but David and Jane were worried. Should they get married? Would it work? Peter did not have a disability but was a low wage earner. He cared for Holly deeply, yet David and Jane wondered if he would always love and take care of her.

The wedding was very emotional. The family invited those who had supported them in raising their special needs children. There were many tears of joy shed as David walked Holly down the aisle. It was a shining moment.

David and Jane also helped the young couple buy a home and taught them basic finances including budgeting. David and Jane lived close enough to support them in person as well as financially. The family recently celebrated Holly and Peter's ten-year marriage with a trip to Disney World, the family's favorite holiday destination, with David, Jane, Joshua, and Drew.

Despite their planning, David and Jane are concerned about the future. Will their financial planning be adequate for their children? Planning for three children with disabilities and their own retirement is exasperating. David is committed to working for the rest of his life to provide a secure future for his children.

"Jane and I will live on bread and water for the rest of our lives if that is what is needed to take care of our children," he said.

Yet financial help has also come from family. David and Jane were very relieved when both received inheritances from their parents when they passed, first from David's father, and then from Jane's family.

David's younger sister Bonnie has been a steadfast supporter for David. Bonnie was born sixteen years after David and has always been close to her older brother. From the start, Bonnie and her husband were very caring toward Holly, Joshua, and Drew, and worried about their futures. They generously purchased a large life insurance policy on David and Jane for the benefit of their children. Even more giving, Bonnie turned over her inheritance from their father in David's favor. David and Jane were truly touched by the selfless gestures on Bonnie and her husband's part. Bonnie also is named the successor trustee of David and Jane's trust as well as the children's special needs trusts.

The Mandy family planning has several complex factors including levels of government assistance. Holly is working and managing well in her married life. Yet both Holly and Peter earn low wages. Holly is considered high functioning with a mild disability. Due to Holly's full-time work, she no longer receives any government benefits either in monthly income (SSI or SSDI) or other Medicaid benefits such as transportation and food stamps. Joshua also functions well in many areas despite his mild cognitive impairment, and he no longer receives any government benefits.

Holly and Joshua's wages unfortunately do not allow them to be financially independent, and they still need their trusts funded by David and Jane upon their passing. David and Jane have amended their trusts as necessary for their children's needs. All three children were equal beneficiaries of their parent's estate when their plan was first set up in 1992. Since then, Holly and Joshua have continued to be employed and do not require as much care. Drew is completely dependent. David and Jane are leaving a greater percentage of their estate now for Drew's trust.

As David and Jane approach retirement and face their own mortality, they think about their children's future constantly.

"What will happen to my innocent children?" asked David in a quivering voice. "Will people take advantage of them? Will somebody steal their money or abuse them? Where will they live and who will take care of them?"

He believes that his God has brought them to earth and will ultimately take care of them. David's faith reassures him that the right people who can be trusted will surround them. Bonnie is their back up. They are concerned about a successor trustee after Bonnie. David and Jane hope David's best friend, Ed Young, and his family may offer to help as they have supported the Mandy family for years through all challenges.

David and Jane do not give up easily. They know they will always need to be resourceful and seek counseling from professionals to revise their plans. They hope Joshua and Drew will continue living in their current home even after they are gone. They also hope Holly and Peter will move back to the family home. They realize the right caregivers are essential to their children's safety and care. They will work with local advocacy groups such as Arc of Macomb and the county Community Mental Health and their list of providers for services to care for their children. They may also consider professional trustees such as CPAs and law firms to work with the advocacy groups.

As much as the uncertainly looms over their future, David and Jane make the most of enjoying their children every moment and depending on each other. David believes strongly he is following the path planned for him in his religious faith. And he has Jane to share that path.

"This is the woman who holds my hand and gets me to go where I need to go," he said.

For David, resiliency, listening and talking to the children, and adjusting is key in keeping their family moving forward. Jane is proud of her children and said their growth sustains her.

"You have to get the children involved early on, you have to share them earlier than you may have planned," David said. "You have to learn to let them go. You have to find a network of friends, teachers who care about your child.

"These children are handicap-able and not handicapped."

David and Jane continue pursuing many activities and hobbies with their family. They are a dedicated Special Olympic family. David is a coach for Special Olympians in several sports, and both serve on the board for one of the area teams. They are musicians and practice weekly. David plays the bag pipes, Joshua plays the base drum, and Jane plays the snare. David and Joshua are active hikers and enjoy adventures in the Canadian Rockies. David also collects historical artifacts including Lionel Trains.

David and Jane will soon celebrate fifty years of marriage, a long journey for an exceptional couple who truly represent their Scottish family motto. BYDAND. Stand Fast. Stand Firm. Stand Together.

Learn early about government benefits for a range of disabilities. The Mandy family shows planning for high functioning or mildly disabled individuals can often be difficult. The children may be able to work but not earn enough to support themselves and yet might not qualify for government benefits. Parents need to consider all wage and potential benefits as the Mandys did for Joshua, Holly and Drew when deciding on funding their trusts.

Understand guidelines for revocable and irrevocable trusts. Revocable trusts provide the important flexibility to make changes where necessary and applicable, including changes in trustees or benefits to beneficiaries. Some states require special needs trusts to be irrevocable. Care should be taken to ensure that all contingencies are thought through before irrevocable trusts are created.

Research long-term housing options from the start. Future residences with care giving for special needs members is often the main concern for families. The Mandys have decided their own home is ideal for Joshua and Drew, and plan to work with Community Mental Health for caregiving for their sons. Housing options may include the parents' home, licensed group homes and take many years to plan.

Ensure whoever is named a successor trustee is aware and willing to assume all responsibilities. The role of a successor trustee of a special needs trust is important, with complex requirements. This includes looking after the best interests of the person with disability and managing the trust assets. The trustee may be given the option to choose a co-trustee including a professional corporate trustee to share the responsibility.

4

When Mental Illness
Crushes Your Dreams

Mental illness is a chronic and often debilitating disease that affects those who are ill and all close to them. Planning for their financial security and lifelong care can be difficult because of their complex personalities and possible lack of cooperation. Family members and professionals need patience and understanding in their advising and caring roles.

As a toddler, Roy Campbell's blond hair and blue eyes were the delight of his doting parents. They enjoyed watching him grow in their suburban Detroit Allen Park neighborhood and encouraged him to participate in sports early. Roy moodily pushed back in elementary school; he had a quiet temperament and did not make friends easily. He began withdrawing socially, preferring reading to after-school activities. Although he was a good student, he was often distracted, skipped school, and preferred to remain alone in his room.

As a teen, Roy became increasingly anxiety-ridden and indifferent toward his appearance and personal grooming. His parents Judith and Leroy were concerned and sought medical help. Roy reluctantly visited their family doctor but refused to take medication.

Judith patiently coped with Roy's stubbornness, mood swings, and emotional ups and downs, hoping to help him find balance. Leroy, a well-educated engineer, was increasingly frustrated and expected more from his son. He held a good position at General Motors and wanted Roy to excel. Roy maintained good grades in school but remained remote, alienating Leroy.

Judith and Leroy believed Roy had a chance for a brighter future when he graduated from high school and was accepted into the University of Michigan. He stayed aloof, was not interested in attending his senior prom, and was forced by his parents to attend his graduation. They encouraged him to move to the campus a half-hour drive away to experience student life, but Roy had difficulty adjusting. He was lonely, missed home, and his anxiety and mood swings worsened until he lost control. Roy had a nervous breakdown at age twenty-one in his third year of college. He had not been sleeping, was hearing voices, and was very agitated and hyper. He felt as if his world was closing around him. Roy was hospitalized and diagnosed with paranoid schizophrenia, a chronic mental disorder that can cause patients to be delusional and lose touch with reality.

Judith was shattered; her worst nightmare had come true. Mental illness was in her family, and she had prayed for her only child to be spared. She knew Roy had a debilitating disease and was in a dark, long journey.

Roy was prescribed multiple medications when he was released from the hospital. He agreed to leave his Ann Arbor apartment at his parents' insistence and move home to attend a local satellite campus. Judith and Leroy were very worried about him and wanted him close in case he had another episode. Roy resumed his studies in political science and graduated.

Roy continued his emotional roller coaster despite his medications. His demons drove him to behave irrationally. He could not hold jobs and was hospitalized several times since the first episode. He began a cycle that included four hospitalizations and a suicide attempt over the next several years. He improved after each hospitalization, felt optimistic about his future, took medications as prescribed and looked for work. He found jobs as a storage clerk, grocery store cashier and in janitorial services. As months passed and his mental health stabilized, Roy became confident and stopped taking his medications. His behavior became erratic and he began hearing voices again. He was forced to quit his jobs and went into downward spirals.

Heartbroken, his parents accepted that Roy's mental illness could be managed but not cured. Roy was diagnosed as mentally disabled. He needed to qualify for government benefits to support himself. He needed a monthly income, health insurance, an independent place to live, and a job. He applied and qualified for Supplemental Security Income (SSI) and Medicaid. Eventually he also qualified for a subsidized studio apartment near his parent's home and a sheltered supervised workshop that he attended three times a week for five hours a day. He worked in the stockroom at a grocery store; it was all he could handle despite his political science degree.

Judith and Leroy were relieved to see him settle on his own and have a routine in his life. They were constantly on edge worrying if they would get another call that Roy was in the hospital again.

I met Judith in 1992 when Roy was thirty-six, a year after Leroy died. I was already keenly aware of the complex needs of those with mental illness – much different than working with families of those with developmental disabilities. Those with severe mental illness can be very bright, educated, and accomplished, but may not be capable of living a normal life. Their debilitating disease creates havoc in their lives as well as in their families.

Judith and I had many conversations about her family during our planning. She was one of three girls; both sisters were diagnosed with bipolar disease and anxiety. One sister never married and died young. The other married early and had children, but the marriage ended in a divorce due to her unstable and abnormal behavior. The children were neglected and suffered from their mother's illness. Three of the next-generation children including Roy were diagnosed with schizophrenia or manic depression. The disease had destroyed their families, their dreams, and any normalcy that average families need.

Judith often wished she had the power to eradicate the awful curse of mental illness from the face of the earth. Despite her sadness about her son's diagnoses, she maintained a positive outlook and her sense of humor. I always found her cheerful, energetic, and eager to help.

Judith became very active in the Alliance for Mental Illness, Dearborn chapter, an advocacy organization for the families and those with mental illness. She formed a support group and remained a dedicated chapter volunteer for the rest of her life. She was secretary and involved in many social and educational chapter events.

Judith was left financially comfortable by her deceased husband. He had worked as an engineer for forty years. Judith had a General Motors survivor pension and a large investment portfolio. She lived modestly and became increasingly concerned about Roy's future and financial security. She also needed help managing her finances. Leroy had managed their affairs, and Judith needed a professional to take over.

Leroy and Judith had left their assets to Roy in wills drawn years ago. Since Roy was now receiving government benefits, any inheritance over $2,000 would jeopardize his eligibility. He could not live in the subsidized apartment or have a supervised job. Judith needed to update her legal documents, including a revocable living trust for her and a separate special need trust for Roy. Her formidable challenge was choosing her successor trustees and a trustee for Roy's trust.

Judith regularly donated to NARSAD – now known as the Brain and Behavior Research Foundation, a nonprofit [501(c)(3)] organization that focuses on mental health research and cures for nine commonly recognized mental disorders. She desperately hoped research would help find a miracle leading to early diagnosis and the ability to treat mental illness successfully.

She had nightmares about Roy wandering the streets as a homeless person without food and medication. Like many families with special needs family members, Judith and Leroy did not have close interaction with their other families and relatives. They felt alone and alienated. She could not think of any family member she could rely on or burden with Roy's responsibility. Roy did not require daily care, but he did need periodic checkups to ensure he was taking his medications, visiting his psychiatrists, and living as healthy a life as possible. After much discussion, we agreed that her CPA Richard would be a suitable successor trustee for Judith's as well as Roy's trust. She had a long and trusted relationship with Richard, the owner of a successful accounting firm. He also knew Roy well. We decided my firm would work with Richard as advisors in all planning matters for Roy and manage the trust assets. Judith felt very relieved and assured that she had made the right decision.

Judith and Leroy had planned well. In addition to investments, Judith had life insurance and a long-term care policy. There was no doubt that upon her death Roy's trust would have a large fund, and Judith wanted the trust income to provide all that was necessary that the government benefits did not. We had another important discussion on how and to whom the remaining funds from Roy's trust would be distributed when Roy passed away. Judith was very clear about that. Except for small amounts for a few people she named, the bulk of Roy's trust would go to a few charities of her choice. The majority would be designated for the Brain and Behavior Research

33

Foundation. She felt very strongly that anything she could do to make mental health of the future generation better would provide her peace.

My team and I continued to meet Judith periodically, and she updated us on Roy. He called his mother every day and stopped at her house twice a week for dinner. They settled into a routine, although ups and downs continued. Roy had additional hospitalizations and at times checked in the hospital on his own. Richard and I had agreed to meet Roy every six months so that he would be familiar with both of us. Roy was also supported by those at his workplace and at his apartment.

In the next several years, Judith began to experience health problems. She began losing her peripheral vision and was unable to drive distances. She could no longer visit us for her review meetings, so we offered to visit her at her home. Within a couple of years, we noticed the changing appearance of her well-kept house. She began to lose important items, could not clean the house, and was not eating properly. She was eighty-four and experiencing confusion and memory loss. She admitted she needed help and wanted to move into an assisted-living facility near her home.

Judith's move to Oakwood Assisted Living was a disruptive change in Judith and Roy's lives. It first meant disposing off sixty years of accumulated possessions. Roy wanted to hang on to too many things, and it was difficult to stop him. One of my staff, Joan, had worked with Judith for many years, and Roy had learned to trust her. Together they carefully picked what Roy could have. It was very emotional for both Judith and Roy. The trustee Richard took charge and arranged for the sale of the home. The sale proceeds were invested to generate a guaranteed income for five years to pay for Judith's assisted-living expenses. Judith settled into her new living arrangement, and Roy went to see her almost every afternoon. It was a highlight of the day for Judith. Many of her friends from the Mental Health Alliance chapter also visited.

Two years after Judith moved to the Oakwood facility, she slipped and broke her hip. She was hospitalized for a few days until she could begin her rehabilitation and move back to the assisted-living facility. Roy was very worried and afraid of losing his mother. Judith was the only constant in his life, and he began to realize that Judith was slipping. His emotions overwhelmed him; he checked into the hospital feeling very depressed and alone. He remained in the hospital ten days, one of the longest stays of his life.

After her surgery, Judith decided to move to a smaller, less institutional facility. Although Judith was frail in her body and mind, she was quite clear in what she wanted. Our firm engaged a geriatric professional to assess her situation and recommend a facility. The recommended home was in farther-away Farmington Hills and operated under the license of Adult Foster Care with six residents. Judith and Roy both felt very comfortable with the home, the operator, and other residents. We were concerned about Roy driving the nearly twenty miles and how he would handle not seeing his mother every day. Richard and I discussed a different approach.

Several years before, I had introduced Judith and Roy to an organization called Kadima. Kadima provides comprehensive residential, therapeutic, and social services to those with mental illness. Roy could participate in their social programs once a week and get to know other residents and members. Roy could also move into one of their supervised apartments in the future, a good option considering their experience and commitment in servicing people with mental illness. Roy had attended the social club a few times but not regularly. He had difficulty attempting anything on a consistent basis. We contacted Kadima to inquire if Roy could live in one of their residential facilities near Judith's new home. An opening was available; the expense of $1,200 a month needed to be paid out of pocket. Roy currently paid $140 a month for his apartment. Richard and I reviewed Judith's finances and agreed the expense was worth enabling Roy to be close to Judith.

Roy moved into the new facility. His other housemates were very welcoming and made him comfortable. Judith was a five-minute drive away. Judith was relieved that Roy would not have to drive far in the winter months. Then Roy became unpredictable. Kadima representatives alerted us that Roy had called a cab and had moved back to his former, familiar apartment. The new place was strange to him, and the unfamiliarity of the surroundings was alarming. Although Judith had described Roy and his patterns quite well over the years, it was our first experience of how Roy's mind worked and controlled his decision making. We realized that despite Roy's mental disability, he could not be forced to do anything. He would do what he wanted to do.

Judith started to experience more physical and mental challenges. She was well cared for at the home, and doctors visited her regularly. Her expenses were now paid with her long-term-care policy. Roy visited her regularly, but at our suggestion he used a cab service instead of driving. Judith's health started failing a couple of months before turning ninety. For the first time, Roy asked us if he was going to be all right when his mother died. We could detect the fear and insecurity in his eyes and his voice. We assured him and gave a brief explanation of his mother's plan for him. We discussed the role of Richard and our firm, but we did not disclose the amount of funds in the trust according to Judith's wishes. Richard's role was to distribute funds from Roy's trust for his appropriate expenses. Judith was concerned what Roy would do if he knew that he had a large trust fund.

Judith passed away one day before she turned ninety. Roy

was fifty-four and with her when she passed. Her service and burial were private. Roy contained himself very well. A dinner after the memorial was well attended by several members of the Alliance of Mentally Ill, in tribute to Judith's dedication to helping those with mental illness.

Our real work as the advisor for Roy's trust, and for Richard as the trustee, began after Judith passed away. After a brief period, we began to assess Roy's needs and were eager to honor Judith's wishes to help him from the trust. It was important to Judith to make sure Roy's living conditions were healthy and clean. We engaged the same geriatric care specialist experienced with mental illness to visit with Roy and assess his living conditions, make recommendations, and hire cleaning services on a regular basis. We also wanted to ensure he had regular medical checkups and ate healthy meals. I noticed that he wore the same clothes and a dirty red jacket every time he came to our office.

We received a very detailed, concerning report from the geriatric care specialist after she met Roy at his house. Roy was a hoarder, and every inch of his apartment was packed to capacity. He had some of his parent's clothes, furniture, and books stacked in already small, cramped rooms. The refrigerator had very little food, and Roy's clothes were piled on the floor. He wore the same clothes repeatedly. The report included several recommendations to ensure Roy would live in a clean place with someone helping him on a weekly basis. His trust could easily afford it.

Roy listened to all the recommendations very calmly. He understood it was what his mother wanted for him. The next day, he called Richard and our office and refused to have anyone enter his apartment and attempt to clean it or help him. His voice was controlled but angry. He said it was his life and his way of living. Nobody was going to change any of that even if his mother wanted it to happen.

We were completely taken aback and realized Roy's mental illness required we approach him differently. We learned to deal with him on a much more gentle and slow manner. Richard and I went over his expenses, items that were covered by his Social Security checks, and additional needs. Richard arranged for Roy to stop at his office every two weeks and pick up checks for his expenses. Roy was very happy with that arrangement. He could do his own grocery shopping and eat what he wanted. He bought new clothes and was excited to afford a new Chevrolet car. The car brought him great joy. We also agreed on a standing instruction for him to call our office every Friday and let my office know how he was faring. Roy had no social life and only visited two cousins on holidays.

Six months after Judith's death, Roy called and demanded to know how much money he had in his trust. It was strange. He had never asked that before and did not have clear concepts about money. He also mentioned a friend of his was visiting and spending a few days until he found a place of his own. This was alarming. His friend was Arthur, an old neighbor who Roy knew growing up. Arthur had his own challenges and often visited Roy asking for money. We advised Roy very sternly to stay away from him. We said he had to ask Arthur to leave his apartment as soon as possible. He seemed to have gotten the message.

Richard and I had a surprise coming. Two weeks later we received a notice from an attorney. The attorney was representing Roy, and the notice indicated that it was Roy's right to know what his trust terms were and what the value was. We knew immediately that it was not Roy's doing. He was vulnerable, and somebody was instigating him. Richard responded giving details of who Roy was and the terms of the trust but stated he did not feel obligated to give any further details. We also let the attorney know that it is very difficult to handle a person with Roy's illness, and we would resign if we felt there were obstacles in our way to take care of him. I personally called Roy to find out why and how he had approached the attorney and learned that Arthur had put him up to it. Roy had no idea what the meeting with the attorney was all about and what was happening. The attorney backed out, and the matter was dropped.

This gave us more insight into Roy's innocence and vulnerability. Arthur never showed up after that. The incident also made me reflect on my role as an advisor to Roy's trust. I specialized in and understood special-needs planning but cared enough to be genuinely interested in his welfare. This meant going beyond the regular management of the trust assets and coordinating with compassion and concern.

Roy called regularly. Politics interested him and yet made him agitated. He always asked me about my travels and cautioned me to travel safely. We developed a regular pattern. Despite our gentle attempts to take care of him, our best way was not his way. It was not our business if he wore his shirts five times or what he ate. He promised us that he was eating healthy. He visited his primary care physician once a year and his psychiatrist on a regular basis.

In 2013, his doctor suggested he visit a cardiologist. He detected irregular heartbeats and was concerned about possible heart problems. The cardiologist conducted tests and recommended a pacemaker right away to prevent a heart attack. Roy mentioned this casually on one of his Friday calls to me. I was alarmed and suggested he take care of it right away. Roy's response did not surprise me but made me sad. He emphatically said that no cardiologist was going to tell him what to do. It was his body and nobody was going to touch or put anything inside his body. Roy was not going to let anybody take care of him. A heart attack was imminent and he did not care.

A year later, I received the saddest and most difficult news. Roy had not reported to work for two days and nobody around his apartment had seen him. The apartment manager called his cousin, Steve, Richard, and our office. They had to report the issue to the police and break open the apartment door. His apartment was full of stench. Roy was found dead in his chair, the television on. He had died at fifty-eight of a heart attack, four years after his mother's death.

Roy was buried next to his parents. A memorial service was arranged and was well attended by the Dearborn Alliance for Mentally Ill family. Roy was tormented all his life with his paranoia and his demons. He lived a lonely life and died alone. He never knew his parents had left a generous trust for him, and he did not care. He lived frugally despite knowing that he could live better. Judith planned well for him and wanted a healthy and stable life for him. Roy's mental illness blocked him from enjoying what most people consider to be the simple and basic things in life. Roy's death was tragic and untimely. But Judith's wish for donations after he died was honored. The bulk of Roy's trust fund was sent to the Brain and Behavior Research Foundation in his memory.

INSIGHTS FROM THE CAMPBELL FAMILY

Ensure that the trustee in a special-needs trust understands the disabled person's needs. Most special-needs planning cases entail creating a special-needs trust, management of the funds of the trust, and protecting the government benefits of the person with disability. But those are just some among many of the responsibilities. Caring for a person with mental illness requires deep understanding and complex resources and needs.

Consider appointing a professional trustee in the absence of family members to manage trust assets and care for a mentally ill person. The role of the trustee of a trust for a mentally ill person is a challenge. Roy resisted being told what to do as an adult, it is not unusual for mentally ill trust beneficiaries to be uncooperative and act against their own welfare. Management of the trust assets and looking after the beneficiary's best interest are two different roles and may not be possible by one individual or entity. Research the possibility of co-trustees, including small accounting firms, law firms, or other independent corporate trustees.

Participate in programs offered for families of mentally ill individuals by advocacy organizations such as Kadima (kamicacenter.org) and the National Alliance for Mentally Ill and their local chapters. (https://www.nami.org). Judith found solace and support by working with the Dearborn Alliance for Mentally Ill. Being part of a support group helps families cope with issues and assist loved ones with debilitating.

5

Where Will Our Children Live?

> *Parents wrestle financially and emotionally with housing options as their children with disabilities become adults. Residential planning takes years and requires levels of care, including changing amounts of supervision, transportation to jobs and help with daily needs. Local Community Mental Health experts and their service providers can help explore residential options early on.*

Life was wonderful and full of love and optimism for Russ and Betty Reynolds when they began dating. They both worked at Cadillac Motor Company in Detroit and met at the General Motor Chorus, a musical group of one hundred singers. Betty was in awe of tall and handsome Russ with his convertible car, and Russ was smitten with Betty, blonde and beautiful. They shared their love for music, church, and family. They married in April 1960 after a three-year courtship.

Betty loved children and wanted to be a mother right away. Unfortunately, she suffered two miscarriages, and Russ and Betty were heartbroken. They decided to become foster parents, with Betty staying home with the children. They looked forward to the pleasure of parenting while waiting to have children of their own.

Their first foster child was a little girl. She was with them less than three months and was adopted by another family. The next child was a feisty four-day old boy. He had an unformed right hip socket and needed to be placed in a body cast his first year. He pulled himself around the floor and grew stronger. Russ and Betty loved him, admired his determination, and grew very attached. They agreed to adopt him. Richard became their son officially when the adoption was completed in March 1967.

Their joy compounded when Betty became pregnant again after four miscarriages and carried the baby to full term. Her pregnancy was normal, but she had significant difficulties delivering their son, David. He was born with a slightly larger head than normal. Although this concerned them, their pediatrician recommended they wait and watch for signs of issues.

"He insisted it was too early to know," Betty said.

They soon saw that David was developing and learning differently than Richard. Their lives were changing in an unknown direction, and challenges in raising David were mounting. They knew he was different, and things were not normal.

"He was very hard to please and seldom smiled," Betty said. "He was slow to crawl, and he didn't walk until he was twenty months."

On the first day of kindergarten, school representatives called Russ and Betty and asked them to come to the school. They were told the news they feared: David did not belong to a regular kindergarten class and should be in a special education program. This came as a jolt as their worst concerns were real. They were surprised the school confirmed his issues rather than their doctors.

Special education in the early 1970s was in its infancy, and programs were in experimental stages. Children were divided among different elementary schools for children of certain ages. David's teacher had never taught special education before. His parents and teacher learned to work with David's challenges at the same time.

David was recommended for evaluation at the William

Beaumont Hospital Neuro-Education Center. A meeting was arranged to outline detailed descriptions of David's challenges with the kindergarten teacher, the school principal, and David's parents. David was immature for his chronological age, had difficulty with his speech, and had issues with large and fine motor skills. He had difficulty in all ways of alerting and processing, including auditory, visual, and tactile. He expressed frustration and preferred to spend time with children younger than him. David continued in special education with Russ and Betty monitoring his plan with teachers. He remained in the Southfield, Michigan, school district for a few more years until the family moved to nearby Farmington. David was categorized as Educable Mentally Impaired or EMI, a special education label used at the time describing the ability to function and learn.

Although David was growing, Russ and Betty worried constantly. His developmental disabilities were taking an emotional toll on them both, especially Betty, who was with him at home. School officials recommended they visit The Institute for the Study of Mental Retardation and Related Disabilities at University of Michigan in Ann Arbor, or ISMRRD. Institute doctors could see that the parents were not focusing on their own emotional needs. As they began evaluating and interviewing other family members, Russ and Betty's pattern of frustration and guarded emotions became clear. Betty was experiencing some level of depression.

"They said that although the parents make great effort and expend a great deal of energy in trying to do the right thing for their children, their own emotional needs do not seem to be provided for," Betty said.

Russ and Betty were taken aback but relieved that the professionals could see they needed guidance and counseling along with their children. The family began psychological therapy in addition to continuing physical, occupational, and speech therapy for David.

Among all the chaos, Richard was a joy to raise, enjoyed having friends over, and supported his brother. He did not know that David had challenges until he started school and was transferred to special education. The family worked together to meet David's challenges and find balance.

"It was our normal," Betty said.

When David was six, Betty became pregnant once more. She did not have genetic testing or counseling and never learned why David was born with disabilities.

"The doctor said I should be fine having another child," Betty said.

Their son Darrin was a healthy and happy baby, much easier to raise than David. Everything appeared normal at first, and then their suspicions began. Darrin walked late and had difficulties with his speech. This time they did not wait and took baby Darrin to the William Beaumont Hospital for evaluation and later to the Institute for the Study of Mental Retardation in Ann Arbor. Darrin was diagnosed with mild mental retardation and macrocephaly, or an abnormally large head. Russ and Betty were devastated and felt defeated and alone. Their faith and love for each other kept them going. Every time they felt themselves sinking emotionally, they found a new determination to keep their family close and move on.

Darrin attended special education from the beginning. Special education had come a long way in addressing special needs since David entered school just six years earlier. One teacher was becoming known for her structured format, non-acceptance of poor work, and regular written communication to and from parents. Darrin was showing results and benefiting from the special education program, which now included speech therapy. He was easier to raise than David because of his pleasant personality. Surprisingly, Darrin was classified as Trainable Mentally Impaired (TMI) a grade lower than his brother David.

Betty and Russ realized they needed to plan for lifelong care for David and Darrin. They knew the boys were going to have difficulties their entire lives and it was up to them to do all they could to carve out a path for their independence.

For most parents of children with disabilities, the journey is arduous, long, and lonely. Russ and Betty, however, felt fortunate to have wonderful neighbors who provided great comfort and support. Betty was part of a babysitting club where each parent earned hours for caring for one another's children. None of the other mothers objected to looking after David and Darrin. The babysitting arrangement gave Betty and Russ much-needed respite and a little time for each other. They could not count on their families as their siblings were busy raising their own children. Richard and Darrin were fairly easy to raise, even with Darrin's disability. David remained a challenge with his inability to perform simple functions and express himself without frustration. Rich continued to have a normal childhood, inviting his friends over to play in the big sand box and the swing set Russ installed, never feeling embarrassed about his two siblings who were different from others.

Although their close friends were very supportive and invited all three boys in family activities, Russ and Betty often believed scant attention was paid to David and Darrin. Russ and Betty were stigmatized. In the early 1970s, acceptance of those with disabilities was poor, although the parents still experience slights even today. Betty remembers one neighbor who refused to let her son play with Darrin, who was the same age as her son and did not allow Darrin to enter their home.

Russ and Betty often felt sad and uncomfortable when David and Darrin were left out of discussions and activities. They felt awkward and distressed trying to take the boys in public places and events without knowing how they would behave. They also refused invitations from others, not knowing how the boys would be received.

"Emotionally, it was very hard to see other kids grow and develop when ours were slow and demanding," Betty said.

Russ and Betty felt blessed to have Rich in their lives as they raised their younger sons with disabilities. Richard spent time with his brothers and was at ease, giving them a break in their emotions and knowing he truly cared. Rich was very aware of his parent's difficulties dealing with his brothers. Russ and Betty feel thankful for God's way of creating a balance.

As a family, Russ and Betty created a safe and joyous environment in their home. Despite their daily challenges in dealing with David and Darrin's ongoing educational and developmental difficulties, they fondly remember happy times and special people they enjoyed in their early life. David was the happiest on his Big Wheel bike and felt a sense of accomplishment as he mastered riding it. It boosted his self-esteem and morale. Later, his greatest achievement was graduating from special education. During the ceremony, he let everybody know about his accomplishment by raising both his arms and letting out a loud yell, much to his parents' and teachers' surprise. Russ and Betty laughed later, encouraged that David could express himself when he wanted.

Darrin remained charming, pleasant, and very social. He had difficulty attaining academic expectations and could not attend the special education high school program. The Farmington School District's special education program provided a workshop and training called Visions Unlimited for students like Darrin who were diagnosed as Trainable Mentally Impaired. Darrin was the star of his small graduating class at the Visions Unlimited special education program. All the teachers competed for who would walk Darrin down the aisle. His parents were proud Darrin was popular and very much loved.

Betty's mother was also instrumental in creating a fun and loving environment for the five years she lived with the family until she passed in 1999. All three boys enjoyed kidding with grandma, and it was a happy time for them. Grandma was very independent. Betty worked at the local YMCA and came home during lunch, enjoying fun times with the boys and her mother.

Russ and Betty believed firmly in community involvement and recognized the need for the family to participate in helping children with disabilities. Their world grew with their commitment to have their children become part of many programs. Russ and Betty chartered a Cub Scout pack for boys in special education after learning one didn't exist. For three years, Russ organized weekly meetings, overnight camping trips, and daily trips while working full time. All eight boys in David's class became Cub Scouts and were allowed to wear their uniforms to school on meeting days. That was very special. The teacher noticed and appreciated how close the boys were once they became Cub Scouts. The meetings were always held at the Southfield Civic Center. The city of Southfield honored Russ with the Citizen of the Year award for his contribution and making a difference in these children.

The Reynolds family was also committed to the Special Olympics. One of the Farmington High School special education teachers obtained permission to start Special Olympics for the district, and Russ jumped at the opportunity to get David involved. David participated in the basketball and swimming programs, and the team achievement and camaraderie made a very positive difference in his personality. Darrin participated in softball, soccer, bowling, and weightlifting with his brother, and together they won many medals.

As the boys grew and prepared to graduate from special education programs at twenty-six, real issues of life began to surface. The parents struggled with many questions planning for their futures. Where will they work, will they earn enough? Where will they live? How will Rich be involved in his brother's life in the future? In the early 1990s, little education was available on planning for adult children with disabilities. Russ and Betty attended a workshop on special needs planning organized by my firm through Team Farmington Special Education in 1994.

David was twenty-seven and had begun working as a courtesy clerk bagging groceries at the Kroger grocery store. Darrin was still in school. They both had already qualified for Supplemental Security Income (SSI) and Medicaid. It became obvious that Russ and Betty needed to create special needs trusts for David and Darrin, rearrange their finances to protect themselves during retirement, and provide financial security for the boys. They wanted to ensure Rich was left with some inheritance and not just the responsibilities of his brothers. They were very aware that their meager employment income and government benefits were not enough to sustain them.

Following the planning workshop, Russ and Betty completed all the legal and financial planning recommended by us. Once parents are educated on planning requirements for their child with disabilities, they typically complete their legal planning, including creating a special needs trust, working on their financial planning, and funding the special needs trust. Like most families, changes have taken place in Russ and Betty's lives since starting, and the plans continue to be monitored. Russ retired after many years of service at Eaton Corporation, and Richard married and moved to Columbus, Ohio. Russ and Betty have experienced minor health issues, and economic challenges and market corrections required adjustments in planning.

Russ and Betty worried most about where David and Darrin would live. They dreaded looking for housing and the day the boys might move to a new home. Despite being aware of their aging, and despite recognizing the importance of David and Darrin's finding their home, they could not bring themselves to be emotionally ready. Residential planning takes years and requires preparedness of parents and children. Most parents have extreme difficulty imagining their son or daughter with a disability moving out of their home. They are usually very concerned about their children's vulnerability and anxiety created by the move. Lack of adequate housing options and caregiving professionals are also major challenges in every state, important reasons why parents can be conflicted over housing decisions. Russ and Betty were no different.

They visited several group homes but were disappointed as none came close to their expectations and what they wanted for their sons. Russ and Betty were convinced no one could take care of David and Darrin the way they did but were realistic they could not care for their sons forever. They also knew that it was not just a question of being well fed and having a roof over their head, but availability of transportation, meaningful activities, getting along well with others, personal hygiene, and many other daily needs.

They needed to learn about housing options, including licensed settings such as group homes or Adult Foster Care homes, and independent living arrangements such as Supported Independence Programs or the Self Determination Initiative to help those with disabilities find the most suitable place at the right age. They also needed to learn about adult caregiving options.

An opportunity arose in 2006. One of David and Darrin's Special Olympics coaches, Pat Forkin, was also the director of Supportive Alternative Living in Milford (SAL), a nonprofit entity that was originally developed as a Supportive Independent Program (SIP). The independent program SIP assisted developmentally disabled adults in moving into their own homes and living, working, and worshipping in the community of their choice. Pat invited Russ and Betty to visit duplexes that could be available for their boys if they were ready. For the first time, Russ and Betty were satisfied with a housing option that could be considered for David and Darrin. The accommodations were good, staff was available daily along with meals, and transportation to take them to work was also provided. Their SSDI payments would pay expenses along with funding from Community Mental Health through Medicaid.

This was just what they needed, yet it was one of the most difficult decisions Russ and Betty ever made. They had many sleepless nights and shed tears. David and Darrin were forty and thirty-four, but in many ways they were still children. The boys were not effective at expressing what they needed or wanted. Their parents struggled with how they all would manage.

They reluctantly agreed to continue, and moving day arrived. Darrin was excited and ready. David wanted no part of it. He told his fellow workers at Kroger he was going to run away but not leave his mom and dad. Once he saw his new duplex, David changed his mind and wanted to live with Darrin and did not want to go home.

"We had a pizza party, and David and Darrin were invited to go next door to watch TV," Betty said. "A bit later we went over to see how they were doing and mentioned we were about to leave. They gave us a hug goodbye and continued to watch TV."

The boys settled into their new homes, adjusting more quickly than Russ and Betty did to their absence. It was quiet in the house, and it took a long time to get used to that. They were relieved the boys were in a safe home if anything happened to their own health. Russ and Betty talked to David and Darrin daily for weeks and visited them, at first daily and eventually less frequently.

It has been eleven years since David and Darrin moved into their home. Adjustments were needed, including in their jobs. Russ and Betty were always there to help any time things went wrong. Darrin was well liked at Home Depot, loading major purchases into vehicles, and slid into his new life with ease. David had loved his job at Kroger bagging groceries and bringing in empty shopping carts near their home. He was transferred to the Kroger branch in Milford near the boys' new home. It was a busier store and very stressful for him. He was also very sensitive to criticism in front of others from one of his coworkers. He was put on probation. David adjusted over time, and his work efforts improved.

Much to Russ and Betty's chagrin, David and Darrin proved difficult roommates and began squabbling, even though they remained close and seemed to enjoy each other's company. When the fights continued, David had to be moved to a house three doors down. They still live apart but get along well.

David and Darrin have learned to be independent and handle their daily problems. They still call their parents first whenever there are problems related to the home or at work. They have been gently but firmly directed to call the staff, and they try. Darrin is always more hesitant to do so due to his speech problems. Russ and Betty worry about the sons' lonely and limited social life. Darrin visits his other neighbors from the duplexes occasionally, but David likes to be alone and watch TV. The parents are glad their work gets them out of the house. Russ and Betty also see a difference in the caregiving staff. Some are genuinely interested in keeping the boys busy with various activities such as bowling, going to shows, to the park or shopping. Other staff members are concerned about the boys' safety and are reluctant to take them anywhere or let them go alone.

Russ and Betty are at peace knowing they have done everything possible in their personal planning and settling their boys in safe surroundings. They worry whether the boys will remain employable and will stay employed in the future. They also worry about the future of Supportive Alternative Living after the director retires. The boys are sensitive, and changes are very hard on them. Their health is also a concern as they age. The boys are insured through Medicare and Medicaid, but

these programs are subject to change due to federal government policies and the economy.

Richard is their hope for David and Darrin's future protection. He calls them regularly to see how they are doing. Unfortunately, David and Darrin cannot vocalize concerns they may
have. Richard lives two hundred miles away and is limited in
visiting and his ability to take them out to eat, go shopping, or
fix things around the house. For now, Russ and Betty take care
of all they can and know Richard is there for emergencies.

"We worry about their vulnerability. They have never been
able to express what they want. We have always mentioned to
them it is better to speak up, but they still don't," Betty said.

"Thankfully, they are concerned about one another's well-
being."

Plan early on for the future home of those with special needs. Residential planning takes years and requires that both parents and those with disabilities be prepared emotionally and financially for young adult children to move out of their parents' homes. Darrin and David were fortunate to find a stable environment although their parents initially dreaded the day they left home.

Learn about housing options that include licensed settings such as group homes or Adult Foster Care homes, independent living arrangement such as Supported Independence Programs, or other initiatives that help determine the most suitable housing at the right age.

Research caregiving and housing. The Reynolds learned much from working with Community Mental Health and their service providers to work toward getting the right amount of supervision and care available for their sons.

Transportation for jobs is important. Community Mental Health can provide programs teaching use of public transportation or can provide transportation as needed.

6

No True Perfection
in This World

Telling others about the challenges of daily life with special needs children is difficult for parents, especially during times of temper tantrums and severe ups and downs. The sense of loneliness can be compounded for immigrant families with all family overseas. This chapter describes outlets easing the burden of responsibility, including writing candidly in blogs and sharing through support groups and friends.

It was a busy time for the Sen Family. The week around Thanksgiving always was, and this year the Sens had several celebrations. Amar and Renu Sen, their daughter Riya, son Anuj, and their three other closest family friends took turns hosting the Thanksgiving dinner. The American holiday had become a very meaningful annual celebration for this group of first-generation immigrant families from India. The Sens also celebrated their son Anuj's and their friend Mala's birthdays the same week. Anuj already had two birthday parties celebrating his fourteen years. Then there was a sleepover on Friday after Thanksgiving extending to Mala's birthday party on Saturday.

"Are we planning anything fun for Christmas break?" Anuj asked after they left Mala's party. He had so much fun the last several days and craved the company of their family friends. He did not want it to end. He was happy and could have high scores for good behavior for the entire week, which was rare. There were lapses, but he recovered fairly quickly.

Anuj was exhausted but content. Mala and Amar let him sleep almost until noon the next day, followed by four hours of study time. Anuj did not argue or complain nor show his usual silliness. He happily did his math—adding and subtracting in scientific notation, composition. He learned about Haiku poetry and prepared to write his own. He studied the middle colonies in the America of the 1600s for history and read two short stories. He obediently cleaned up his messes and even helped put clothes from the washer into the dryer. He spent the rest of the evening watching his and his sister's baby videos in the basement.

Renu wrote gratefully and cautiously in her blog that night about the week's events. She ended with, "I feel tearful as I write this. I cannot remember when Anuj has been so good and so happy."

Anuj was born in 1999 and his fourteen years included more turbulent days than calm and happy ones. He was diagnosed with Autism at age ten, although he had many classic symptoms very early on. He began saying a few words between twelve to eighteen months and repeated rhymes. During that time, Renu took Riya and Anuj to Kolkata, India, Renu's native home for six months while Amar studied for his Master's of Business Administration at the University of Michigan. Anuj was in a day care program a few hours a day before the age of two. But he stopped talking completely after returning from Kolkata. Renu and Amar suspected he was confused by learning two languages. Bengali and English were spoken at home; Bengali was spoken exclusively in Kolkata. Within a few months, he began speaking in English again to his parents' relief.

Their reassurance was short lived. Anuj's language skills developed much slower than children his age. He also had difficulty interacting with other children, disrupted their activities and hit them out of frustration. The director of the day care program suggested Anuj be evaluated. His parents began a stream of visits with pediatricians and speech therapists. No one diagnosed Anuj with Autism. He was social, liked people, loved giving and receiving hugs. The pediatrician diagnosed him as developmentally delayed. Anuj had other issues that concerned his parents. He was not toilet trained until age five and did not respond when called, although there was nothing wrong with his hearing. Renu and Amar were bolstered by Anuj's love of animals. He knew their names and could point to the right toys from his animal collection. Amar and Renu hoped if he could learn about animals, he could soon learn other things as well.

They became anxious when Anuj was six years old and showed no progress. He was not catching up with his peers. They consulted specialists at the University of Michigan Hospital known for cutting-edge research. They needed to determine the type of therapy and treatment to help Anuj. They were referred to a professor but instead were seen by a post-doctoral student who conducted a single evaluation. The memory of her conclusive test followed by her comments still pierces Renu's heart. She said Anuj had mild retardation and that there was nothing Amar and Renu could do but to join a support group. "Don't kill yourselves trying to do anything," the student said.

Renu and Amar asked if they should consider Dr. Stanley Greenspan's DIR/Floortime therapy, a successful learning program for children with autism and other developmental delays. They were told again that Anuj did not have autism.[1]

Renu and Amar's experience with the University of Michigan professional was the low point in their research to find help for Anuj. Renu spent several sleepless nights after that

---

1 Greenspan, Stanley, Wieder, Serena. *Engaging Autism: The Floortime Approach to Helping Children Relate, Communicate and Think*. Perseus Books, 2003.

episode and felt devastated, more so because both parents were still in denial about Anuj's situation hoping that this was a long but temporary phase and Anuj would become normal. She wished she received encouragement about possible progress through therapy. Every parent needs that hope—something to hang on to and a belief that there is indeed light at the end of this journey.

Renu's frustration was mounting. She often felt alone. Amar and Renu did not have any family in the United States. They were typical first-generation immigrants who left their families behind to further their education and career goals. Renu was an only child, and Amar's older sister and both their parents lived in India. They met other young families who were in similar situations, also immigrants from the state of Bengal in India. Three of those couples--Ruma and Deb Mitra, Mala and Sunil Ray, Suma and Kavi Guha—were their core group of friends.

Asians experienced exclusion by law from the United States between 1880 and 1965, and were largely prohibited from naturalization until the 1940s. Since the Immigration and Nationality Act of 1965, the United States invited South Asians to migrate to the U.S. provided they were physicians, engineers, research scientists, pharmacists, or registered nurses. As a result of this law, the majority of immigrants from India and other Asian countries were highly educated and accomplished professionals.[2] Amar and Renu and their friends had similar educational and professional backgrounds in engineering, medicine, research, and academics. Most importantly, they were all from the same geographical location in India and spoke the same language, Bengali. Being together made them feel at home. They raised their children with similar cultural and academic values.[3]

2 Lee, Erika, Legacies of the 1965 Immigration Act, South Asian Digital Archive, www.sada.org, October, 2015.
3 Alba, Richard and Victor Nee. *Remaking the American Mainstream:*

Renu began to write her blog when Anuj was about six years old. Writing regularly about her challenges dealing with Anuj's progress or lack of it gave her an outlet to express her feelings. She was a talented writer, and her ability to narrate important incidents of their lives expressively and emotionally provided her with the calm she needed. She shared her blogs with her core group of friends and kept them informed of Anuj's status. She wrote about Anuj learning to play simple pieces on the piano from Riya, learning to tie his shoes, as well as about throwing tantrums in public places and creating embarrassment for her. Her blogs became her "Letter of Intent," an important non-legal document to record everything about a child with disability that is extremely helpful for the future caregivers. Their friends were genuinely interested in Anuj's development and were Amar and Renu's sounding board and objective when the parents had to make certain important decisions about Anuj. They rejoiced with the Sen Family at Anuj's smallest accomplishment and stood by Amar and Renu when they felt broken after disappointing incidents involving their son. They were extended family in their adopted home, and the Sens depended on them.

Renu recorded heartfelt and painful moments in her blog, such as this when Anuj was seven:

My dark double life, November 20, 2006

As the author of this blog I am all-powerful. I can portray my kids, their teachers, our friends, myself any way I wish. More often than not my own image is that of the long-suffering but patient and loving mother worrying about her son's future, looking out for him at school, trying hard to find the right balance between discipline and indulgence in handling him.

Assimilation and Contemporary Immigration. Cambridge: Harvard University Press. 2003.

While all of that is true, equally true is another side of the picture that only gets mentioned in passing, the details often being glossed over or smoothened out with attempts at humor or semantic tricks such as substituting "smack" for "hit." "Smack" sounds more like a friendly pat than an assault. It's probably shame more than the intent to deceive that sweeps under the rug episodes such as the times I've yelled at my son, "You are a bad boy and the police will come get you." (the most recent instance took place today) or sent him for a time out on the deck in the cold November weather. Today he fussed and screamed all evening, dropped his pants, scratched and hit while grocery shopping in the pre-Thanksgiving crowd, while friends were visiting, when I made an innocent statement at bedtime that he took exception to. I finally lost it when he was brushing his teeth and "smacked" him on the leg. "You hit me," he wailed. "You hit me." Somewhere in the flurry of emotions I noted with pride his improved use of the pronoun "you." Just a few days ago he would have said "Ma hit me." "Sorry," I said tearfully. "I just don't know what to do with you. You screamed and screamed and pinched me. How do you think that makes me feel?" "I just want to go away and live with my mom." I said, skillfully turning myself into the victim. Is that enough confession of my diabolical deeds for today? Or should I tell how quiet he became and how he wanted to get under his comforter and turn off the light, how much he wanted that particular scene to end?

Amar and Renu's daughter Riya was a little over three years older than Anuj and was sensitive to her home environment and her parent's challenges with brother Anuj. She grew up resenting that Anuj always got much more attention. She found her brother annoying and difficult to tolerate, let alone love him. How could you feel any affection for someone who once bit you in the arm in the middle of the night? Riya was only six when the experience of being awakened during a deep sleep at night deeply frightened her; she remained scared for days. And yet she cared for her little brother. She worried about him getting lost when he went on his first field trip at age two with other day care children and felt protective toward him when she found other children bullying her little brother.

Renu described one incident about their relationship in her blog:

> *And then there was the day before yesterday. Unable to bear his whining, I sent Anuj out to sit on the deck quietly for a while. It was a warm day and with his grime-streaked face and faraway out-of-favor-with-mom look, he seemed so forlorn that even his very irate sister's heart was touched. She gazed at him for a while through the patio door and then said something I couldn't hear. "O-range" he said loudly, separating and stressing each syllable solidly as he is wont to do. A few minutes later I saw him biting into a whole peeled orange, leaning over to keep the juice from spilling onto his clothes, looking a shade less bereft – fortunate recipient of his very annoyed but teeny bit loving sister's gracious bounty.*

Anuj's journey from a happy first grade with a wonderful and patient teacher who helped him read and write to a miserable second year with an inexperienced teacher of a crowded class jeopardized Anuj's progress and made him vulnerable. He was bullied, but the teacher never noticed. He kept running out of the class and was often punished. He was transferred to a special education class for some of the time, but the teacher could not handle him there. At home, everybody walked gingerly when Anuj was home. He could be quiet one moment, and a slight and simple comment could set him off completely.

He was six when Renu wrote:

Today it was "You don't need your jacket. It's warm outside." And there he was screaming in what I call his "animal" mode. It's when he gets a hunted and desperate look in his eyes, loses all control over himself and starts fighting for his life. That's just the time for me to lower my voice and talk soothingly and the effect can be magical — if I do it the right way. Unfortunately, his screaming releases my inner animal too. All my fears for his future, what people will think of him, whether he will ever be anywhere near normal come rushing in from their hiding places and there I am screaming beside him, a quivering mass of terror just like him. Today I yelled, so loudly the neighbors must have heard, "STOP SCREAMING RIGHT NOW." So much for setting an example of appropriate behavior.

Leaving an impression that he is an unrepentant screamer would not be fair. As he has grown he has become more self-aware and learned to do post-mortems on his behavior just like any adult. After all the screaming is done, he will come sidling up to me and look up into my face with an embarrassed smile on his tear-stained face. "I screamed at home. Not good. Use your words." My fears fade away like the phantoms that they are. I know he'll be fine when he grows up. Maybe a little eccentric. But he'll be fine.

That year Renu decided to homeschool Anuj. She was losing her confidence in the school's ability to cope with Anuj's moods and provide him with the right structure. She felt confident that she would be able to handle him a lot better at home, in a controlled environment. She looked up online resources and found educational materials. She took Anuj to soccer, karate, and music. The speech therapy continued at home. Renu later joined a homeschooling group in the third year that met once a week with group classes taught by parents. Anuj also started to go to school again for a couple of classes like music and gym. Renu could not tell if full-time homeschooling was helping him. Anuj had anxiety and was prescribed Prozac, a medication for attention, anxiety, and aggression. The medication helped but also had side effects. Renu was very stressed and desperate to find anything that could help Anuj with his behavior and what troubled him.

Amar and Renu's initial episode with the University of Michigan almost four years ago kept Renu away from approaching any professional for many years. She was not prepared to deal with insensitive professionals who pushed her in a dark world. The parents continued his speech and physical therapies hoping for progress in Anuj's speech and motor skills. Renu did her best for three years but was becoming exhausted with Anuj's anxiety. He could not handle school, and Renu could not tolerate him at home. Amar finally insisted on finding the right medical help for Anuj. They went back to the University of Michigan when Anuj was ten, this time to a well-known physician at the Autism Clinic. It took weeks to get an appointment; they had a completely different experience than before. The clinic did extensive evaluations using multiple sessions with different specialists. At the end the doctor confirmed the diagnosis of Autism, something Amar and Renu suspected all along. The doctor recommended therapy and introduced them to the therapist. Renu and Amar also talked to Anuj about the diagnosis. Anuj was aware that he was different but could not understand the reason. They were relieved that they had a diagnosis and were hopeful that the therapies would help Anuj overcome many of his challenges.

Having a diagnosis and a treatment plan was not an assurance of an easy life ahead for the Sen family. Anuj continued to vacillate between highs and lows in his behavior and yet also progressed in certain areas of academics, language, and motor skills. Renu was determined to work with his strengths and exercise as much patience as possible to see her son continue to move forward at home or with the help from school. Amar and Renu worried about Anuj's future. Will Riya stay involved in her brother's life despite the barriers his behavior creates? Will Riya and the children of their friends grow up and continue to accept Anuj the way they do now? They suspected all would be likely to move forward in their lives to achieve their dreams just as Amar and Renu did when they left India for their dreams.

Amar and Renu met at Indian Institute of Technology (IIT) in Kharagpur, one of the most prestigious engineering schools recognized worldwide. They were academically high achievers. Both grew up in the state of Bengal and had middle class upbringings where education achievement was a priority. In a conservative society where young men and women did not date, they were good friends with hopes of a long-term relationship. Amar graduated in mechanical engineering, and Renu completed her undergraduate degree in physics a year later.

Several of Amar's friends had moved to the United States for higher studies. United States universities were welcoming overseas students with a promising future. Amar enrolled in the master's program at the University of Kentucky followed by a PhD program at Iowa State University. Renu followed him to pursue a doctorate after completing her master's degree at Purdue University. They were finally in the same place after three years and were married a year later, in 1989.

Amar completed his PhD in 1991 and accepted a position with General Motors in Detroit, but Renu stayed behind for three years to complete hers. Those three years were lonely for both as they started jobs and finished school. Once Renu completed her doctorate, she joined Amar in Detroit, and they finally began to grow roots.

While Amar settled down at General Motors, Renu was not sure about pursuing a career in physics. Instead she worked part time at Ford Motor Company writing minutes for meetings. Then the children were born, first Riya in 1996, an absolute joy, and Anuj in 1999—the unsolved mystery of their lives. Renu found motherhood extremely satisfying and a more meaningful purpose than pursuing any career path, despite her education.

Soon after they moved to the suburbs of Detroit, Amar and Renu looked for other Bengali families and connected with the three couples who have been there for each other through the various phases of their lives. Each of the couples had a daughter close in age, and they grew up like sisters. Anuj was the only boy in the group. Their gatherings began with birthday celebrations of their children, weekend outings and picnics, celebrating Indian holidays, or just meeting for dinners at each other's homes. They made every effort to keep a balance between the western culture of their adopted home and the Bengali-Indian culture. They introduced the music, art, and literature of their homeland to their children. They cooked their favorite Bengali and other Indian recipes together on special holidays.

Each of them visited their families in India periodically. As time went by, the trips became somewhat more frequent as their parents in India aged, needed more help, and in some cases passed on. Losing a loved one is always sad; it is even more difficult when the distance between the oceans is so wide and the farewells are said from so far. The pain of not having closure is also felt by the close friends. Immigrant families often bear the stress alone and silently, whether it is the loss of a loved one back home or the challenges of raising a child in a different environment or work-related issues. Amar and Renu's core group of friends made sure they were not alone battling their challenges. Their involvement in Amar and Renu's lives and their genuine interest in Anuj's well-being had been a life support for Amar and Renu.

Amar decided to take a leave of absence from General Motors in 2000 to pursue his MBA at the University of Michigan to enhance his career. Renu decided to spend several months in Kolkata with her children at her mother's home. When she returned, Anuj's challenges with language, fine motor skills, and behavior began to grow, and Renu immersed herself in her children's care with complete focus on Anuj's development. She reduced her work hours and later quit completely. She tutored high school students at home in math and science subjects and enjoyed it. She realized that she was not using her education and could be a financial contributor to the family finances, but focusing on Anuj was her priority, and Amar supported her in her decision.

Amar and Renu's most challenging years with Anuj occurred while he was six and seven years old. Because Renu was home, she experienced more of the daily behavioral issues of Anuj and worked with the school teachers closely. Several individuals including professionals created a team to help raise their son. Renu wrote about heartfelt and difficult moments in her blogs during those years, yet she never stopped hoping for improvement or loving Anuj.

She wrote on November 11, 2006:

Every time I remember his teacher saying "He gets back on track when I manage to stay calm." I can feel my heart lurch. As a parent I am "allowed" to lose control sometimes but, as a public employee, she's not. I'm almost twice her age and have only two kids to handle. She's barely out of college and has to deal with a gaggle of kids all day in addition to Anuj. Maybe I won't send that long e-mail with good advice that I was planning to write to her. Maybe I'll just let her know that Anuj went to see his musical hero Billy Jonas last Friday and that he wrote a letter to the tooth fairy so she would give him a treat despite the fact that he lost the tooth he was supposed to hand over. I'll let her know that he counted the dimes and quarters the tooth fairy gave him and got some practice with the money concepts that are so hard for him.

Anuj was also developing an obsessive behavior pattern of curiosity and repetitiveness. His mind worked in strange ways, and it was impossible to guess what he was thinking and what his next question would be. Renu experienced excitement every time Anuj showed interest in something new or said something intelligent. But her heart fell when he reverted and had sudden temper tantrums, ignored her requests, and hit or bit her. Another blog describes Anuj's curious mind and personality at age seven very well:

December 5, 2006

Embracing (or not) the whole of it, uncertainty and all.

It's hard. Unless you are a Buddhist or some kind of mystic. You would think it would be easy for me to look at my child and see a whole person; Anuj, a seven-year-old boy with his quirks and his mischief, his questions and his syntax. The Anuj who just is who he is. The whole radiant being. But the fact of the matter is that, most of the time, there is a continuous ticker tape running in my mind that keeps switching between two states "He's normal, he's normal, he's normal" or "He's autistic, he's autistic, he's autistic."

In so many ways he's the typical seven-year-old, fighting imaginary enemies with his Jedi sword or whispering to me with mischievous sparkling eyes "I said touching butt in recess today." When his sister wants juice, he wants it too. When I ask him to do his homework he says "Not now." At times like these the "normal" ticker tape takes on a comfortable background quality like the hum of an old refrigerator.

But the switch often comes without warning. There we are engaged in friendly banter and casually I say something like "Anuj put on your shoes" and he explodes. He screams, scratches, hits and bangs the door. Maybe he already had his shoes on and I didn't notice or maybe it was something I should have remembered related to shoes. Nothing that, in my mind, justifies this betrayal of the conviviality between us. Suddenly he's alien, strange. And the other ticker tape starts up loud and ominous, "He's autistic, he's autistic, he's autistic." There are other times too. When his eyes somehow lose their luster. He ignores someone's question and starts off on something else. "Can I say I love you" he says and brings his face close to mine. But his voice is a monotone and he does not smile.

Today, after several days of the same "What will happen" and "What color hair will that man have when he is sixty-eight" questions, with the "autistic" ticker kicking into action multiple times, he finally asked me a new one. He wanted to know where the food goes when he eats. Greatly relieved by the change in topic, I told him about his esophagus, stomach and intestines. He said he saw it at the store (his dad confirmed later that there was a model at the toy store. I hotfooted it to the library after dropping my daughter at dance class and got a couple of books with vivid illustrations that, to my deep satisfaction, he was entranced by as he ate dinner. We're off to the museum this weekend. He needs more stimulation.

The sincere and honest posts were fascinating, and Renu and Amur's core group of friends watched for Renu's blogs and questioned when there were none for weeks. Did that mean Anuj was behaving well or was Renu too stressed to write anything? They offered more than a friendly support on the phone or kind words of solace. Soon after the episode at the University of Michigan when Renu felt helpless, Amar was traveling for work and Anuj was constantly unpredictable, friends made sure they were there for the family. Ruma and Deb lived in Dearborn, about twenty-five miles southeast of Farmington Hills, the suburb where the Sens lived. Ruma, a busy executive at Ford Motor Company, visited the family every Tuesday evening to spend time with Anuj for months. She had a nine-year-old daughter at home, and yet Renu and Amar felt grateful every time Ruma visited.

Anuj had the most difficult phase of his young life during his upper elementary and middle school years. After being home schooled for three years, adjusting to a school and classroom environment was very challenging. Middle school was the worst. Anuj often became aggressive and hit other students. Renu had to pick him up from school frequently. She was always nervous after dropping him off to school wondering if and when she was going to get the dreaded call from the principal saying Anuj was in trouble again and had to be taken home. He was on medication for anxiety, but the additional aggression was creating havoc for Anuj and everybody in the family. He was not able to express himself, but his demeanor showed he needed help. Later the family learned his extra aggression was a side reaction of his medications.

Renu still remembers a painful incident from when he was twelve. Her blog that evening was heart wrenching:

Thursday, January 13, 2011

"There is no god but there are some evil spirits who lie in waiting for someone to say 'I am at peace.'"

Today was a low point . . . and since low points come in a variety of flavors, it's no surprise that today was something new yet again.

Anuj actually had a decent day in school despite having been upset in the morning. But he came home upset about something his teacher said and all the other things that happened in the last few days and he went on and on. He seemed to quiet down for a while and asked how he can earn some extra tokens to make up for some of his consequences. I asked him to read the first chapter of Charlotte's Web *after which I would ask him three questions. He read it and, as usual, was unable to answer the questions. He usually can answer questions after a second or third reading and after hunting through the pages, a process he prefers to avoid. As usual, therefore, I suggested that he read the chapter again with the questions in mind. Then he snapped and started whining. He didn't even stop when my student came for her lesson.*

He knows that when someone comes to our house it's like a public place and he has to keep quiet and behave. So far he has honored this, which makes it possible for me to tutor. But today he went on and on, threw some mail on the floor, and then took off his pants (and underwear) and then actually came to the doorway of the room where I was teaching. Needless to say, I lost it at that point, asked my student to call her mom to pick her up and grabbed him and promised to punish him.

Well, that's about it. I totally lost control for about an hour. I told Amar that he had to take the rest of the week off and take Anuj to the doctor and manage things somehow because I was giving up and he should just pretend that I was not there. Amar tried to convince me that this was just another thing and nothing different from what they were already dealing with. For about an hour I lay in a fetal position and wailed and meditated on what would be a good poison for a quick death. But then I got up and finished cooking and called him and gave him more consequences and made him read and answer the questions.

He is going to be quiet and sober for the next few days. But the thing is, I can't trust him anymore. He has been quite good for the last couple of months, very good in public and at home. But it doesn't mean anything. He could be good for years and it wouldn't mean anything. At any time he could do anything. He's a crazy person with an erratic brain. There is no such thing as trust or logic or sense that one can rely on. He may be wonderful ninety-nine percent of the time but that doesn't mean anything.

There are all these wonderful, deeply patient, deeply loving people who care for their impaired children year after year without complaint, without breaking down.

Renu's anguish was felt by everybody. Kavi and Suma, one of the three couples of their core group stopped by the very next day after reading Renu's blog. They were sympathetic but they also agreed with Amar. It was one more of Anuj's behavioral pattern. It was more important to focus on what was bothering Anuj so much so that he felt compelled to remove all his clothing. Together, they counseled Renu and encouraged her to put this episode behind.

Anuj's ongoing challenges were at their worst in eighth grade when even the principal did not want him in school for more than a couple of hours. Most of his other classes were taken online. He was unpredictable most of the time and stressful for Anuj's teachers and family. Renu tried very hard to be rationale and be tolerant of the wide swings in his behavior. He was an innocent child one moment and a devil the next. The good days raised Renu's hopes, and she was not willing to give up on her son. She wrote when he was twelve:

Monday, October 3, 2011

A kind of perfection

There is no true perfection in this world. But every time we step back from the brink of the abyss and resolutely turn our backs on it, every time we lie abed all morning depressed and eating donuts but spend the afternoon walking outside and singing along with the chores, every time we fall and get up again — it's a kind of perfection. Anuj's day in school was fine today; but after a long time he suffered a meltdown in the car on the way back home. The trigger was trivial; I made a "mistake" and then yelled at him for whining while I was on the phone. Afterwards he himself was quite shaken by how upset he'd been and by the fact that he had reverted to many old behaviors such as throwing things in the car and opening the car door while it was moving. "I did this after a long time," he said. "Do you think I will do it again?" "Ma, I'm sorry I opened the door." "I promise I won't do it again." That's the perfection part that I was talking about - he screamed and kicked and threw and got consequences . . . but he stopped soon and he was genuinely contrite. I'm not sure if it's the long-term effect of the medication or maturity or both . . . but he's distinctly getting better at bouncing back. That's the best we poor flawed humans can do.

Anuj improved in high school, which he attended four hours a day. The special education teachers, the personal therapist, and the social worker worked together to help Anuj, and he began progressing steadily. The high school classes include cooking classes and "On My Own," a program designed to prepare the special education students for life after school.

Renu wrote when he was fourteen:

TUESDAY, SEPTEMBER 3, 2013

First day of school

It wasn't that bad actually. I sent an e-mail to Mr. Smith in the middle of all the screaming and he wrote back and said that overall Anuj did okay most of the time even though he was silly and said bad things some of the time. My mistake was asking questions.

Anuj came out after school quite calmly and sat in the car. (Riya got out later today than usual so she was in the car as well — in general she won't be there. Then I asked "How was your day?" "Good." "What happened?" "I laughed when Jaren cried." "Why did you do that? What was your feeling?" "Are you going to be mad?" "No, I just want to know." But in view of the fact that I've been mad on previous such occasions I guess my "no" was not believable and he suddenly took off screaming about Riya trashing his beard, then he started kicking her, scratched her, all in the moving car. Riya threatened to kill him. I cancelled stuff. All hell broke loose. Some of you know because you got calls. Anyhow after talking with you and me and some more screaming he calmed down and is fine now.

One is never too old or too experienced to learn. My learning for today:

Don't ask questions to a person who is stressed out and is liable to have an outburst.

Make sure that said person has nails trimmed.

3. Have protocol for outbursts in moving car: Stop as soon as possible and don't start again until all are calm.

Anuj will be eighteen soon. He has continued to make progress in the last few years; his silliness continues from time to time, but aggression is nowhere near what it was before. Overcoming the hormonal changes during his puberty had taken a toll on him and his family, but the dark clouds have lifted, at least for now. Although he is not anywhere near other children, Amar and Renu are very optimistic about his progress. His language skills have improved; he can read and spell well, although he still does not comprehend as well. His vocabulary is somewhat limited, and the syntax of a complex sentence can throw him off. His math skills are much better than any other subject. He can calculate fast and can also grasp mathematical ideas easily, including solving equations.

Anuj's motor skills have improved considerably. He learned to ride a bike much more easily, but it took him forever to tie his shoelaces, and his handwriting is still childish. He is a much more pleasant person now and can be fun to be with.

Anuj is nearing an important age where a lot of important decisions will need to be made. Amar and Renu attended one of my workshops in spring of 2014 and have completed their financial plan with the help of my firm and created a special needs trust along with their own trusts and wills. Their trusts have appointed their close friends as successor trustees (Sunil, followed by Mala, followed by Suma until Riya is thirty-five and willing to be the trustee.) They did their financial planning very carefully and purchased life insurance for Anuj's trust to help with funding. Per our recommendation, Amar is contributing the maximum allowed amount in his 401(k) plan as well as in their after-tax savings. Renu is considering working part time again to add to the family's financial savings plan. Their plan will continue to be monitored as Amar and Renu plan their retirement and Anuj's future housing arrangement. They are giving a great deal of thought on whether they should have partial guardianship over Anuj. Renu does not like the idea of taking over Anuj's rights in any area. Amar has always been more practical and believes that Anuj's vulnerability and irrational personality cannot be trusted.

Renu's persistence in keeping up with Anuj's education had paid off. He is on track to graduate from high school, although Michigan Special Education is available until age twenty-six. Anuj has declared that he will leave school in June 2019. What after that?

What is the future is a question constantly on Amar's mind. Renu handled all of Anuj's day-to-day challenges, meeting with his education requirements and medical matters, yet she was always more focused on the present and somewhat optimistic about the future. Amar is more realistic. He is proud of Anuj's progress and Renu's determined efforts in caring for their son. He wonders about the right path for Anuj after high school, whether they should try community college or job coaching. He worries if Anuj will be trainable, find employment and last in a job long enough if he is hired. Renu believes they have to try all their options and hope that something will work. They cannot give up hope.

As she wrote in her blog in 2011:

> The reason low points are low points is that there are high points to compare them with. There are pluses and there are minuses, but they always add up to something positive, maybe teeny-tiny but positive. Baby steps but forward, always forward.

Riya is nearing completion of her undergraduate degree. She plans to pursue her master's degree in math. Her relationship with Anuj is typical of siblings. She is more tolerant of Anuj's silliness since she has been away at school in Ann Arbor at University of Michigan. She has accepted that she will always be in Anuj's life looking after his best interest and protecting him.

It has been more than thirty-five years since Amar and Renu as well as their friends came to the United States. They are all American citizens. They have benefited greatly in their respective careers and have prospered in many ways. They have also contributed a great deal to their new country. Their children are achieving their dreams while this first-generation group of immigrants is slowly progressing toward retirement. They are still bonded deeply, but their lives are moving in different directions. They may not always live in Michigan when they retire. Who will be in Anuj's life? Their friend's children as well as Riya will have their own lives and families to focus on. There are no definite answers. Renu is right in believing that they will do the best in finding whatever is available for Anuj and for his future and will always remain optimistic and hopeful. She has been impressed by the work of Dr. Stanley Greenspan, who pioneered the Developmental, Individual-Difference, Relationship-based (DIR) Floortime approach in treating children with Autism. She is grateful to Dr. Greenspan for writing the following because it gives her needed hope:

"If we start working with a twelve-year-old boy who behaves like a four-year-old and keep going for as long as his learning curve is going up, by the time he is sixteen he may function like a six-year-old. He'll have made significant progress! If by the time he's twenty-two he behaves like a ten-year-old, he'll be able to live semi-independently rather than in an institution. If by the time he's thirty he can function like a fifteen-year-old, he'll be able to go to a two-year college, have a girlfriend, get a job, live a good life. Is this possible? We don't know. The experiment is yet to be done. But we do know that the brain and the nervous system are much more elastic than formerly thought, and we are now seeing large numbers of children who develop skills at later ages than once thought possible."[4]

---

4 Greenspan, Stanley, Wieder, Serena. *Engaging Autism: The Floortime Approach to Helping Children Relate, Communicate and Think*. Perseus Books, 2003.

Consider several ways of expressing ongoing challenges and engaging others in support. Renu's blog posts offered a personal outlet and helped her close friends know when she needed them, along with providing details and chronology of Anuj's Autism.

Look into alternative methods of education for children who cannot handle a regular school environment. Renu focused on home schooling and online education in addition to regular special education classes to ensure Anuj achieves all he can academically.

Think beyond immediate family for the role of a trustee for the special needs trust. Many families do not have members to take on the complex role of a successor trustee. Consider friends, extended family members or professionals such as a trust company, small CPA or law firms for this important role.

7

Our Beautiful Daughter,
Autistic and Bipolar

Dual diagnosis is the co-existence of the symptoms of mental illness and intellectual or developmental disabilities such as bipolar disorder and autism. The symptoms can also be in a combination of substance abuse or alcoholism with other intellectual disabilities or mental illness. Each separate illness requires its own complex treatment plan. Finding services and resources from Community Mental Health requires patience, diligence, and persistence.

The home phone was ringing again. Brenda Bentley tried to ignore the sound and go back to sleep, but a bad feeling made her sit up and check the time. It was 10:30 a.m. She jumped out of bed and grabbed the phone. She suspected correctly . . . school officials were calling. Annie, her young teenage daughter, was sick again, and the school asked her mother to take her home. This was the fifth time in the past two weeks.

Annie had started a new pattern. As soon as she returned home from school, she preferred to isolate herself in her room, rock and listen to music, sometimes all night long. She would not sleep and was exhausted when she went to school the next morning. She complained almost daily about being sick or too fatigued and begged to be sent home. The teacher did not know how to handle her and asked that Brenda be called to take her home. This time Brenda was exhausted from an almost sleepless night, despite taking Xanax, from hearing Annie's restless movements and her music. Brenda had just gone to sleep after watching Annie board the school bus. The last two nights, Annie had added one more unusual habit. Brenda found all of Annie's clothes on the floor in the morning. She had tried every outfit during the night unable to decide what she wanted to wear to school the next day.

Annie was a difficult child from her birth in 1988. Now as an early teen she was becoming unpredictable and it was taking a toll on Brenda. Her husband, Paul, had his own way of coping with Annie's issues. When he was not traveling for work, or entertaining clients as a sales manager for an engineering company, he stayed in bars until late at night. Alcohol was his way of keeping Annie out of his mind. Annie worried about Paul, imagining him in an accident and stayed up waiting for him. It was a punishing family cycle, with all three members circling around Annie's personality, strange behaviors, and a diagnosis of autism.

Brenda knew Annie was different from the moment she was born.

"From the time they wheeled her into my room in the bassinet, she never slept. Her eyes were wide open all the time," Brenda said.

Annie cried incessantly and slept on and off for short periods. Brenda's six weeks of maternity leave slipped by very quickly, and she was frantic when the babysitter she hired couldn't handle Annie. Brenda had to quit her job at General Motors Proving Grounds where she worked as the director's personal secretary. She loved her job and was looking forward to returning to work.

Paul had left General Motors for greater opportunities with a mid-level Fortune 500 company in sales and marketing. His work with military customers for specialty electro-mechanical systems entailed extensive traveling and entertaining clients.

"It was a very difficult time for me," Brenda said. "Paul traveled a lot, and I went from being very social in my job to being home by myself with a baby that never slept."

Brenda and Paul were high school sweethearts and married soon after high school graduation. They tried to have children for years. Finally, Annie was born fifteen years later. Now home with her difficult baby, Brenda began to have crying spells and experienced severe postpartum depression. Her ob/gyn was alarmed to see Brenda's condition at her six-week check-up and prescribed antidepressant medication.

Paul and Brenda struggled throughout Annie's childhood. She did not start talking until she was three. Brenda worried Annie wasn't talking and took her to their pediatrician at the children's hospital. He assured her there was nothing wrong.

"He said she's just not talking because she's an only child and you meet all her needs, so she doesn't need to talk," Brenda said.

Although she was a happy child before she began school, she needed to be kept occupied, whether it was with a balloon while they shopped or with a toy at home. In nursery school and kindergarten, Annie wouldn't sit still, pay attention, or play along with other children. She preferred to be alone but needed to be busy and was obsessive. She loved riding the mechanical horse at the grocery store and wanted to continue for hours. Paul and Brenda believe that she realized even as a young child that she was different. Though it seemed she was acting out, she was likely seeking attention.

Annie's behavior did not improve when she reached first grade. She was talking and communicating well by then, but her social skills were very poor. The teachers complained that Annie hid in play structures during recess and refused to come back in. She ran away from school at every opportunity and threw tantrums. School social workers visited the Bentleys to check on their home environment. Paul and Brenda took Annie to Beaumont Center for Human Development, where she was diagnosed with Attention-Deficit/Hyperactivity Disorder, or ADHD, and prescribed Ritalin. Annie rocked constantly and flapped her hands. Brenda asked the doctor if she could have autism. The doctor did not believe so, since Annie was talking, but suspected that Annie was developing a mood disorder. Paul and Brenda were confused and felt helpless. Annie was difficult and drove them crazy, but she was just a little girl. They couldn't fathom what was happening inside her brain.

Annie was recommended for special education by school officials in Livonia, where they lived in suburban Detroit. Her parents were relieved because the mainstream kids in school and on the school bus often bullied Annie, causing her to have meltdowns. Special education classes were smaller and better supervised than regular classes. Annie was showing more disarming and unusual behaviors. She lined up all her toys but never played with them. She climbed on furniture, rocked for hours on her bouncy horse, a big therapy ball, and her rocking chair, and laughed and laughed while rocking. She was obsessive and compulsive. Noise bothered her.

"When the furnace clicked on, she wanted to go downstairs and look at it. If she was asleep and we sneezed in the other room, she would wake up," Brenda said.

Brenda tried to invite her friends or take them to McDonald's, movies, parks . . . anything to get other children her age to be with her.

"Ultimately, she would have meltdowns and frighten the kids," Brenda said.

After a major meltdown during her seventh birthday party, Annie was admitted to Havenwyck Psychiatric Hospital. She was there for seven days and was prescribed Risperdal, an anti-psychotic medicine. Risperdal works by changing the effects of chemicals in the brain, and that finally helped Annie sleep. She was referred to University Hospital – managed by the University of Michigan Health System – for further testing and diagnosed with autism. Brenda and Paul felt defeated and hopeless, yet relieved to have a diagnosis. From then on for years they tried many therapies in hopes of helping Annie, including psychiatric, sensory integration, vision and art therapy, socialization groups, and music classes.

The Bentleys continued to struggle. Brenda dreaded not knowing what each day would bring or if she was going to have the energy to deal with Annie's issues and manipulation.

"She needed me to meet her 'needs.' She learned how to manipulate her 'wants' to 'needs,' and we accommodated her every wish that we possibly could to avoid conflicts," Brenda said.

When Annie was fifteen, her medications abruptly stopped working. She stopped sleeping again. The family car keys had to be hidden to stop her from sneaking out at night. She knew how to drive but was not old enough for her license. She managed to apply for charge cards and got them. She bought strange items such as hockey skates and variations of wigs that Brenda returned. She dressed very revealingly and strangely. If Brenda did not allow her to dress skimpily before school, Annie snuck the clothes in her school bag and changed in school. She started acting violently and broke a door, kicked in a cabinet, and fought with her parents constantly. Paul and Brenda tried very hard to be patient but lost their temper often. They felt the whole family was being sucked into a hopeless vortex. Desperate, they called Annie's psychologist and at his recommendation, Annie was admitted back to the Havenwyck Psychiatric

Hospital. This time Annie was diagnosed with bipolar disorder. Annie, their beautiful, troubled, only-daughter, had the dual diagnosis of autism and bipolar disorder at fifteen.

It started to make sense. Brenda had been trying to learn as much as she could about autism, and some of Annie's strange behavior still wasn't explained. Annie was in the Autism Impaired program when she started Livonia High School's special education. The program had just begun in many districts due to the rising population of students diagnosed with autism. Brenda met the five other students in the Autism Impaired program and occasionally compared notes with the other parents. Most with autism had many issues but none like Annie's. Brenda often wondered if Annie's illness was genetic, since one of Paul's aunts had mental illness. Brenda's father suffered from depression and anxiety, and committed suicide at fifty-seven. The two years following Annie's diagnosis of bipolar disorder and autism were the worst her parents ever experienced as they tried to cope with all aspects of both illnesses, each needing its own complex treatment plan. Along with her treatment, they worried about what her future would be after they passed. They sought help from professionals specializing in special needs planning. We worked with them to address their financial planning needs and their legal planning, including coordinating a special-needs trust for Annie.

Annie did not read well but was articulate and worked hard at areas that interested her. Her greatest achievement was passing driver's education and getting her driver's license, a difficult achievement. She was still undergoing occupational therapy, and her fine motor skills were weak, yet she played piano and wrote poetry. She excelled at performing at various music functions. Even though she was in special education, Annie asked to try out in the school's Creative and Performing Arts Program. She did well and was the first special education student to be admitted. She outperformed everyone and was very comfortable performing on stage. She also sang a song she wrote, called Bipolar Blues. Paul and Brenda also took her to FAR, a Therapeutic Arts and Recreation program where she played the piano for their annual fundraising performance at The Country Day School in front of seven-hundred people. Annie performed very well. It was a proud day for Paul and Brenda.

Annie eventually graduated from high school with a diploma. Paul and Brenda did not want her to graduate, preferring she get a certificate of completion and continue in school until age twenty-six as allowed under Michigan special education rules. They felt that she would be protected under the school system; Annie was not ready to be out in the real world. Annie refused to wait, she thought staying in school until twenty-six was just for what she called "slow kids." She did not think she was as needy as the other special education students. Annie attended a nearby community college, Schoolcraft, and took beginning courses. The counselor was very accommodating but one day called and told her parents she was good when she attended classes, but that she was never there. Paul and Brenda were surprised as they thought Annie drove to the college every day. Instead she visited shopping malls and coffee shops and hung around with boys. The college lasted a short time.

Annie attempted to work at McDonald's, volunteered at a senior center and charmed everyone at each, but no job lasted long. She was a beautiful girl but appeared lost and nothing made her feel good, nothing made her feel better. She was in and out of St. Mary's Hospital because she wanted to kill herself, cut herself, or drive her car into a tree. She wanted to numb her pain and drive away her demons. She just wanted to feel normal. She continued to receive therapy as an outpatient after each hospitalization.

Paul and Brenda were victims of trauma caused by Annie's illness and continued having difficulty coping. Brenda said it was a miracle their marriage survived. Brenda sought medical help while Paul took solace in alcohol. Brenda fought depression and was on several anti-depressant medications and gained weight in the process.

"It was rough on both of us. Paul was drinking heavily and many times wouldn't come home until 2 a.m. Annie would wait up for him, then get angry when he came home intoxicated," Brenda said.

Paul chose to stay away from home, often hanging out in bars. He changed jobs a few times as his drinking got in the way of job performance. He often chose to go up to the family cottage in Alpena in northern Michigan for the weekends by himself. Staying close to nature, fishing and being alone helped him recover from his work and family stress. Being away from Annie and Brenda for a couple of days helped him cope during the work week.

Brenda decided to take positive steps in her life. She went through the Weight Watchers program, lost thirty pounds and joined the program as a counselor. The job gave her an outlet to escape her constant problems, and she made new friends who are still part of her close circle. Paul and Brenda were often sad thinking that they could no longer attend outings as a family. Their attempted vacations were very stressful due to Annie's unpredictable behavior. They remember fondly Annie's happy times as a younger child at the family cottage in Alpena in summer. They went there most weekends, and Annie liked the continuity of going to the same familiar place. She loved the water and the bouncy horse she had there.

Annie was descending into the most difficult time in her life with attempted suicides and hospitalizations. With each attempted suicide, Paul and Brenda felt part of themselves dying with her. During her third visit to St. Mary's Hospital, the psychiatrists made the important decision that she could not be allowed to return home. Her life was in danger. She was recommended to be transferred to Rose Hill Center in Holly, Michigan, a residential treatment facility dedicated to helping adults with mental illness achieve a better way of life.

Rose Hill Center is well known for its success in rehabilitation of people with mental illness. The center's psychiatric rehabilitation program is based on the belief that recovery takes place when people receive professional psychiatric care while participating in meaningful activity. All work is done in a consistent, compassionate, dignified environment. Rose Hill opened in 1992 and provides residential care paid privately by the patient's family for a few months with the goal of transitioning patients into the community with supervision.

Paul and Brenda were hopeful Annie's life would finally be saved at Rose Hill Center. They didn't know how they could afford the cost. Paying privately cost three hundred dollars a day in 2008, the equivalent of four hundred dollars a day in 2017. That was out of the question, although Paul and Brenda were ready to do anything to save their daughter. Their only resource was to find public assistance if provided by a mental health authority. The Bentleys live in Wayne County, Michigan. The Community Mental Health of Wayne County would have to approve this cost for Annie to receive residential treatment in Oakland County, over fifty miles from where they lived. They began a tireless effort to plead with Community Mental Health to approve Annie's admission to Rose Hill with the help of their doctors. The hospital officials, psychiatrists, Paul, and Brenda cited Annie's mental illness diagnosis. Finally, Annie was approved through Gateway, the provider for mentally ill adults under Wayne County Community Mental Health.

A new chapter began for the Bentleys with desperate hope for change. Annie's stay had challenges, but she gradually adjusted to her new environment and responded to the psychiatrists, therapy, and medications. Rose Hill Center is in a peaceful setting, with four-hundred acres of land including woods, lakes, and fields. The tranquil setting provides grounds for healing. The residential care included safety and supervision, a huge relief for Paul and Brenda. Annie visited home a couple times a month, and Paul and Brenda also visited her periodically. She still had behavioral issues and was overly friendly with men. She was inconsistent in following rules and instructions at the center.

Yet life was calm and stable for almost eight years. Annie's being away in a safe setting brought some stability in Paul and Brenda's lives. Then, she started smoking and chain smoked; as a result, her multiple anti-psychotic medications became less effective. She takes Risperdal, Clozapine, Lithium, Ativan, Clonidine, and Trileptal. Annie began not completing her required chores and instead sat on the porch and smoked all day. This was not acceptable by Rose Hill standards. They warned her, but she did not change and was moved from the residential program to the extended living program, a more supervised program more like a group home with other men and women.

Annie's moving to the extended living arrangement was a huge disappointment to Paul and Brenda but it was a safer place for Annie. They also began to worry if the Rose Hill program would come to an end for Annie, and if Community Mental Health would stop paying for her treatment. Brenda went into a deep depression worrying about Annie and ended up requiring months of treatment and therapy. The psychologist suggested Brenda attend Co-Dependents Anonymous as she believed that Brenda had difficulty separating herself from Annie.

"It was like grieving. I think I had to finally accept she may never be normal. I always felt that maybe, maybe one day, she will be okay," Brenda said.

Annie's case manager also feared for her safety even though she was in a more restricted environment. Annie often misused her privileges and made unpractical decisions such as leaving the premises for long periods of time and hanging out with unknown people. She also skipped taking her medication from time to time. When reprimanded, she usually retorted that she was old enough to do what she wanted. Options for her care were worsening. The case manager suggested Paul and Brenda attain partial guardianship for Annie through court appointment. This would allow them to make residential and medical decisions for her, and Rose Hill staff and doctors could be open in sharing Annie's medical and personal matters with her parents.

Paul and Brenda were very hesitant to take this difficult step. Guardianship permits the state of residence to remove a person's legal right to make decisions for his or her own good. It pits the person's rights of autonomy, self-determination, and self-definition against the state's interest in protecting people from personal and financial harm when they are incapable of making sound decisions. Annie resisted, and it was painful for her parents to go through the process of taking certain rights away from her. They knew it was necessary for her safety. Paul and Brenda are now Annie's full guardians, and Annie has accepted and gotten used to the arrangement.

During the process of obtaining Annie's guardianship, Paul and Brenda had to declare her either a developmentally disabled or a mentally ill adult. They were advised by professionals to choose Developmental Disability (DD) as that was her primary diagnosis. This created several difficulties. Rose Hill Center specialized in recovery for the mentally ill. With a DD status, Rose Hill Center could refuse to have her as part of the program. This also changed her service provider to Community Living Services (CLS) from Gateway. CLS provides services and primarily funds and manages group homes for the developmentally disabled and does not handle homes or treatment for the mentally ill. CLS officials wanted the Bentleys to visit and consider a group home for Annie under their management. The Bentleys were very disappointed when they visited the group homes. The residents had cognitive impairment of different levels and were not compatible with Annie; she functioned at a much higher level and would have been miserable. Paul and Brenda couldn't imagine her living in the group homes for those with developmental disabilities.

Paul and Brenda have wondered if they should change Annie's status to Mentally Ill, or MI, but have been advised against doing so as autism is her primary diagnosis. She still has all the characteristics of a bipolar individual. Lithium keeps her stable, without which she reverts to erratic bipolar behavior. Another challenge for Annie is also that her community mental health service provider is in a different county than Rose Hill. Although Community Mental Health of Wayne County paid for her stay in Rose Hill in Oakland County for eight years, Paul and Brenda are very concerned they may eventually back out. They are tired of opinions between various professionals and confused about what direction to take if or when Community Living Services refuses to fund Rose Hill. This is not uncommon for individuals with a dual diagnosis. The complex and separate treatments can mean a lack of continuity of care, and those with a dual diagnosis tend to be bounced between programs and family care due to the misalignment of services relative to their needs.

Paul and Brenda have managed to continue CLS paying for Annie's stay at Rose Hill Center but the future is unknown. Rose Hill Center now has other patients with a dual diagnosis, some of them with autism. Some are from other states and pay on a private basis. An autism specialist visits with them regularly. Paul and Brenda have to pay privately to use their services.

Annie's stay at Rose Hill Center has given Paul and Brenda

time to think about their future as well as revisiting planning for Annie after they are gone. They were saving for their retirement and concerned about what will be left for Annie when they pass. Annie qualified for Supplemental Security Income (SSI) and Medicaid at eighteen, and Medicaid had been paying for her health benefits including her stay at Rose Hill Center. Although Medicaid has been covering many of her needs, the Bentleys have created trust documents for themselves as well as a special needs trust that will be funded upon their death to supplement her government benefits. My firm monitors their plan on an ongoing basis. Paul is now retired and spends time between their cabin in Alpena and home in Livonia. Brenda accompanies him to Alpena from time to time. She retired from Weight Watchers after working there for many years.

Annie is almost thirty, attractive but in many ways is like a child. She worries about her future, especially life after her parents are gone. She has worried about this since she was thirteen years old. Men at Rose Hill Center are attracted to her and she leads them on, but becomes bored with her suitors in a few weeks and breaks up. These men are on emotional roller coasters themselves and go through a difficult time after a break up with Annie. Brenda keeps hoping that someday she will gain maturity and not make irrational decisions. Annie recently met a young man with Asperger Syndrome who adores Annie. He is an engineer, holds a job, and was in the air force. He seems devoted to her and has never been happier. No one knows how long this will last, but Annie has not been this happy in years.

Paul and Brenda find thinking of Annie's future after they are gone depressing and discouraging. She is an only child and there is nobody in the family that is close to her. All uncles and aunts are older, and the cousins are busy with their own families. Although one of her male cousins is named as her trustee for the special needs trust, Annie and her cousin don't have much of a relationship. If necessary, Paul and Brenda may research hiring a professional trustee to work with the nephew named as trustee.

Brenda sometimes wonders if the best solution is for Annie to leave this earth before her parents. She will mourn her death but will be relieved. Paul disagrees. He still hopes that she will be okay, and although she could not live alone, their home will always be open for her.

Learn about coordination of benefits for adults with a dual diagnosis from local Community Mental Health. An individual with dual diagnosis can have a developmental disability and mental illness like Annie or substance abuse and other disabilities. The Bentleys learned it is challenging to coordinate benefits and find community-based programs for an adult needing separate treatment plans due to lack of collaboration. Systems must be arranged to meet the needs of people with chronic reoccurring diagnosis.

Consider whether a guardianship is necessary for a mentally ill person. As with the Bentleys, the process can be complex. Symptoms may be intermittent, and those with mental illness may resist legally imposed assistance. This makes it hard for a court to consider whether they can care for themselves. The goal is not to interfere with a person's independence, as Annie's parents wanted most. There are also concerns on managing government benefits. In some cases, appointing a health care proxy, granting financial power of attorney or establishing a "representative payee" may work but may not be enough. A growing number of states have established psychiatric powers of attorney which, once signed by an individual, enable the agent, with agreement from a doctor, to admit them to a psychiatric hospital despite their objections.[5]

Learn about types of guardianships. Full guardianship generally invests an individual with responsibility for medical, residential and a wide range of personal care decisions. In some states, limited guardianship invests the guardian with specific responsibilities—such as health care and housing—with the ward retaining all other decision-making authority. Temporary or partial guardianship may be granted for a limited period in response to an emergency. Obtaining full guardianship can be a time-consuming process and requires planning.

5 Salzman, Leslie. Guardianship for persons with mental illness, Association of American Law Schools, 2011.

8

Daddy, Please Don't Go

The burden of parenting a special needs child can increase the amount of stress on a marriage. Additional issues can arise in determining which parent shoulders the primary responsibility and the different ways each parent handles emotions. The divorce rate in families with a special needs child is about the national average, yet it can be higher depending on the degree of disabilities, available resources, and others to help.

It was a beautiful fall morning in October. Melony was waking up to a busy day ahead. She slowly woke and removed the curtains to look outside. The fall colors were brilliant as far as her eyes could travel throughout her yard. This was her favorite season of the year. Both her daughters were born in fall, and their birthdays always coincided with visits to the cider mill, hay rides, Halloween parties, and their birthday parties. She took a moment to reminisce and wondered how the years had gone by.

Today was very special. Julie, her younger girl, was having her thirteenth-birthday party. They had talked a lot about Julie becoming a teen this year. It was a time to become more responsible, practice things she had learned in the past year such as making her own sandwiches, taking showers without help, helping with household chores, and staying home by herself after school until her mother or her older sister Megan got home. Julie had come a long way in her overall development since she was first diagnosed as Autistic around her third birthday. Although she was turning thirteen, she acted like a seven-year-old in many ways.

Julie wanted the party near their home, at the club house of their subdivision. The theme was balloon and bubbles, her two favorite things. Melony had found a young man who made many figures and shapes with balloons, and she also ordered a bubble machine. She invited a few of Julie's school friends from the Plymouth Canton Autistic Impaired (AI) program, some from her swimming program, a few from the subdivision, and her two cousins. Melony's parents and her sister and brother-in-law were also coming for the celebration. Melony was excited but a little anxious because she had not heard from her husband Matthew in several hours. He was traveling abroad for work and was scheduled to return that afternoon well before the party.

Julie was daddy's little girl. Julie and sister Megan, who had just turned fifteen, were very close to their dad. Matt, unfortunately, did not always have the luxury of time for his family, especially since he was promoted to vice president of sales and marketing in a computer engineering company two years ago. His company was based out of Austin, Texas, but Matt worked at their office in Novi, Michigan. The promotion gave him the challenges he loved, the recognition he deserved, and a substantial pay raise, bonus, and other benefits. It also came with the responsibility of looking after the growth and profits of the company. He oversaw twenty national managers from various regions within the United States as well as Canada, Mexico, United Kingdom, and the Netherlands. The company was very pleased with his work ethic, his capabilities in juggling various time zones for meetings, and maintaining his travel schedules. The company was making steady progress under his leadership.

Balancing work and family life was getting harder for Matthew. Melony was increasingly impatient and often wondered where their careers would lead. She had a pretty responsible job at Ford Motor Company as an electrical engineer. Both Megan and Julie were involved in various activities, and Melony was tired of being in charge of all their commitments. Julie had speech therapy, Applied Behavior Analysis (ABA) therapies, and doctor's visits. Matt was a loving husband and dad, but even before his promotion he was dedicated to his work and extremely ambitious. Melony found herself changing her commitments and meetings at work to accommodate Matt's schedules. She often relied on her parents who lived in nearby Ann Arbor, Michigan.

Matt felt guilty all the time. He was very torn between his family's expectations and needs and those of his company. He was always stressed after returning home from late meetings past Julie's bedtime, letting Melony handle the parent-teacher meetings for both the girls and missing special occasions with the family. Melony and Matt had not had any personal times or dates in months. It was not always Matt's work that came in their way. Julie had difficult days quite often, and Melony was worn out. Either Melony was too tired or at times angry for no discernable reason. Megan and Julie also missed their dad and wanted his attention when he was home. Melony and Matt often discussed their challenges behind closed doors after the girls went to sleep. There didn't seem to be any resolutions, and they knew Megan and Julie sensed some of their tension.

The party was at 4 p.m. and scheduled to last two hours. Matt's flight was scheduled to arrive at 1 p.m. from Amsterdam. Melony and Megan were concerned Julie might throw a tantrum if Matt did not arrive in time for the party. The festivities began on time with Julie's friends enjoying the balloons and bubbles. Julie clapped and giggled throughout the evening and was enjoying her special day. She asked about Matt when it was time to cut the cake. Megan had tears in her eyes, and Melony controlled hers. Melony promised that even if Matt couldn't come to the party, he would be home soon. In her mind, this was an addition to the layers of disappointments and frustrations built over the last few years. Julie held her composure, seemed to have a great time, and did not ask about him again. Megan was sad, and Melony was disappointed one more time.

Matt finally arrived and stood over Julie's bed late that night after she had gone to bed waiting for her dad. Megan was still studying in her room. Melony was in their bedroom and heard Matt return home minutes before. She was afraid of her reaction. She was sad, angry, distressed, yet screaming and fighting were not her style. She wanted to maintain her composure for the sake of her two precious children who were at a very sensitive stage of their lives. She was also trying to be reasonable and knew Matt wouldn't miss Julie's party if he could help it. Somehow nothing made her feel better. She tiptoed to Julie's room. Matt stood there with tears in his eyes and gently stroked her forehead.

"Happy birthday sweetheart, I am so sorry," he said. Julie stirred briefly, opened her eyes slightly and whispered, "I love you, Daddy," and went back to sleep with a smile on her face.

In the living room, before Melony could say anything to Matt, Megan stormed in the room and quietly and fiercely whispered "How could you, Dad? Is your work more important than Julie's thirteenth birthday?" They all had tears in their eyes . . . Megan's were of anger and betrayal, Matt's were of guilt, and Melony's were of sadness. Melony also sensed a silent, invisible gorilla in the room that night; it was an omen of something onerous unfolding soon.

Matt had experienced a series of travel problems and missed his first flight, barely making it to the next. His battery was dead on his phone and he could not call Melony. His reasons were genuine, but it did not matter. Matt couldn't sleep that night, nor could Melony. He had been giving a great deal of thought to his life, his family, and his career. Melony was trying to read his mind while nursing her own emotions and thinking about Megan's words and anger. Julie had spared everybody by not reacting and breaking into sobs. She had come a long way in these past two years in controlling her emotions, but she still had her up and down days.

The morning seemed normal on the surface. Julie was overjoyed to see her dad and could not stop talking about her party. After sulking initially, Megan came around and joined the family for breakfast. Matt asked Megan if she could spend the evening with her sister while he took Melony out to dinner.

They had an early dinner at their favorite seafood restaurant. The conversation was guarded but casual. They avoided talking about Matt's job, his travels, and Julie's birthday party. Melony looked at Matt and saw the same deep blue eyes that made her fall in love with him twenty-two years ago. Matt was handsome, and his slightly graying temples made him look even more attractive. She wondered if Matt still thought her to be as attractive. He always said he was smitten by her long neck, auburn hair, and hazel eyes.

They met in their junior year at University of Michigan's School of Engineering. Matthew Ward was a computer engineering student and Melony was studying electrical engineering. Melony Cook grew up in Ann Arbor; her father was a practicing physician and a professor at U-M School of Medicine. Both her parents were Michigan graduates and so was her sister Jackie, two years older and a student at the Michigan Law School. Both Melony and Jackie were talented and well-rounded students. Matt's father was a mechanical engineer, a retired naval officer and had settled in San Diego working for a large engineering company. His mother Jane was a retired schoolteacher. Matt and his younger sister Lara, a software engineer in Silicon Valley, grew up in many cities and attended several schools due to their dad's postings. He was an exceptionally bright student and chose University of Michigan over many others with a scholarship. Both Matt and Melony were close to their families and had comfortable upbringings.

Melony's sister Jackie introduced them. It did not take too long for them to realize that there was a strong chemistry there and a lot of common interest. They started dating. By the time they graduated the following year, Matt had a job offer with IBM in New York but Melony decided to pursue her master's degree at University of Michigan. Matt traveled to Ann Arbor once a month, and Melony flew to New York occasionally. It was difficult for them to stay apart; they were best friends and madly in love. Matt proposed to her just before she finished her degree eighteen months later. Melony was in seventh heaven. Life was wonderful and promising. She had just been offered a job at Ford Motor Company, and Matt was trying to return to Michigan.

Matt and Melony were married two years later on a beautiful spring day in 1993, and life couldn't be better. They bought a home in Plymouth and lived their dream life of love, fun, travel, family, friends, and great careers. Matt joined a mid-size, fast-growing computer company and worked out of its Novi office. Melony loved the challenge and excitement her job at Ford Motor Company offered.

Melony was methodical and organized in everything she did. Matt always looked at the big picture and planned ahead. They were close to their parents and sought their advice on many matters as they settled down. They enjoyed a good income and balanced finances between enjoying their young lives and saving for the future. They frequently complimented each other Their occasional arguments were on inconsequential matters.

A little over two years after their marriage, they were blessed with Megan, a beautiful blue-eyed baby, just like her father. Life became busier managing a child and their careers. Melony's sister Jackie was also now married to Daniel, and they lived in Birmingham. They had a son just a little older than Megan. Melony's mother was thrilled at being a grandma and visited and helped both Jackie and Melony often whenever she was needed. Fifteen months later, Melony was expecting again. They were thrilled. This baby would complete their family.

Julie was born near Megan's second birthday in early fall. This daughter was born with her mother's hazel eyes. She was beautiful, healthy, and a good baby. Megan welcomed her baby sister with excitement but was also jealous of all the attention Julie received. Melony loved being a mom to her two babies, and Matt was a great dad. Life was fulfilling.

Matt and Melony agreed to have a full-time nanny for their two girls when Melony went back to work after her two-month maternity leave. The nanny Eva was a loving woman in her mid-forties with an early education background and loved children. She fit into her role in the Ward family very quickly and made Matt and Melony's lives easier to manage.

Both Melony and Eva noticed some concerns about Julie around the same time. Megan was born in 1995 and Julie in 1997. They started observing issues with Julie developing slower than Megan when she was six months old. Melony remembered how excited Megan was when she picked her up at the day care. Julie showed no reaction or sign of excitement or recognition when Melony saw her at the end of the day. Eva felt the same way. At seven months, she did not respond to her name. She showed no interest in wanting to sit up and when she did, she sat in one place for long periods of time. She did not babble like Megan did at her age. Melony was becoming concerned as she watched Julie develop more slowly than her sister. At her six-month check-up, her pediatrician suggested the parents be patient but asked that they report back in a few months.

In the months following the pediatrician's visit, new discoveries about Julie changed the Ward family forever. Julie demonstrated more signs of aloofness, lack of interest in playing with any toys, and even in eating food. Eva found feeding Julie challenging. Julie rarely made eye contact, and they noticed her rocking gently whenever she was in a sitting position. Melony and Matt met with the pediatrician again and asked if Julie had Autism. She said it was early to tell but it was possible.

Melony felt devastated and Matt handled the news more restrained. Although this was not a firm diagnosis yet, Melony and Matt both knew that this may not change, they may have to accept the reality and plan their lives around Julie's needs. Eva's care of Julie was a blessing for Melony and Matt as their career demands grew along with the need to also focus on sister Megan. Matt noticed certain unfamiliar things about Melony. Melony often wondered if she did something wrong during her pregnancy that could have prevented this. Did she exercise too much, could the few times she had wine during early pregnancy be the reason for Julie's issues? She became obsessed about learning more about Autism and if there was a cure. She loved her work, but Julie's problem became her priority. Nothing else mattered.

Melony and her sister Jackie grew up in a very loving but strict disciplinary environment. Their father Dr. William Cook was a renowned physician, a specialist in nephrology. Their mother Brenda was a registered nurse but quit working after Melony was born. Both the girls were involved in various activities and were expected to be the best in whatever they did. They both excelled in academics as well as music and sports. Melony was a perfectionist and Julie's possible diagnosis of Autism was hard to accept in her perfect world. Matt was more balanced and took life as it came. He excelled in school and college but was easy going. It was difficult for him to see Melony's anguish and disappointment.

Julie did not walk until she was almost two and had not said a word. Melony's parents were equally concerned. They came from the world of doctors and specialists and suggested Melony and Matt visit neurologists and genetic specialists at the University of Michigan hospital. Additional testing confirmed that Julie indeed had Autism Spectrum Disorder (ASD). Melony accepted the reality of the confirmed diagnosis, but in many ways it changed her. Matt noticed she was quiet and non-communicative and broke into tears very easily. Melony's parents and sister noticed the changes, too, and suggested Melony visit a psychologist. It was obvious she was experiencing depression, not uncommon for parents of children with disabilities. Matt agreed to visit the psychologist as well; they were partners in this battle and Matt was behind Melony every step of the way.

Melony and Matt also started Julie in the Applied Behavior Analysis program (ABA) and speech therapy and enrolled her in the preschool program. Julie was three and Megan had just started kindergarten. Julie was having frequent temper tantrums. She began to say a few words but banged her head and cried nonstop until they figured out what she needed. Eva was very patient with her but at times was worn out. In the middle of all the chaos and challenges, Megan was a joy for the family. At times she became scared when Julie threw a tantrum, but she was always the first to hug her and calm Julie down.

A few months before Julie started preschool, Matt was asked by his company if he would consider enrolling in the executive Master of Business Administration program at the University of Michigan. It meant a time commitment to study and attend sessions once a month. Matt was excited but also concerned how he and Melony would handle the added pressure with Julie's demands, including frequent ABA and speech therapy sessions. Melony's parents encouraged Matt to sign up for the program and offered to help as much as they could. Matt and Melony were fortunate to be able to afford the expensive ABA therapy;

they knew for most families this was a huge financial drain. ABA therapy focuses on positive behaviors and reducing those causing harm; without insurance it can cost up to $45,000 a year.

For almost two years Matt traveled for work and spent extensive hours completing his MBA. Melony managed the household, their children, and her career. Matt, Eva, and Melony's parents helped as much as they could, but Melony often silently felt that she shouldered the major responsibility. Matt often felt guilty about not contributing enough. Their family times were stressed not knowing how Julie's behavior would be, and Melony was detached when Matt and Melony were together. They did not realize a gradual rift developing between them. Matt had difficulty understanding Melony's inability to accept Julie's diagnosis and how it was changing her as a person. Melony felt that Matt did not take Julie's issues as seriously and remained more dedicated to work than the daily challenges caring for Julie.

Julie began the regular special education program at five. Both Matt and Melony attended a workshop on special needs planning that my firm had presented through the school. Matt was a planner, and they both agreed that they needed to do their financial planning, create their living trust, a special needs trust for Julie, and other related documents. It was important for Julie to be eligible for any government benefits for which she could qualify. They both felt Jackie and then Daniel would be the best choice as a guardians and future trustees for their two daughters. Matt's family, including Lara, lived too far but Lara was listed as a guardian and successor trustee if Jackie and Daniel could not fulfill the role. They had a savings plan for retirement and college education for Megan in place. It was recommended that they not start a savings plan for Julie yet. They had adequate term life insurance for the surviving family in the event of an untimely death of either one of them, and they also purchased a life insurance plan for Julie's special needs trust called Second to Die Whole Life insurance. The Second to Die policy insured a tax-free benefit for both Matt and Melony for Julie's special needs trust. All the trusts were revocable, allowing the family to make changes as and when necessary. They also made sure both Matt and Melony's parent's planning were coordinated with their own. Julie's planning was done in anticipation of her qualifying for SSI and Medicaid at eighteen and other benefits as needed and available.

Matt's absence from family dinners and some special occasions were not unusual, and the family had accepted that. Matt was very conscious of this and tried to make it up by spending as much time with the girls whenever possible. While Melony took charge of the household matters and Julie's weekly therapies, Matt handled all the financial matters of the family. Both Matt and Melony made a priority to keep each other informed on updates as best as possible and as time permitted.

Melony endured several incidents when she found dealing with Julie almost impossible. One evening when Julie realized her favorite macaroni and cheese was unavailable for diner, she lost her temper completely. She threw her dinner plate on the floor, ran all over the house screaming, banged her head on the wall constantly, and finally laid on the floor wailing. Nothing could calm her. It took over an hour to settle her down, and Melony was exhausted. She had a long day at work and Matt was out of town. Julie was ten. Megan had gotten used to her sister's temperament but was always scared when Julie was out of control. Melony remembered crying several hours after the tantrum, feeling alone in her battle and missing Matt terribly.

Melony also remembered another incident at her sister Jackie's house. They were invited to Jackie and Daniel's for a family dinner. Melony and Jackie's parents were there, too. Megan, Julie, and Jackie' son Aaron were playing outside after an early dinner. Matt had just left for the airport after eating. Julie was about nine years old. Suddenly, Megan burst inside the house saying that Julie was upset with them and had run away from the house. Aaron was following her. Melony immediately got in her car and started looking for them. She found Julie several blocks down screaming and crying, with Aaron trying to catch up to her. Melony parked her car ahead of Julie and caught up with her, hugged her, and calmed her down. It was scary; she could have easily run into the oncoming traffic. Melony's family was there to calm all of them down, but Melony was angry and frustrated. Why do awful episodes happen when Matt is away?

Julie's thirteenth birthday was special. Julie had worked very hard on many of her difficulties for the last two years. She was now much more in control of her emotions, and her temper tantrums were rare. She spoke in clear sentences and was able to express what she wanted. Melony, Eva, and Megan were her safety net, but she was happiest when she was with Matt. Julie was very excited about her birthday, was counting days and could not wait for her Dad to be there. Melony's disappointment was deeper because of Julie's hope to see her Dad on her special day being crushed. She was just relieved that Julie did not make a scene. She knew she and Matt needed to face their issues.

Matt asked Melony if they could go for a drive and talk. Melony agreed, they both wanted to clear the air and bring out unsaid feelings that had been piling up for months. Their home was not the right place to talk without worrying about Megan and Julie listening. Matt had given a lot of thought to what he was going to say and struggled to find the right words. He explained to Melony why he felt their marriage had serious challenges, and it would be best if they separated.

Melony was stunned but not surprised. She had sensed both their unhappiness for a long time. But she wondered if they had really reached a point of no return. A few years ago they sought counseling when Melony was having difficulties with Julie's daily tantrums and refusal to eat, compounded by not always having Matt around when she needed him. The counseling helped bring out issues of expectations, communication, sharing responsibilities, and dealing with a difficult child. Matt and Melony were both equally intelligent and accomplished professionals but were experiencing major challenges in their marriage brought about by raising a child with a disability and the other demands of life. Counseling and efforts in communication were not helping enough to overcome the anger, sadness, difference in opinions, and how each accepted Julie's disability.

Melony accepted this new reality calmly and realized that despite their respect for each other, the last several years had separated them in a way that was impossible to glue back. She remembered a number of incidents when Matt had tried hard to live up to her expectations, deal with her emotions, and urged her to accept the fact that Julie had a disability. She knew Matt was a loving father and would do anything for his daughters. Somehow, their nest was broken with all the tumultuous challenges and was not strong to enough to hold its own any longer.

Matt was tired of the silent tension between Melony and him. He was a good father and had been a good husband but was not able to fulfill all that was expected. Was that enough grounds for a separation? A divorce? Was he being selfish? Was he being fair to Melony? She had suffered a great deal from the day Julie was born, but so had he. They were different people now, and life had to go on.

The months that followed were rough on the whole family as Matt moved out. They attended family counseling and endured Megan's anger at both parents, Julie's lack of understanding of why her dad was not living at home anymore, and her crying spells every time Matt left after each visit. They experienced disappointment and sadness, and both sets of their parents tried to help. Melony and Matt needed to sort through how best to see and take care of the children and a division of assets.

Their divorce was a mediation proceeding where Matt and

Melony worked with a neutral third-party mediator on all matters including division of their assets, custody of their children, child support and maintenance, retirement plans, and taxes. They also followed recommendations and worked with a mediator familiar with special-needs planning. Although there were no open arguments or fights, both Melony and Matt experienced tremendous sadness and a sense of failure. Melony felt bitter but controlled her emotions. The post-divorce settlement and agreement went as smoothly as possible given their inner struggles.

Matt and Melony had accumulated assets over the years and had similar amounts in their individual retirement accounts. They divided their other savings equally. Melony wanted to continue living in the same home, and Matt bought a home a couple of miles away. His income was higher than Melony's, and he offered to pay a portion of their mortgage as well as any additional expense for Megan's college beyond her college savings plan. He was very fair with his child support, and they arranged joint custody of the girls. They also agreed Matt would let Melony know ahead of time about his work travel plans. He would have the girls full time every other weekend and visit them as often as possible.

Julie's special-needs planning needed to be revisited in light of her parent's divorce. They had a stand-alone revocable special needs trust and were co-trustees. The Second-to-Die life insurance policy would fund Julie's trust, and upon their deaths their other assets would be divided equally between Megan and Julie's special needs trust. Megan's inheritance would be held in a trust until she reached thirty-five. Matt and Melony agreed to leave the terms of agreement the same. There was no need for each parent to create a new trust for Julie. They would each pay fifty percent of the premium for the insurance for the special needs trust. Matt trusted Jackie to be ideal as a successor trustee, and that did not have to change either.

Matt felt that his responsibility toward Julie's financial needs would not end when she turned eighteen and qualified for SSI and Medicaid. He wanted to continue contributing toward her support. They were advised by our firm and their attorney that any financial support after she qualified for SSI and Medicaid may be deemed as Julie's income and may reduce or jeopardize her SSI income. It was better to create another special-needs trust called a first party D (4) (A) trust and deposit the support funds in that trust. According to the terms, any assets left in that trust at Julie's death would be subject to recovery by the state according to the amount of Medicaid benefit received by her. Yet it was still a good plan.

Matt and Melony worked hard to not make their parting uglier or harder on the family than it already was. They witnessed plenty of couples go through misery over asset distribution, child support, and parenting time. There was no bitterness, malice, or anger between them, and that was hard to believe. Melony, however, often wondered what she could have done to prevent this. Were they one more family with a child with disability adding to the statistics of divorce?

Megan did not handle her parent's divorce very well. She was almost sixteen by the time the divorce was finalized, in high school, and close to both her parents. She loved her sister but also had difficulty at times during her early teen years with Julie's odd and embarrassing behavior. Julie's moods had stabilized with ABA therapy, and Megan had also learned to accept Julie's disability and grown protective of her. However, when Matt and Melony first announced their divorce, she broke down completely and at first blamed it all on Julie and her disability. She was a very perceptive child and had seen how Julie's disability had changed her family. It took her a long time to accept this dramatic change in her family.

Julie seemed to have matured during the months before the divorce. She made steady progress in her speech, social skills, and communication. Melony insisted on continuing with the ABA and speech therapy despite the cost, and Eva remained with the family doing her part. Julie was able to express herself reasonably well and had a decent vocabulary. She loved working on her iPad on things she learned at school. She loved music and attended music therapy. Her life was busy and full. At first, she did not understand what her parent's divorce meant. Once she comprehended, she broke down and had difficulty deciding whose side she should take. Matt and Melony assured her that they both loved her and she would always be their daughter. Julie was devastated at Matt's moving out of the house permanently and cried for days. Matt stopped by often when he was in town to spend time with Julie and Megan. It broke his heart every time Julie clung to him and teared up, saying, "Daddy please don't go."

Acceptance gradually set in and slowly the family began to adjust to a new life and routine, at least on the surface. It has been almost seven years since Matt and Melony divorced. They have remained friends and worked at not letting their differences affect their children. Neither of them has remarried, although they have dated occasionally. Megan recently graduated in Biomedical Engineering from University of Michigan. Her parents couldn't be prouder of having one more U-M graduate in the family. Matt's parents and sister along with the entire Cook family attended the graduation celebration. Matt took Megan on a weeklong trip to France as her graduation gift. Melony and Matt make every effort to do things together as well as separately with their daughters.

Julie qualified for SSI and Medicaid at eighteen. She received a certification of completion from school but is now attending the post-secondary program offered by the school and will remain there until age twenty-six. Matt and Melony have agreed to review her options once she is twenty-six. She is a beautiful twenty-year-old, innocent, and a little shy. It is hard to tell what goes on inside her brain, but she seems happy. She has come far.

Matt has continued to move ahead in his career. He turned down an opportunity to move to London for his work as he believed it would not be fair to his daughters and Melony. He still feels sad about the changes Julie's disability brought in Melony and their lives, but he is also proud of what both his daughters have accomplished, especially Julie. It would not have been possible without Melony's dedication, devotion as a mother, and determination in finding and continuing the best treatment for Julie.

Melony often reflects on her life. She had a happy childhood and accomplished a lot as a high school and college student. She is very respected and liked at Ford Motor Company. Her happiest part of the life, however, was falling in love with Matt and having her two daughters. How did Matt slip away from her life? What could she have done to manage her emotions better about Julie? She wonders if her need to be a good mother failed her in being a more understanding and patient wife. She knows she is strong and will work hard to move on, but nothing can replace what she has lost.

INSIGHTS FROM THE WARD FAMILY

Every marriage has challenges and coping with a special-needs child requires frequent checks on who is carrying responsibilities. Couples can work on open communication; consider frequent counseling, date nights or time away to work on their relationship. Matt and Melony did not discuss their mounting issues often enough and began drifting. It is also important to develop additional support systems to ease daily parental responsibilities.

Divorces require review of all special needs, legal, and financial planning. Planning created prior to a divorce in most cases needs revising. Each parent must create new individual financial and legal plans for their special-needs child. Matt and Melony proceeded with new coordinated plans for Julie and Megan, an essential step to ensure that updated conditions are not jeopardized by the other parent's specifications. For example, if Matt's financial and legal plans were not updated and coordinated, they could jeopardize Melony's plans created by Julie.

9

He May Never Walk Again

Even the most promising future can change drastically by a life-threatening event. A healthy individual may require around the clock care and supervision after an accident. Families may need to seek government benefits for long-term health and special needs to avoid financial depletion and personal exhaustion. Business succession and career planning for parents and children may take unexpected turns as families cope with illness and recovery.

The close-knit Thorne Family awaited each Thanksgiving with great anticipation, and this year was especially elaborate for the parents and their three children. The extended family had many milestones to celebrate along with their grandparents, Aunt Pamela, and her family. Their oldest son Andrew, twenty-two, and daughter Michelle drove home from college on Wednesday, joined younger sister Isabella, and everyone pitched in for the Thanksgiving feast. It was nearly Grandpa Newton Thorne's seventy-fifth birthday and the fiftieth wedding celebration of Newton and his wife, Barbara. Isabella was in her high school senior year. The Thorne parents, Philip and Janet, were about to be empty nesters. The family all felt especially warm and close and had a beautiful celebration with much to be thankful for.

The day after Thanksgiving was traditionally a big shopping event for Janet, Pamela, Michelle, and Isabella. They planned to leave early for the nearest mall. Andrew, an avid cyclist, cross-country athlete, and engineering student, had brought his bicycle with him. He had not had a chance to ride in the last couple of weeks and planned a forty-five minute ride in the morning before the other family members awoke. He hoped to spend time later with his girlfriend Jill and her family. Andrew left a note by the kitchen telephone for his father, Phil, saying that he was out on his bicycle and would return in one hour. It was 6:30 a.m.

The phone rang around 7:30 AM. It was still a little dark outside, and everyone was slowly getting ready to start the day. Phil was still upstairs and answered. It was the Bloomfield Hills police. There was an accident. A bicyclist had collided with a deer on nearby Franklin Road at Maple Road and had been rushed to the Beaumont Royal Oak hospital. Philip froze momentarily and felt light headed. He sat down, took a deep breath, and yelled for Janet and Isabella. They were all getting ready to leave for the mall. He tried to explain about the accident but he could barely speak.

"We need to go to the hospital," he said, shaken.

The family waited in the waiting room for hours before the doctors met the family. The emergency medicine physician, the neurologist, and an internist first met with them. The news was not good. Andrew had a catastrophic injury to his spinal cord. His helmet had protected his head, but the impact of his fall had fractured his C5 vertebrae and had caused an open injury to his spinal cord in the neck region. Everybody was in shock. What did this mean? Phil felt numb, and Janet's heart was sinking. Both Michelle and Isabella held their parents' hands as they prepared to hear details. Jill was quiet but nervous. Andrew was in surgery to remove a bone fragment and replace a portion of the fractured vertebrae. His breathing was labored due to complications in his pulmonary functions.

Then came the worst news: The doctors said that they could not tell if Andrew would walk again. He would most likely be in the hospital for weeks. Phil felt faint; Janet suppressed her sobs and tried to remain strong.

Andrew was on mechanical ventilations while repeated CAT scans and MRIs were performed to assess the damage caused by the spinal cord injury. He lost sensation on both sides of his lower half of the body as well as in his wrists and hands. His pain was monitored, and a team of orthopedic surgeons, neurologists, pulmonary specialists, internists, psychiatrists, and rehabilitation specialists were in and out of his unit. The Thorne family members took turns staying in the hospital around the clock during the weeks Andrew was in the intensive care unit and later in a regular room recovering and awaiting news of his future.

After twelve weeks, his recovery, future, and quality of life remained uncertain. He left the hospital and was transferred to a rehabilitation facility for further physical and occupational therapy. He was paraplegic and had loss of function in the legs and lower body. His pain was manageable and his breathing improved.

It was difficult to know Andrew's feelings and reaction in the beginning. He was prescribed extensive medication, and it was difficult to talk to him. Sadness and anger started to surface as the reality began to become clearer. He tried to conceal his feelings, but his frustration was very obvious. The doctors wanted him to start seeing a psychiatrist right away, and Andrew agreed. He was diligent in his rehabilitation and gradually improved his wrist and hand movements but not his legs. He hated to be incontinent and wear diapers. He was strong but was also human. As a child, he had disliked when his sisters cried over petty arguments or other small matters, and he always maintained that only weak people cry. He was not weak and did not want to shed tears, but he only saw darkness in his future. During one family visit to the rehab facility, he broke down and said he wished he had a head injury and did not have his mind anymore; he just wanted to die. It was unbearable to see him suffer bodily and emotionally. His parents and family had no words to console him.

Every family member grieved in their own way and made adjustments in their routines and schedules. After the accident, Michelle came home from college in East Lansing every weekend. His girlfriend Jill came most weekends as well. She and Andrew had unspoken words, and they were both hurting. Andrew's best friend Stephen was steadfast and strong for all of them. Stephen had met Andrew in their freshmen year in high school, and they were like brothers. He had become more like a son to the Thorne family and was more important than ever as they all looked to him for encouragement. He was a constant source of support and did not let them down.

Philip and Janet had always felt blessed with their three children. Andrew was their oldest, followed by Michelle, two years younger, and Isabella, four years younger than Andrew. Janet played a major role in raising them while Philip grew his thriving family business, Thorne Plastics Design, Inc. Yet both parents were involved in raising their family. Andrew showed great athletic ability early on, with a passion for cycling. He also maintained good grades in school and excelled in math and science. Michelle was outgoing, and even as a child she made friends easily. She loved languages and was always well organized; she could not stand messy things from when she was a child with her toys to her books and closet as a teenager. Isabella, the baby of the family, kept her family laughing with her ongoing jokes and cheerful personality. She was a talented debater and participated in forensics at school. Janet disciplined them with a firm and yet loving hand and made sure they all focused and excelled in academics and pursued other interests to be well-rounded.

As Thorne Plastics Design prospered, Philip and Janet's personal wealth grew as well. The family moved to a larger home in Franklin, a northwest suburb of Detroit, when Andrew began high school. They also bought a home in Sarasota, Florida, for winter retreats. Their Franklin home was within the Birmingham School District and offered Andrew the sports opportunities he excelled in. He was a distance runner and part of the cross-country team. He trained hard every day with great discipline and made it to the varsity team, hoping to run in college. As part of his fitness training he also swam regularly. His best sport activity, however, was cycling. He found cycling relaxing and yet invigorating. He dreamed of participating in a Grand Tour in the future.

Andrew and Stephen shared the same interest in cross country and were part of the varsity team. They were buddies in their daily training and often ended up in each other's homes to study together. In their junior and senior years, they had similar advanced placement courses in physics and math. They both planned to study engineering and agreed to enter the same college.

Michelle was a freshman when Andrew and Stephen were juniors in high school. She idolized her brother and secretly admired Stephen. She was absolutely thrilled when Stephen asked her to the junior prom. Michelle introduced her friend Jill to Andrew and suggested he ask her to the prom. This was the beginning of a long-term friendship for them.

Andrew and Stephen both graduated with high grade point averages and ACT scores. They entered Michigan State University in the mechanical engineering program. They continued running for the cross-country team. Andrew cycled whenever he could and as much as he could. He was proud of his new

Enigma Elite Road racing bike his parents had given him as a graduation gift. The pressure of the studies along with keeping up with the cross-country training was getting harder and did not leave enough time for cycling. They saw Michelle and Jill occasionally but remained great friends. Michelle and Jill were freshmen at Michigan State University at the time Andrew and Stephen were in their junior year.

The summer before the end of his sophomore year Philip and Andrew had a serious conversation about his future career options. Philip was pleased with his son's choice of career path in engineering and hoped for Andrew to be part of the family business. He felt, however, that Andrew should have summer internships in the engineering industry and then work for a large company just as he had done at Chrysler. Andrew respected his father's opinion and admired him for his business acumen and success he had achieved. Interestingly, Stephen approached Philip to see if he could intern at Thorne Plastics the following summer. The Thorne family had become very fond of Stephen over the years. He was not only Andrew's best friend but was now dating their daughter, Michelle. Andrew interned at Johnson Controls, a global company manufacturing automotive parts, the summer before his junior year and was invited to return the following year.

Andrew and Jill's friendship blossomed and they were together every minute they could. Jill was studying international relations at the James Madison College and was considering law school after graduation. They were both serious about their education and future careers. Jill enjoyed running for pleasure and exercise, and they often ran together.

Andrew, Jill, Stephen, and Michelle wanted to make the summer of 1998 memorable. Before their internship and before the school began, they took a two-week trip to the national parks through Yellowstone and Grand Teton. They had two weeks of fun, love, excitement, and hope for the future. Both couples felt that their relationship was meant to be permanent.

As Andrew and Stephen's senior year started, they began to be buried in academic pressure. They knew that soon they needed to apply for jobs and seriously plan their futures. Andrew wondered if he should accept a job at Johnson Controls if it was offered. He had interned there two summers and was well liked. Stephen was hoping to get a job at Robert Bosch.

After the accident, Stephen drove home every evening from Michigan State in East Lansing for weeks until Andrew was stable. He spent hours every weekend at the hospital and later at the rehab facility. They were a semester away from graduating, and Stephen wanted to postpone his graduation until Andrew could graduate with him. They had done everything together since they first met in their freshman year in high school. He did not want to graduate alone. Andrew talked him out of it and promised him that he would not be too far behind, that he would finish his engineering degree somehow. Isabella chose to live at home and attend Wayne State University instead of attending Michigan State where both her siblings attended. She wanted to help Janet care for Andrew as much as possible once Andrew came home.

Philip had other challenges. The business had to be managed. Larry Huff and Frank Barton, his two key people, were managing the business as best as possible, but he needed to get back to work. Phil was also thinking about Andrew's future care, their ability to care for him at home, the cost of the medical treatment, and the care covered by insurance. Janet could not care for Andrew around the clock. They were advised to apply for SSI and Medicaid, but more importantly for a Medicaid waiver for home health care. Phil was aware that the Medicaid waiver program would take a long time to be approved. They could pay for Andrew's care for a while, but although they were comfortable financially, they could not pay for Andrew's around-the-clock care indefinitely.

Andrew qualified for a Medicaid waiver almost fifteen months after his accident, and it was a huge relief. Andrew's becoming eligible for Medicaid made Philip and Janet realize that they needed to plan for Andrew's future differently based on laws related to special needs planning. It broke their hearts to think that Andrew would be on the welfare program instead of becoming a successful engineer. They did their estate planning soon after that and created their own revocable trusts to hold all their estate. They also created a separate stand-alone discretionary (special needs) trust for Andrew. They chose to leave forty percent of their estate for Andrew's trust and thirty percent each to their two daughters. Andrew's trust assets were designed to supplement his government benefits and pay for things that were not covered by the government benefits. They asked Philip's sister Pam to be the trustee until Michelle and Isabella were at least thirty years old. Their legal plan was revocable as Philip and Janet wanted to remain flexible and be able to make changes when it became necessary.

Philip's business was an important component of the family estate, and Andrew's accident created a challenge and confusion in Philip's mind about his estate and business planning. Although Phil and Janet completed their basic estate planning to protect Andrew's government benefits in the event of their untimely death, they knew their plan would need to be adjusted in the future.

The company was started by Philip's father, Newton Thorne, in 1960, when Phillip was ten. The company went through many changes and transformations over the years and survived several economic ups and downs. Newton was a tool designer and started his own company after working for General Motors for several years. Phil worked at the shop after school a few days a week and in summer during high school. He was greatly influ-

enced by his dad's work ethics and love for design and manufacturing. He had a keen mind and was drawn to engineering.
He graduated in mechanical and manufacturing engineering
from Lawrence Tech and worked at Chrysler for three years
before joining the family business full time at age twenty-five.
He developed many contacts and gained valuable experience
during his few years at Chrysler.

Philip was also a visionary from a very young age. He
introduced to the company the manufacture of custom injec-
tion-molds for the automotive, medical-devices, and residential
industries. The name of the company changed from Thorne
Tool Industry to Thorne Plastic Design, Inc., in 1977. The company initially focused on low-volume projects with faster turn-
arounds and gradually developed the capacity for larger projects. Over the years, the company gained respect in the industry
as a small but dependable and trustworthy manufacturer. The
company continued to grow with both father and son working
side by side with several key people in the company. They also
addressed their business plans for Philip to succeed Newton
when the time was right, getting the proper buy-sell agreements
and funding the agreements with life insurance. Newton was
proud of his son's leadership skills and how far they had come.
When Philip turned forty-five, Newton handed over leadership
of the company to his son and decided to retire. Philip bought
out Newton's interest in the business over ten years and used
the profit from the company to do so. Philip also hoped that
someday the business would have his children playing key roles.
Philip continued to expand his business and had customers in
the United States and Canada. Rockberg Engineering Company
was one of their long-term customers.

Stephen accepted a job at Robert Bosch after graduation
and continued to visit Andrew regularly. A year after the accident—when Andrew had stabilized in his routine including
therapy and doctors' visits—Stephen insisted that he complete

his last semester and get his engineering degree. The year had taken a physical and emotional toll on the entire family. It had really impacted the grandparents. This shock at their stage in life had broken their spirits. Phil tried to focus on business matters, but Andrew was always at the back of his mind. Michelle and Isabella managed a brave front but hurt for their brother and grieved over the loss of who their brother was. Janet was the backbone of the family. She shed many silent tears but remained the anchor of the family and a rock for Andrew to lean on. Stephen was the other rock for Andrew and for the family. Stephen made arrangements for Andrew to study for the remaining credits at home online. Andrew could not focus well and was tired easily. Stephen was patient and insistent. He continued to encourage Andrew until he graduated a year later, two years after the accident.

Once Andrew earned his degree it became important for Philip that he give Andrew an opportunity to put his education to work at Thorne Plastics Design. He was qualified, but it would be difficult for him to work in a traditional employment setting. He needed to work in a friendly and less regimented environment. He needed help with toileting, and although his wrist and hand movements had improved with routine therapy, he needed assistance in feeding. At home, a caregiver from the Community Mental Health provider arrived at 7:30 a.m. to help him with his morning routine. Philip suggested Andrew start working a few hours at a time and learn the business structure, the manufacturing process, the roles and responsibilities of the seventy-five employees, as well as the sales, revenue, and profitability aspect of the company. As Andrew became familiar with the work pattern, Philip suggested he focus on the aspect of operations he most enjoyed. Philip and Janet had purchased a van with a lift for Andrew, and his caregiver drove him to work and back home. He started with two or three hours of work per day and gradually increased to a manageable schedule.

Andrew's career aspirations were further complicated by the income limitations imposed by the government programs that provided him with the personal care he needed to dress, bathe, use the bathroom, and move around. If Andrew's income exceeded the guidelines for these programs, he would lose his eligibility. Andrew's professional assistance was valuable but difficult to compensate, since he couldn't work a full-time schedule and sometimes had medical issues that interfered with his work. Philip explored options under the governmental benefit programs where certain employment-related expenses could be offset from Andrew's income.

Jill and Michelle graduated before Andrew earned his degree. Michelle had majored in business and Jill was accepted in several law schools. Michelle and Stephen were a couple, and the family tragedy had brought them even closer. Jill remained very committed to Andrew, but Andrew accepted that there was no future for them together. Jill believed Andrew was brave and competent, but Andrew knew he was physically disabled and felt he could never be the man Jill deserved. It was the saddest day for both of them when Andrew ended their relationship and urged her to move on. Jill entered University of Chicago Law School that fall. Andrew battled deep depression, anger, frustration, and sadness as he faced a bleak future. What is the purpose of an intellectual mind caged in a worthless body? It would take a long time before he could believe that his mind was intact and a gift and needed to be used.

Andrew gradually became an important presence at Thorne Plastics Design. He used his wheelchair to move around the plant carefully and easily. He was involved in design of the products as well as strategic planning and supervision with Jim Huff. He still tired easily and needed frequent breaks. He still suffered from spasticity, a urinary tract infection from time to time, and also had muscle and joint pains. He was on several medications including anti-depression. The care-giving team from the Community Mental Health provider worked well with his challenges and schedules. They helped him change and dress in the morning, dropped him at the plant and picked him up in four hours to take him back. They helped him keep his room in his parent's house clean and took him to all his medical appointments. Janet supervised Andrew's caregiving and accompanied Andrew and his caregiver to most medical meetings. Philip and Janet were thankful for the waiver program. They could not possible manage to care for Andrew without that.

After working for a steady two years, Andrew asked his parents if he could have his own residence. Philip and Janet were surprised but agreed. They wanted to reward Andrew's contributions and commitment, so they purchased a small ranch in Farmington Hills between their home in Franklin and their plant in Wixom. Philip and Janet owned the home, and it would be deeded to Andrew's Special Needs Trust at their demise. They made arrangements with Community Mental Health to increase the hours they needed for staffing after Andrew returned home and for the night. Andrew would always need care and supervision, and the financial value of the benefits received from the government could never be replaced by any assets they could leave for Andrew.

Thorne Plastics Design expanded steadily. Philip felt the need to add another engineer, an operations person, and a human resource person. He discussed this with Andrew, Larry, and Frank. It was Andrew who suggested Phil approach Stephen and Michelle. They were engaged to be married soon, and the Thorne family could not find more appropriate people. Stephen was hesitant at first. Andrew convinced him that it would be good for his career and a big help to him and his family. Stephen became a member of the Thorne family after he and Michelle married in the summer of 2005. Michelle, Andrew,

Stephen, Larry, and Frank handled the key aspect of the Thorne Plastics Design under Phil's leadership.

As years went by, Philip and Janet began realizing it was time for them to begin their retirement and business succession plan. Philip knew he was fortunate to have succeeded in his business, but what he was thankful for was having Janet by his side as a true companion since they married thirty-five years ago. He was approaching his sixtieth birthday and wanted to make important decisions regarding the continuity of Thorne Plastic Design Inc. Every time he thought about it, though, a stabbing pain went through his heart, and he had a sinking feeling. His father had helped him mold his career and destiny. Would he be able to do the same for Andrew? What about Michelle and Stephen, who were now key components of Thorne Plastics Design?

A new development had occurred over the last few months. Phil, his accountant and attorney had been in conversations with the Toronto-based Rockberg Engineering Company for the last few months about Rockberg's interest in acquiring the family business. A meeting was arranged for Phil and Janet to meet the executives of Rockberg Engineering Company.

The years flashed back in Philip's mind as Janet and he prepared for their meeting with Rockberg representatives. Philip had discussed Rockberg's proposal—to buy out and have Thorne Plastics Design be a subsidiary of Rockberg—in great detail with his children. He also consulted Newton, who was still very sharp at eighty-five despite his failing health. They were offered an excellent valuation for the company and wanted some of the key people to stay on. Philip felt honored and gave it a lot of thought. He knew what his decision was going to be, and Janet was in complete agreement.

The Rockberg Engineering Company CEO was surprised when Philip declined the offer to merge. Philip explained that

Thorne Plastics Design was not just a family business; the company leaders also believed in taking care of the family. It was unanimously decided by the family members that it was unlikely that Andrew would have been able to continue his unique role in the business despite the Rockberg CEO's assurance he could. Limiting Andrew's work and compensation in a manner that preserved his benefit eligibility was simply too complex. Rockberg was a big company and likely could not make the constant adjustments and accommodations that Andrew would need. Philip and Janet would have to work differently to protect his future. The family recognized that they were turning down a tremendous opportunity, and Michelle, Stephen, and Philip would have all done well with Rockberg. But they also concluded that their journey could not continue without Andrew.

Philip celebrated his sixtieth birthday in 2010 with a quiet celebration with his family. Grandpa Newton turned eighty-five the same year. Philip recalled that his father began his successions plan at age sixty, and he was anxious to put his own plan in place. Phil was challenged by several personal and business planning objectives and the complex tax and Medicaid laws. My firm became involved in their financial planning and Andrew's planning soon after Andrew's accident in 1998. The family now needed a team approach of other professionals to put all the components together and plan for Andrew's future.

The same law firm that did the Thorne family estate planning introduced us to their tax and business-succession planning attorney, who was also knowledgeable of special needs planning. Philip's CPA also was a certified business valuation expert, an added value. As a team we assessed the Thorne family estate. This included the value of Thorne Plastics Design, Philip and Janet's financial needs in retirement, Janet's income needs as a survivor, and their thoughts on dividing the estate between their children, other family members, and charities. It also was important to consider Newton and Barbara's estate.

Phil and his sister Pamela were heirs to their parent's assets, but the grandparents also wanted to leave assets to their grandchildren, including Andrew.

Philip and Janet wanted to treat their three children equally. The youngest Isabella was not part of the family business. Bella was finishing her doctorate in psychology and married to Ryan, an IT specialist. Phil and Janet had good investments in Phil's retirement account as well as in their trusts. They owned the building housing Thorne Plastics Design and received rent from the company. These along with Phil's life insurance would be adequate to provide financial security for Janet at Phil's passing. They both had long-term care insurance as well. They continued to make their own calculations of the intrinsic value Andrew added to the company, and set that aside in a separate account to be "Transferred on Death" to Andrew's Special Needs Trust.[6]

Phil was insistent upon using simple planning strategies for his business succession. He wanted to include Larry Huff and Frank Burton, the key people in his plan. They had remained by his side for many years through difficult and challenging times. They knew his children since they were young and understood Phil's sentiments about his business and anguish over Andrew's situation. He did not want to include Isabella in his business succession plan and wanted to consider Michelle and Stephen as one unit. Isabella's inheritance would be a third of the estate but be distributed from assets outside of the family business. Phil and the planning team's greatest challenge was including Andrew in the business succession plan and making him a stock holder of the company. Phil and Janet also gave a great deal of thought about whether Stephen should be a stockholder. They loved him, and he had done more for their family

6 Estate and business planning strategies for the Thorne family were reviewed by Lauretta Murphy, Doctor of Jurisprudence. She is a member of the Special Needs Alliance and chairs the Trust and Estate Practice Group at Miller Johnson law firm, Grand Rapids, Michigan.

than they could ever ask. And yet they wondered what would happen if Michelle and Stephen divorced.

The business valuation along with the other assets including investments, retirement plans, life insurance, and possible inheritance from Newton and Barbara amounted to a size that could be subject to estate taxes at both Phil and Janet's deaths. Although there wouldn't be any estate taxes in 2010, the laws were about to change, and they hoped to avoid the taxes if the new law increased the exemption allowed per person for estate taxes.

Many tax-saving strategies were discussed such as creating an Irrevocable Life Insurance Trust, Intentionally Defective Irrevocable Trust, and a Family Limited Partnership. Phil reviewed them all carefully but decided against a strategy that would be irrevocable and could not be changed. Their lives had changed in a fraction of a second when Andrew was in the accident, and it was important that their plans be flexible enough to adjust with changes in circumstances.

Philip and his CPA agreed that the profits of the company each year could be given as a bonus to Larry, Frank, Michelle, and Stephen to buy the corporate stock of Thorne Plastics Design each year for ten years or until they owned the amount Phil had planned. Phil and Janet also decided to include Stephen in the stock purchase plan and hope that their daughter and son-in-law would stay happily married. Phil decided that Larry and Frank should each own five percent of the stock, and Michelle and Stephen should own twenty-two-and-a-half percent each. The remaining forty-five percent of the corporation stock would go to Andrew, the greatest challenge for the planning team.

Phil and Janet often questioned if they could replace Andrew's Medicaid-provided caregiving and all other benefits he received. It would be easier to plan their estate and business succession if Medicaid was not an issue. They wondered if Andrew's inheritance, social security benefits, and income he could earn would not interfere with those benefits and be sufficient to take care of him. They concluded the government benefit was irreplaceable and too risky to give up. It also meant that Andrew could not be treated the same as their other children. He could not own or earn more than what the Medicaid eligibility rules allowed. He could not own any part of the Thorne Plastics Design directly. Phil and Janet were also aware of the budget constraints of the government programs and the future governmental funding of programs that would provide for Andrew. It was difficult to predict his life expectancy, aging process, and future needs. The team advised they should assume a normal life expectancy for Andrew and to fund his special needs trust supplement enough to cover what the government benefits did not. The Thorne Plastics Design stock would need to be owned by Andrew's special needs trust.

Phil could not plan on providing Andrew a bonus to buy company stocks every year as he did the others. This would be treated as income, reducing or eliminating Andrew's eligibility for the essential benefits that allowed him to live independently and work. The planning team considered the pros and cons of gifting the company stocks to Andrew's special needs trust each year until the trust owned forty-five percent of the company.

They also considered sticking with the original plan of Phil continuing to own forty- five percent of the stock, passing it on to Janet, and then to Andrew's special needs trust . They wondered how Andrew would feel and who would be the ultimate trustee of Andrew's trust. Michelle and Stephen succeeded by Isabella seemed the appropriate choice. But that would make Michelle and Stephen combined owners of forty-five percent of the company, and trustee of another forty-five percent. They could become majority stockholders, and the parents wondered if that was safe for Andrew.

The special needs trustee could not name Andrew as a

trustee. However, Andrew could act as "investment advisor" for the trust. In this role, he could direct the trustee on the management of the business assets held in the trust as long as he had no authority to make distributions on his own behalf. He could sit on the board of directors, continue to lead discussions regarding the company's strategic direction, and continue to contribute both his technical expertise and valuable personal insights. Phil appreciated the fact that this solution gave Andrew credit for the role he continued to play in the productivity of the company and allayed the concerns about interfering with his income-tested governmental benefits. As the company grew and prospered, the profits directed to Andrew's special needs trust could be used for Andrew's benefit and to enhance his independent and quality of life.

Ultimately, Phil chose to gift company stocks to Andrew's special needs trust each year until the trust owned forty-five percent of the company. The gift would become irrevocable at Phil's death. Phil was the initial trustee of Andrew's revocable special needs trust. Since this was a revocable trust, it was not considered to be a completed gift, and Phil could overrule Andrew, but Andrew saw this gesture as evidence of Phil's intent to include him in his planning in a tangible way and reward him for his valuable contribution to the company.

It took almost eighteen months to complete their business succession and estate plan. Philip and Janet were pleased and relieved to have a well thought out plan for their family that was also flexible and could be changed if necessary. The estate exemption was increased by Congress, and further changes were anticipated.

Newton, Phil's father, mentor and founder of Thorne Plastics design, passed away in 2013 at the age of eighty-eight. He remained Phil's life counselor until his death. Andrew's accident hit him hard, he loved his grandson and was his biggest fan. Newton called Andrew daily, chatting about all that was happening in their lives. Andrew always felt secure in expressing his insecurities and fears to his grandpa. Andrew lost his best friend and confidant when Newton died. Barbara, Philip's mother, died eighteen months later after a short nursing home stay. Their assets were then divided between Phil and his sister, then their five grandchildren. Andrew's share was given to Philip to be added to the account Philip and Janet were maintaining for Andrew's special needs trust.

Andrew no longer questions his fate. He is grateful for his family business and the opportunity to work and have a routine in his life. He meets with a support group of accident survivors from time to time. Grandpa Newton had suggested many years ago that he speak publicly about his experience as an accident survivor with a spinal cord injury. He started speaking with his support group and now speaks periodically at various other groups such as the Rotary Club, Veteran's Groups, and other support groups. He looks forward to these opportunities.

His family remains devoted to him but also have their own lives. Stephen is his loyal buddy and visits every weekend. His caregivers change from time to time, but they are his companions. Both his sisters have their own children and careers to manage. His parents are aging and now spend their winters in Florida. It is difficult for Andrew to travel, and life is lonely. He still experiences pain and fights sadness and depression despite psychiatric counseling and medications. He has great days and not so good days. He wants to be stronger and have purpose in life. His efforts will be ongoing and lifelong.

INSIGHTS FROM THE THORNE FAMILY

Unexpected accidents can mean every aspect of financial planning and anticipated job security must change. Family can apply for appropriate government benefits and review financial aid considerations carefully.

Accidents can create both permanent physical and mental disability, changing the life of the injured individual as well as of the family. The psychological impact of a possibly lost future is unmeasurable.

Business succession plans combined with special needs planning create added levels of complexity and require professionals from various disciplines to work together. The value of the government programs for most people as seen in Andrew's case is irreplaceable, and the planning has to be designed to protect the eligibility of the benefits.

Keeping the plan flexible and revocable is often important for many families and outweighs the importance of tax savings. If tax savings plans are more important, more flexible language in the trust documents may be necessary as well as giving certain powers to a Trust Protector. That is another individual appointed by the trust creator to make adjustments as necessary.

10

Finding Support When Hope
Seems Lost

*Families can create careful plans for their special needs
children and yet face obstacles created by longer life
expectancy of the parents or untimely passing of future
trustees. Teams of experts are needed to help when
situations grow desperate and designated caregivers and
finances are at risk. Professional experts can be enlisted,
yet it is important that a relative or person familiar with
the family is involved in ensuring quality care.*

Carl Shuler called my office three days after Father's Day in
1995. It was difficult to understand him between his muffled
and quivering voice and sobs. I was shocked when I finally
comprehended what he was saying. His son Charles died on
Father's Day of pulmonary embolism on a golf course. Carl was
despondent over his profound loss and also confused. He was
eighty-six and now the sole caregiver of Susan, his daughter
with a developmental disability.

I met the Shuler family four years earlier while planning
for Carl and Noreen Shuler's daughter Susan. Both Susan, forty-eight, and Charles, forty-four, lived with the parents. Carl was
usually quiet in our meetings. Noreen did most of the talking,
providing details of her family and about Susan. I remember
her as a very meticulous and methodical person with attention

to details in her descriptions, the way she dressed and provided her financial and family information. She dedicated her entire life to caring for her two children.

Charles was single when I met the Shulers in 1991 and worked at St. John Hospital in their central supply room. He was known to be very sensitive but hid his feelings behind his poker face. He developed ulcers at a very young age. He had a difficult time in school due to dyslexia but graduated from college and overall had a friendly personality. He was a loner with a handful of friends but loved golf, food, and hunting guns. His love for food showed in his heavy size. He did not seem to mind living with his parents at his age. Charles was committed to his older sister's caregiving. Although his parents were concerned about his somewhat lonely life, they took comfort in the fact that Susan would be cared for after their passing. Carl and Noreen made Charles promise that his sister would never live anywhere but their own home. She would never live in a group home. Charles was committed to honor that.

Noreen and Carl worried about putting their affairs in order for the benefit of their children, but did not have any directions. Special needs planning was not discussed much in the early nineties, and very little planning information was available. Noreen and Carl were seventy-nine and eighty-two, with two simple wills that were insufficient and incorrectly drafted for their needs. They both had health challenges. Carl was an insulin-dependent diabetic, and Noreen had a major surgery two years earlier to remove a malignant tumor in her stomach.

After learning and understanding the planning that was required for Susan, they immediately created a special needs trust for Susan with Charles as the successor trustee followed by Henry Gabler, a young man and a friend of the family. The Shulers were not wealthy but were financially comfortable. They had saved as best as they could and hoped they could continue to live on their pension and Social Security alone and leave a large part of the savings for Susan's trust. They lived in a modest but comfortable home on Lake St. Clair where Charles and Susan could continue to live. Susan received Social Security Disability income and contributed her share to the family finances, as did Charles.

Noreen's cancer spread to other organs within a few months after she and Carl completed their planning. She passed away in 1992, leaving her husband and son to take care of her beloved daughter Susan. Carl and Charles did their best to take care of the house and Susan. Life went on for a few years until the phone call I received in 1995 after Father's Day.

Both my firm's and my personal role had been to determine the Shuler family's financial and legal planning needs, to understand Susan's disability, her future planning requirements, and help them implement as well as monitor their plan. Carl's desperate situation after his son's death and inability to make any decision forced me to step out beyond my role as their wealth advisor. I requested and arranged a meeting the following week between Mary Ann, the director of Macomb Arc, an advocacy organization for the developmentally disabled population in the same county that the Shulers lived in. I also invited Henry Gabler, the future successor trustee.

The meeting was held at the Shuler home. I was the first to arrive and shocked to see the state of the home and both Carl and Susan's appearances. The sink was full of dirty dishes, and belongings were scattered all over the rooms. A laundry basket with dirty clothes lay in the middle of the family room. Carl was so tired he fell asleep wherever he sat down. I was not sure if he was taking his insulin shots. Susan appeared disheveled and had not had a bath in days. They had not been eating well. The only food in the refrigerator was a half a can of spam, a half a loaf of bread, a bottle of ketchup, and milk. Noreen would be horrified at the sight of her beautiful home and the plight of her loved ones.

Mary Ann, an experienced and knowledgeable professional in special needs individual's caregiving, assessed the situation very quickly and determined that Susan and Carl could not be left alone to fend for themselves. We asked for Henry's input as he was the future trustee of the Shuler family Trust as well as Susan's special needs trust. The trust also allowed him to step in to be a trustee immediately if Carl could no longer handle his role as the trustee and manage his finances and other important affairs. Henry appeared overwhelmed and unsure of what he should do. Mary Ann agreed to have the Macomb Arc advocacy organization arrange for help three times a week. This included a person who could take Susan and Carl for grocery shopping, help them keep the house clean, remind Susan to take her bath, and remind Carl to take his insulin shot. Susan was capable of doing many things but needed direction and supervision at times.

Henry resigned as the successor trustee a week later. He apologized for his inability to help Carl and Susan and explained that he had offered to step in in case Charles could not be the trustee but never anticipated that it could actually happen. He did not feel he was capable of handling the task. Carl was completely shaken by Henry's resignation. His grief over losing his wife first and then his son compounded by worries about his own health, his imminent death, and Susan's care and well-being began taking a toll. He started to call our office asking what to do next, worrying what would happen.

Working with the Shuler family made me realize that my decision to specialize in special needs planning could not rest after helping the families create their legal documents and a financial plan. From time to time, I had to reach out to other professionals and family members and create a team of support to assist a desperate family. In Carl and Susan's case, an easy solution would have been to appoint a corporate trustee such as a bank or a trust company. Yet it was more important to have someone familiar with the family who could have patience caring for Carl and Susan. In addition, the corporate trustees required larger assets to manage than what the Shulers owned. A professional/corporate trustee would be the last option to consider. Other options needed to be thought through.

Carl was one of eight children in his family, and three of his siblings and their children lived in the area. Carl was known to have a gruff personality and attitude and was not particularly close to his siblings, nieces, or nephews. When the children were younger, Noreen made attempts to keep the family connection by inviting them to summer picnics on the lake where they lived and during holidays and other celebrations. As Susan's care and Noreen's career demanded more time, socialization became less frequent, and the family kept to themselves. Noreen had a small family. Her only brother Glen was single and never had children. I connected with Carl's siblings with his permission and arranged for a meeting. Two of his siblings were older with health issues and could not attend. Jane Gilin, Carl's sister, attended with her husband and their son, David.

I explained Carl and Susan's situation to the Gilin family and requested to see if any of the younger members could step in to be the executor of the Shuler estate as well as trustee for Susan's special needs trust. It was obvious from the ensuing conversation that it was a lot to ask from anybody, especially because of a lack of true relationships. David's parents wanted to understand what the trustee's role would be after Carl's passing. They had not kept up with Susan's level of functioning or her medical condition. They were concerned about the financial management responsibility as well. David's parents seemed hesitant about their family stepping into this role. David listened to the conversation and remained mostly quiet. At the end, he came forward and offered to be the executor of the Shuler estate and the trustee of Susan's trust despite his parent's hesitation and concerns.

David lived within two miles from Uncle Carl and Cousin Susan in St. Clair Shores but rarely visited since his childhood. He remembered their family reunions on Uncle Carl's lake home, but that was a long time ago. He was younger than Susan and Charles and had not had interacted much with them. David appeared kind and considerate. He was concerned about his uncle and cousin and believed he had a duty to step in and help. He was in his early forties and felt sorry and compassionate toward the father and daughter who were vulnerable and forlorn. David's wife Dianne supported her husband's decision whole-heartedly.

David began immediately understanding and assessing the Shuler family affairs and creating a plan of action. First, he and his wife needed to help Carl settle Charles' affairs, liquidate his investments, sell his hunting guns, and donate his clothing. Carl and Susan's trust documents were revoked to name David as the successor trustee followed by Dianne. The most pressing decision was what to do with the family home. Although it was not a very big house, it was too large for two people and difficult to maintain. Noreen's brother, Gary Cooper, had left a small two-bedroom ranch home within three miles of Noreen when he passed away. Carl and Susan decided to move to the more manageable ranch, and the sale proceeds of their home added to the size of the funds from which they could later benefit. During their visit with the attorney to make the changes and their move to the ranch house, Carl reminded David that Susan would always live in their home and never in a group home. She would just not survive there.

Managing both Carl and Susan's needs required David to understand their personalities, idiosyncrasies, habits, medical information, and their finances. Fortunately, they had the "Letter of Intent" that Noreen prepared. During our initial meetings, I asked Noreen if she kept any records of Susan's development as she was growing up and had documented other details about her. To my surprise, she presented during the following week one of the best "Letters of Intent" I had seen, with many details described methodically. A neatly typed journal of about twenty pages covered significant events since Susan's birth until the time we met. Reading this document provided David the much-needed background for him to move forward in directing Susan's caregiving. The reality also was that Susan and Carl were in similar difficult situations. Susan had developmental disabilities, but Carl was deteriorating in his physical and mental ability due to his age and grieving from the loss of his loved ones.

Noreen had a difficult pregnancy with Susan, her first child born in September 1942. She was a beautiful baby with no obvious signs of trouble. But Susan suffered brain damage due to lack of oxygen during birth and was slow in some of her physical developments. Although she appeared mentally alert and began speaking at a normal age, Noreen was concerned. Carl had to leave to serve in the armed forces for two and a half years during World War II. Noreen lived with her parents in their country home. Susan received attention from her grandparents and other doting adults. She did not experience the usual give and take of a peer group but developed a pattern of preferring to be with older companions. Among Susan's challenges was her inability to tolerate unexpected movements and sounds of babies; the noises terrified her.

Noreen moved back with Susan to their own home in a neighborhood of young families after Carl returned. Charles was born in 1946 when Susan was four years old. She continued to panic and cried every time her baby brother cried. Her reaction to noise was extreme. She also walked and ran awkwardly and stared blankly for short periods. She had an unofficial diagnosis of petit mal seizure resulting in brief, sudden lapses in attention and mental confusion that medication helped control. She began attending a kindergarten program in the neighborhood school. Susan learned to read and work with numbers but had poor coordination and difficulty in writing, fastening garments, tying bows and catching balls. Her poor sense of direction made it unsafe for her to walk anywhere alone. She could not muster the skill of riding a bike. The noise in school and in the school bus continued to terrify her.

Despite her lack of coordination and inability to participate in physical games, Susan made friends who enjoyed her company in quiet ways. She became a member of the Brownies and the Campfire Girls, yet withdrew from activities that she could not handle. Susan always displayed honesty in refusing to pretend or take credit for qualities she did not possess. Most of her friends had parents who were understanding and sympathetic, and this influence showed in the children's attitude toward her. There were, however, some children who reacted to her clumsiness with disdain and ridicule. Sometimes her school supplies and money were stolen, adding to her feelings of insecurity.

Noreen and Carl agreed that high school was not a safe environment for Susan due to less control and supervision. Instead, she enrolled in the White Special School for Epileptics in Detroit. An electro-encephalographic testing had confirmed a diagnosis of epilepsy. Susan was happy and felt secure learning in the company of other students with disabilities of various degrees and under the guidance of trained teachers. She gained more confidence as a result of feeling accepted. She began to take interest in her personal appearance and became much more positive in her personality. The burden of always feeling inadequate began to lift off her shoulders.

The White Special School for Epileptics option unfortunately closed for Susan a year later due to a school transportation cost-cutting. Susan returned to South Lake High School and managed to get through classes. The stress of becoming lost in the school, noise in the lunch room, and losing her belongings frequently weighed heavily on her. Her petit mal seizures occurred throughout the day, and her medication caused drowsiness. The teachers were understanding and allowed her to assist in the library to avoid the noise created by other girls at the Girl's Glee Club practice. The library was a haven for Susan, and being in a library continued to provide her peace and calm.

Carl and Noreen joined the Greater Detroit Council for Epilepsy and benefited from their support, advice, and participation in programs of mutual interest. Meeting with other families and adult children with seizures helped Susan and her parents. She graduated from high school and continued to meet with a social worker to find an occupation. She had come a long way in her personal growth and was now ready to adjust to a world after high school. Unfortunately, the family was soon jarred with setbacks.

Susan scalded the upper half of her body except her face while taking a shower at home. She was used to baths but had started to learn to use the shower. The accident precipitated a drastic change as the shock of the pain and accumulated distress caused her to have major convulsions. She remained in the intensive care unit at Bon Secours Hospital for days and then in a private room for three months. She endured excruciating pain and suffering during her five surgeries for skin grafting. Her seizure medications had to be stopped during her treatment, which caused her to have both petit and grand mal seizures with loss of consciousness and muscle contractions— both worse than before.

By the time Susan was discharged from the hospital, she had regressed emotionally and was extremely weak physically. She started walking backward and bumped into objects. Some of her medications for seizure were restored, but it could not completely prevent her shaking. The research department experts of the Lafayette Clinic in Detroit tried a combination of many medications to help. Finally, a new doctor at the clinic tried a medication called Diamox that provided noticeable relief. Her seizures diminished to a point that she could walk more normally. She remained a young girl emotionally, and that did not change.

Noreen and Carl consulted psychiatrists to help with Susan's emotional scars caused by her trauma and seizures. They were not reassured about Susan's progress and ability to reclaim her coordination, except that over time she might be able to perform a few minor tasks well. Noreen decided to take charge and work with Susan. She was a middle-school teacher but retired early to work with Susan at home and also with Charles, who had dyslexia. Noreen also started a graduate course in library science at Wayne State University. Once a week, she visited the university library for research and took Susan with her where she could explore many books in a quiet environment. She pretended she was "going to college," and was very enthusiastic.

The family moved to the lake home in 1965. There were many play and work opportunities in the area. They enjoyed outings on their small boat and picnics with friends, families, and neighbors. Carl and Noreen also invited Carl's family to have the annual reunion on their lake house every summer. Although many cousins attended, they mainly stayed with their own family groups. Charles and Susan did not always feel included but still had a good time. Everybody enjoyed swimming in the lake, but Susan was reluctant to expose herself to public scrutiny in a bathing suit because of her scars from burns on her chest, arms, and back.

Noreen tried to find a job for Susan with the help from Mount Clemens Social Services. There were a few interviews and a few promises, but nothing worked out other than a few volunteering positions. People lost patience with her lack of coordination and slow way of doing tasks. But she enjoyed attending adult education classes at the local high schools on subjects such as art and psychology. The family also took vacations together, and Noreen sometimes travelled with Susan on shorter trips. Wherever they went, Susan's favorite pastimes were browsing through the bookstores and eating in nice restaurants. She often ended up ordering too much food, which started to become a problem. She could not always finish what she ordered and began gaining weight.

Susan's seizures never left her completely. She continued to have petit mall seizures but would go for months before a grand mall would occur. The doctors tried new, sophisticated medications as they were introduced in the market. Susan's mood swung drastically from joy to despair, which was often overwhelming, requiring additional medications. Finally, Depakote, a drug that had been used very successfully in Europe to control seizures became available in the United States. Depakote worked like magic for Susan, and she slowly stopped having seizures. Her cheerful and generally pleasant personality returned. After suffering from seizures all her life, she was finally able to find relief at age forty.

Noreen and Carl assigned Susan certain household chores. They hoped her chores helped her learn to perform better and to make her feel that she was contributing to the family welfare. Susan unfortunately faltered; she was never able to master or complete projects. If she did dishes, they were left still wet. If she dusted, she spent an entire day on one room. Trying to make a bed resulted in a twisted heap of covers. She had no interest in doing or learning new things. The only pastime she enjoyed was reading books and eating. She loved mysteries and adventures, and brought home several books a week from the library. She could not wait to go back to get more books.

When Noreen underwent surgery in 1989, the family recognized the need to redistribute the household chores and lower standards temporarily. Susan learned to pitch in more. Carl and Susan learned to shop for groceries and make some simple meals. Susan was impatient and often frustrated when things did not turn out well, but she was learning. Noreen's illness made Carl and Charles realize that Charles would face many challenges once Noreen and Carl passed away. They wondered if Charles could care for Susan the way his parents wished. Susan was very high functioning, but living with her was not easy.

After Noreen's passing in 1992, Charles and Carl managed as best as they could. It was not Noreen's standard, but life went on as normally as possible. Then Charles died, and David realized he had a very difficult task on his hands with medical, financial and caregiving responsibilities. David and Carl had no one to help with the day-to-day challenges even though David did not need to be responsible fully until his uncle passed. Then he would be the executor of Uncle Carl's estate.

The help of Mary Ann from Macomb County Arc worked very well for several weeks. Guidelines restricted her from helping with insulin shots for Carl or other medical matters. Although he still managed to take shots, Carl needed to be supervised and reminded. David looked for alternatives and contacted an agency that provided home care for the elderly. Arrangements were made for a person to visit them every day for a few hours. Tony Girten, who began working with Carl initially, also helped Susan with some of her needs. Tony took them grocery shopping, to doctor's visits and the library, and helped them plan their meals. Their dinners were healthy but were ready-made meals from grocery stores. David stopped by every other day on his way home from work.

Finances became a concern. Private home help was expensive and adding to the monthly cost. We reviewed all of Carl's investments, income sources, and expenses, and adjusted investments to increase the family income. The investments performed well in the late nineties since my firm took over the Shuler family finances. Carl worked most of his life at General Dynamics in the accounting department and had a modest pension. He also received Noreen's survivor pension from the State of Michigan. He had adequate savings, but we were concerned about preserving them for Susan's future.

Several family-life, world terrorism and financial changes took place between the years 2000 and 2002 that challenged the Shulers. Carl's health deteriorated, and he began requiring full-time nursing home care beginning in late 2001. The economy worsened when the internet bubble burst in 2000, and the terrorist attacks on September 11, 2001, created a heightened sense of threat. Then major financial companies were convicted with fraud in 2002. These incidents impacted the world economy, and the financial markets took a major loss. David worried about the Shuler family finances along with other priorities.

Susan could not be left home alone while Carl was in the nursing home. Tony offered to care for Susan alone under the same terms for the same hours and charges as he did for Carl. David also approached Community Mental Health seeking home help for Susan. She received Social Security Disability Income and Medicare. She was also eligible for Medicaid, and David hoped she could be eligible for a caretaker at home. The cost of a privately paid nursing home for Carl and care for Susan at home was mounting and could not be managed indefinitely.

Tony drove Susan to the nursing home every day to visit Carl. He was almost ninety-three and had multiple medical issues. He had no desire to continue living. He wanted to be in heaven with his beloved wife Noreen and son Charles but had tears in his eyes every time he looked at Susan. David and Tony assured him that Susan would be well looked after. Carl passed away within a few months in 2002. Susan took his death in a very matter of fact way. David and Tony had cared for Carl and Susan well for almost seven years, and Susan had become dependent on both.

Planning for Susan's care became a challenge both financially and in caregiving. The Community Mental Health denied home help care for Susan. She was too high functioning and did not have any physical disabilities. She did not qualify for the program. Susan was now sixty and able to take care of herself in many ways. Yet she was also like a child and vulnerable. She could be home on her own occasionally but needed care and supervision. David appealed the Community Mental Health guidelines through a well-known attorney, but Susan was denied home help again. An important decision had to be made if Tony should continue to offer his services through the agency where he worked. It was cost-prohibitive. Susan sensed the dilemma David faced and was worried about her future.

Susan's trust assets were reviewed again. Carl's life insurance proceeds helped recover some of the market losses and cost of his care before his death. The question was whether Susan's trust had enough to pay for Tony's full-time care on a private-pay basis. Tony was fifty, single and lived with an older sister not too far from Susan's home in St. Clair Shores. He analyzed his own situation. He could quit the agency job and work independently. He offered to do that and become Susan's full-time care giver. He needed a fixed salary and health insurance.

Tony's salary was not the only expense for the trust. The trust funds would also be needed for ongoing maintenance of the home including property taxes, utilities, and repairs. David had worked for several years to look after Carl and Susan's needs. He had a right to trustee fees. There were concerns about future market fluctuations, increase in cost of living, and unexpected emergency expenses. Carl lived until ninety-three.

Susan at sixty could live that long as well. David worried that the trust would run out of funds. He also knew he had assured Carl that Susan would continue to live in her own home.

Tony and David agreed on a workable arrangement to ensure Susan could remain at home. Some days of the week he spent most of the day at Susan's home. Susan's favorite outing was still vising the library once a week followed by lunch at her favorite Chinese restaurant. Reading continued to be her passion, and books were her best friends. She also had occasional doctor's visits and trips to museums and grocery stores. Susan was comfortable living alone at night. She knew how to operate the alarm system and call David, Tony, and 911 for emergencies. She had not had a seizure in many years but still wore a medical alert bracelet. She sometimes stayed the night at Tony's home with him and his sister. David was greatly relieved by Tony's sincere and trustworthy work ethic as well as his commitment. David and Dianne always included Susan and Tony at Thanksgiving and Christmas dinners, and Susan was never alone on her birthdays.

Financial matters continued to be worrisome. The recession of 2008 impacted the trust fund to a certain extent. Other factors such as a new roof, new windows, and repairs in a leaky bathroom over a period of time required invading the capital. Interest rates were greatly reduced on bonds, but the expenses kept increasing. David occasionally took modest trustee fees but most years did not take any. The fear of Susan outliving her trust fund was real.

Earlier in 2017, Susan was diagnosed with cancer of the roof of her mouth. After complaining of chronic ulcers in her mouth, she went through tests followed by a surgery to remove part of the roof of her mouth. It was a difficult process for Susan. Her post-surgical pain and inability to speak has been frustrating. Her prognosis is not very promising. She may overcome this life-threatening disease and live longer, but it could also result in death in three to four years. There are enough funds to last just a few more years.

Susan is seventy-five and has been cared for well. David has not let her down and has fulfilled his duty as well as the promise he made Carl to look after his daughter. David could not have managed without Tony's help and his wife Dianne's support. Susan has battled many challenges in her life but is blessed to have a good plan set by her parents and a trustworthy person with a team of planning professionals to execute the plan.

INSIGHTS FROM THE SHULER FAMILY

Adults with disabilities are living longer due to medical advancement and will require more care during their aging process. The government benefits may not be adequate to support the cost of care. Many higher functioning individuals with disabilities may not qualify for much needed benefits. Families may need to plan carefully and arrange for funding of the special needs trust considering higher cost of care in the future.

Families may need to plan for successor trustees beyond their immediate family. There may be a person like David in many extended families who may step forward and honor the wishes of the family and care for a loved one.

It is important to have flexible terms for caregiving, housing and other trust matters. The trustees must use their judgment and arrange for the best care available for the disabled beneficiary within the budget the trust fund allows. David's predicament of maintaining Susan's care in her own home is a difficult promise to keep.

11

Please God, Help Him Remain Stable

Mental illness can cause immeasurable devastation in a family. The illness often surfaces during teenage years or later and is not easily diagnosed. Denial and lack of cooperation from the mentally ill person can make treatment, caring, and financial planning more difficult. Those with mental illness may not be cured but can remain stable with medication and counseling.

It was the darkest night of Filip and Helena's life. They were forced to admit their son Adam to the hospital after an excruciating manic episode. Adam was twenty-years-old, diagnosed with bipolar disorder and also had obsessive compulsive disorder. His behavior had become increasingly unusual the past few days. Adam had insomnia, paced the house all night, and had not been eating well. It was painful for Filip and Helena to watch him suffer.

Adam was obsessive about cleanliness. It was common for him to take three to four showers a day, wash his bed sheets every day, wipe his bedroom furniture several times a day, and wear double socks all the time. Lately, he had become phobic about germs in his hands and washed them every ten minutes. He became dissatisfied with soap and hot water and began using Clorox bleach. Filip and Helena's fear mounted, and they begged Adam to visit his psychiatrist to no avail. They were alarmed when he demanded they buy him long rubber gloves but believed they did not have a choice and hoped it would help him. Adam tied rubber bands around the opening of the gloves and his elbows to avoid letting germs enter the gloves. It was late July and a very hot summer in Detroit. Adam showered and ate with his gloves on for three days. Helena was very concerned how the heat was impacting his hands and begged Adam to remove them. Adam became furious, began pacing the floor of their small home, and started screaming. He pointed fingers at his mother and used extremely foul language. Filip, usually a patient man, became irate and pushed Adam in a corner with all his strength and held him down. Helena cut the rubber band with scissors and pulled one of the gloves.

The scene was horrific. Adam's fingers and arm were blistered from the bleach. Some were infected from the heat inside the glove, and the smell was foul. Adam lost control, shook loose from his parents, and let out a wail. He panicked, opened the front door, and ran out of the house with Filip in pursuit. It was late afternoon on a Saturday, and some of the neighbors were in their yards. Helena sat down helplessly, then knew instantly that she had to take action and called 911. The EMS arrived followed by a police van. The police found Filip with Adam still agitated and out of breath and brought them back to the house. Adam was scared and needed to be calmed down. The EMS team asked Adam if he was ready to go to the hospital. Filip and Helena were concerned if he would resist. They had chosen not to be his legal guardian when he turned eighteen and could not force him to be hospitalized. Adam protested but finally relented, and Helena and Filip followed the ambulance. Adam was admitted to the hospital in the psychiatric ward for an acute case of manic depression.

Filip and Helena had faced many challenges in their lives since childhood. They fled communist rule in their native

Poland with their families to become educated, have stable jobs, and a home in the United States. Nothing had prepared them, though, for the anguish of their beloved only son's illness.

Filip and Helena migrated to the U.S. after World War II. Poland had become a communist-controlled satellite of the Soviet Union, prompting a large wave of immigration. Filip was ten and Helena was eleven. Filip's family spent the first year in the Chicago area and later moved to Detroit, where his electrician father had a better chance of employment. Helena's family settled in Hamtramck, a community bordering Detroit with a large Polish population. The familiarity of the Polish culture established by the earlier immigrants in this town was comforting to Helena and Filip's family. Michigan's weather was similar to Poland and also made them feel at home.

Filip and Helena met in middle school in Hamtramck. The school was attended by many Polish immigrant students along with students from a few other ethnic groups. Many including Filip and Helena struggled to adjust to their new environment and learn the English language. They were haunted by the memories of war and the efforts of migrating to the U.S., leaving behind the only world they knew. Their parents found employment, and the families slowly established roots in their new homeland. The Polish population in Hamtramck created a little Poland right near Detroit. The various bakeries, produce stores, butcher shops, restaurants, and tailoring shops owned by Polish immigrants and serving the local population made the new arrivals feel at home. The Catholic churches also offered services in Polish, and the Polka Clubs were very popular.

Filip was the youngest of three boys in his family. His father was a well-trained electrician and easily found employment in the automotive industry. His mother was an excellent baker and worked for a bakery near their home. Filip's brothers saw the benefits of working for the automotive industry and began working on the assembly line as soon as they finished high school. Helena was an only child. Her father was a construction worker. The post-war construction boom helped him find a job very quickly. Helena's grandmother, a widow, also lived with them. Helena's mother was a seamstress and cared for Grandma Babcia and Helena. She took orders for alterations and worked from home when she could.

Helena loved math since she was in elementary school in Poland. Her teacher recognized her natural talent and encouraged her to take on extra assignments to get ahead. Helena learned high school math easily and was asked to help out a few struggling students. Filip did not need help but accompanied his friend Micha after school one day. That introduction was the beginning of a long friendship between Helena and Filip. Helena was a very attractive girl but shy. Filip was a cheerful and hardworking young man, the joking boy of their class. They often hung out together during lunch break and occasionally after school. They attended the same church and often ran into each other socially. They were young, but the war and their transition to this new world had matured them quite early. Their goal was to assimilate in the American world as quickly as possible and yet maintain the culture they were proud of.

Filip and Helena graduated from high school at the same time. Filip found a two-year apprenticeship in an electric contracting company; his goal was to work for the automotive industry just like his father. Helena decided to pursue an associate degree in accounting at a local community college. Only a handful of girls from their graduating class went for further studies, but Helena was ambitious. They were both busy pursuing their career goals and establishing themselves and helping their families. Helena helped her mother with some of her sewing and cooking. She spent as much time as she could with her grandma and adored her Babcia. Filip and his brothers were close to their parents, and they all shared a common mission. They worked for everything America had to offer with determination and honesty.

Filip and Helena remained great friends, but it was another two years before they admitted that their feelings for each other were more than just friendship. On a spring Saturday evening, Filip asked Helena out to a Polka Club for Polka dance and music. They both loved Polka; it was part of their history, their culture. They were feeling nostalgic, and during their emotional moment, Filip asked Helena to marry him.

Fifteen years after they arrived in the United States as children, Filip and Helena were married at their church in Hamtramck surrounded by their friends and families. They moved into a small home in Detroit, close to Helena's work but not far from their parents.

Helena and Filip felt blessed to have their home and steady jobs. Filip was employed by Ford Motor Company and Helena was in the J.L. Hudson Co. accounting department. Their home was tiny, a seven-hundred-square-foot ranch, but it was their own. Helena dreamed of having children and hoped to have two or three. She did not want her children to feel the loneliness she experienced as an only child. Life did not move in the direction Helena and Filip hoped.

A little over a year after they were married, Helena caught a bad cold with a sore throat, fever, and runny nose. She had trouble swallowing but did not pay much attention; many people were experiencing similar symptoms at work. It was getting close to the end of the year, and work was busy. She nursed her cold for a day and went back to work. Christmas was near, and she looked forward to time to rest and be with family.

Helena did not improve by Christmas morning. She had a fever and severe muscle aches. She had attended midnight mass the night before and was very tired. She worsened as the day progressed, and Filip recognized that she needed to see a doctor. Her joints were swollen and painful; she still had a fever, and a rash developed over her body. The doctor was concerned and suspected that her cold a few days prior may have been strep throat and her symptoms were that of rheumatic fever. He typically saw this happen to children but rarely in adults. He ordered lab tests to confirm the diagnosis and treated Helena with aspirin, steroids, and penicillin. She continued the penicillin for several months.

Helena recovered after two weeks and life went on normally for a while. Filip and Helena agreed to wait a little longer to have a family. That wait ended up taking years. When they were ready, Helena had difficulty conceiving, and it made her sad. Most of her other friends had children by then as did Filip's brothers. Her parents and grandmother Babcia were eager to have a baby in the family. Her grandma was aging and quite frail.

Two years after her rheumatic fever, Helena complained about lack of stamina and fatigue. She did not have much strength to do household work. Filip was a caring and loving life partner and picked up a lot of the home responsibilities. Helena could not imagine having a child with her current health condition. Months went by, and when things did not improve, she was referred to a heart doctor at the Detroit Receiving Hospital. Helena was diagnosed with rheumatoid heart disease, most likely caused by an undiagnosed strep throat years ago. There was no treatment prescribed, but she was cautioned that over the years her condition could worsen.

Helena decided to work part time.

She found a job at a family-owned accounting firm close to her home. The four-hours-a-day work pattern helped. Helena felt healthier and again hoped and prayed for a child. Helena and Filip consulted doctors; both she and Filip were healthy and medically fit to have a child

Nine years after they were married and given up all hopes of having a child, Helena became pregnant. Filip and Helena were overjoyed and grateful. Helena was thirty-five and a little concerned she might be too old to have a child. Her heart condition had not worsened, but she was not very strong. She wondered if she would be able to handle raising a child—and if she would need to give up her work. She loved her job and the income helped, although Filip earned a reasonable amount as an electrician. Both Filip and Helena's parents assured her they would help out when the baby was born.

Adam was born in the spring of 1970, a beautiful and healthy baby. Filip and Helena felt truly blessed to complete their family. Filip's parents welcomed their sixth grandchild and were very happy for their son. Helena's parents were thrilled to be grandparents. Helena thought of her grandma often; she had passed away several years ago and would have loved to meet her son. Helena stayed home for six months and went back to work in the fall. Her parents watched Adam while Helena was at work. She had survived her pregnancy and childbirth well but still felt exhausted easily.

Adam brought laughter and joy to the family. Filip and Helena's lives revolved around their work and family but mainly their son. Their own childhood had lost some of the innocence and was marked by the ugliness of the war. They wanted to raise their child with love and peace. The 1967 riots in Detroit had brought back some of the dark and buried memories for them. A lot of families had begun to move to the suburbs. Filip's parents were considering moving to Sterling Heights northeast of Detroit. Filip and Helena agreed to move as well before Adam began kindergarten; they moved to Warren.

Adam was a sweet boy but also had a stubborn streak and occasional temper tantrums. He was usually a little quiet and did not always enjoy being with other noisy children. Adam was very bright and, surprisingly, loved learning numbers just like his mother did as a child. Helena also made sure that he learned to speak both Polish and English. Filip had a very special bond with his son. Every Sunday after church, Filip and

Adam were either at swimming or soccer or some other activity. Helena was involved in his educational activities and more of the disciplinarian.

Helena noticed that his temper tantrums became more frequent once Adam started first grade and attended school full time. He did not always want to speak Polish at home and answered Helena and Filip in English whenever they spoke to him in their native language. His teacher also mentioned that he often threw a tantrum if he did not like a project the class was doing. After his eighth birthday, Filip and Helena had their first major concern about Adam's temper. They were about to start their dinner when Adam reached for his third cookie from the plastic cookie jar on the kitchen counter. Helena asked him to stop in a stern voice. Adam had already been warned when he had reached for his second cookie. Adam threw the jar at the coffee table in the family room and shattered a glass vase in shards throughout the room.

Adam screamed at his mother, "You are mean and I hate you and I am not Polish like you. You cannot make me a Pole."

His parents were stunned. Adam was confronting them with their proud Polish heritage, their culture, and their lives. Filip rose from his chair still in shock, picked Adam up, and locked him in the bathroom until he calmed down and apologized. Helena could not sleep that night. She worried where the anger was coming from and whether something deeper was wrong. Helena and Filip were a loving couple and never raised their voices. Filip did not think it was serious and said it may just be a passing phase.

Unfortunately, Adam's moods continued. At times he was affectionate and tender, and then he would rage over trivial matters. Helena and Filip began to receive complaints from his teacher. They reasoned with him and also punished when necessary, but it did not seem to make a difference. They discussed his behavior with his pediatrician, but the doctor assured them that his aggression could subside as he got older. They wished their doctor was right.

Helena and Filip's first glimpse of real danger happened when Adam was thirteen. Helena and Filip were watching the news in the family room after supper. Adam finished his homework and joined them. He started to get restless after a few minutes and asked them to change the channel. Filip told him to wait until the news was over. Adam got up and began pacing the floor. He stopped after a few minutes and demanded the channel be changed. Helena recognized the same underlying tone of his voice and expression on his face that warned her of looming danger. Filip ignored him, and Helena remained silent. Adam's anger was mounting. He screamed one more time and approached the television to change the channel himself. Filip rose and held him by his shoulders in an attempt to calm him down. He was no longer a child to be locked in the bathroom for a time out. Adam wrestled from his father's grip, turned and punched a framed family photo on the wall with all his strength. The glass broke in pieces, and Adam's hand started to bleed. All three stood stunned. Adam started to calm down and began crying. Helena vacillated between being angry and feeling sorry for Adam. Filip sprang into action and wrapped a wet towel around Adam's hand. Adam needed stiches, and Filip rushed him to the emergency room at the nearby hospital. Helena broke down and sobbed in anguish when they left. This was not normal. Something was terribly wrong with their son.

Helena had a serious conversation on the phone the next day with Adam's pediatrician. He recommended they see a psychiatrist right away. Adam did not resist; he was usually reasonable most days until his mood changed. The psychiatrist met with Adam regularly and suspected he had a mood disorder and possible manic depression. He suggested regular counseling for a few months and then medication if Adam's behavior did not change.

Adam worsened and began to have difficulty focusing at school. He had always maintained good grades, but he complained about not enjoying some of his classes, did not like certain teachers, found several classmates to be annoying, and often did not want to go to school. Helena did not want to leave him home alone, and she could not skip work that often. Helena's parents were much older now and helped but were limited. Just before Adam turned fifteen he again declared one day that he did not want to go to school. Helena could not miss work, her mother was not well, and Filip had already left for work. Adam assured he would be fine by himself. Helena came home from work in the afternoon a bit nervous, not knowing what to expect. The entire main floor of the house was in complete disarray. Adam had taken out dishes from the kitchen cabinets and thrown them on the floor; he had ripped the pillows on the sofa and tossed them. He was pacing the floor and had a devilish look. He began screaming at Helena and called her names. Helena called Filip to come home and contacted the psychiatrist's office. He asked her to call 911 and admit him to the hospital.

Adam was officially diagnosed with bipolar disorder, anxiety disorder, and prolonged mood swings. He was prescribed with Lithium and other medications. Helena and Filip were devastated to learn about their only son's mental illness. They knew this illness could not be cured but wondered if he could live a normal life. Could he finish high school, go to college, marry and have a family? The hospital's psychiatrist was very kind, with years of experience working with young adults. He assured them it was possible for Adam to achieve a stable life as long as he continued to take medications and continue with his counseling. His parent' support and patience were critical.

Adam was scared but accepted his diagnosis and agreed to take the medication regularly. The medicines made a huge difference, but Adam hated the side effects of Lithium. He lost his appetite and felt nauseous most of the time. He did not want his classmates to see the tremors in his hands. He managed to stay focused in his studies. Helena and Filip were relieved when a year went by with only minor and manageable episodes. Their relief was short lived when Adam became convinced that he had recovered from his illness and did not need medication or counseling any longer. Helena and Filip made sure he took his medication. When he had another episode and hospitalization, they learned Adam pretended to take medication but flushed it down the toilet. Adam had one more hospitalization following an acute anxiety attack a few weeks before high school graduation. The pressure of finishing high school and entering the unknown world of college was too much for him. He did not feel ready. His mind was clouded by repetitive thoughts of failure, getting lost and fear of being alone.

Helena and Filip had joined the Alliance for Mentally Ill (AMI) in Macomb County. The organization is a nationwide grassroots advocacy group, representing families and people affected by mental illness. Their mission is improving the lives of individuals and families affected by mental illness by providing support, education, awareness, advocacy, and research. Helena and Filip felt desperate and lonely in their journey with their son's mental illness. Filip's family members did not understand what was wrong with Adam. Filip's brothers felt that he was too easy on his son. Helena's parents mostly expressed their sadness and concern. Filip and Helena began attending the AMI support group meetings regularly and were comforted by the support of other members and sharing the stories of their children.

I met Filip and Helena at one of the AMI meetings where I had presented the Estate and Financial Planning concepts and strategies for children with disabilities. The presentation included the importance of qualifying for government benefits and planning around maintaining the qualification for the benefits. I remember Helena asking me after the workshop what would happen if they did their special needs planning needlessly if their son improved. I recognized that they had not accepted their son's illness and were hopeful for his complete recovery. They attended two other workshops organized by other entities, and each time they asked me the same question.

I met Helena and Filip again, this time in my office, three months after Adam was hospitalized for the severe manic attack and infected blisters on his hands. They wanted to discuss Adam's future plans. When I asked what prompted them to begin his planning, Helena could not control her heart-wrenching sobs. Filip shed silent tears as he held his wife's hand and narrated the episode with the rubber gloves.

Adam had graduated from high school but was not ready to start college. He was not sure what he wanted to study. His parents were very patient and gently encouraged him to take a few classes at a slow pace. He attended Macomb Community College one class at a time. He started with calculus and then accounting. He preferred evening classes as he often slept during the day. Adam was not confident about driving to school for his classes, and his parents were not comfortable either. They drove him three times a week and waited in the car until he finished. They were devoted parents and were ready to do anything for him. He had to take a break from his studies after his last episode. Adam realized after his last hospitalization that he could not take chances with his medication, and Helena and Filip realized that they could not trust him.

Helena and Filip did not want to be Adam's legal guardian. They did not think it would be fair to him despite his illness. Adam applied for SSI and Medicaid and was approved based on his diagnosis and records of his several hospitalizations. His parents created a revocable special needs trust for him as well as their own revocable trust, pour-over wills to ensure transfer of any assets not part of the trust with ease, and powers of attorney. Filip's two nephews, Ryan and Peter, were listed as successor trustees after Filip and Helena's passing. Helena and Filip both were convinced that this was only temporary. Their son may never need all of this planning or the government benefits for long.

Filip and Helena were concerned about Adam's financial future even if he improved or recovered. They were not sure when he would graduate from college, if at all. Would he get a job and be able to get along with other people? They wanted to leave as much as they could for his trust. They had modest assets and needed Filip's pension and savings for their own retirement and old age. They liked the idea of using permanent life insurance to fund the special needs trust. Buying a second-to-die life insurance policy, which insures two people under one policy, was not an option; Helena was not insurable due to her rheumatic heart condition. A policy on Filip's life alone was expensive. They decided they did not have a choice and had to do the best they could. Their completed financial and legal plan provided them with a foundation for their son and immense relief.

Adam took six years to get his degree in accounting but lacked people skills and the ability to work forty hours a week. Helena made arrangements for Adam to interview at the firm where she had been employed for many years. They knew his medical history and were empathetic. They agreed to hire him on a part-time basis. His earnings were just enough to maintain his SSI and Medicaid benefits. He drove to work, worked three hours a day, and was able to manage the work environment as well as the type of work. He had a corner table at the office overlooking the window. He was not social, minded his own business but did his work well. His medications and psychiatric counseling were absolutely essential for his physical and mental stability.

Adam had several minor episodes but stayed out of hospital for many years. His life was not exciting, and he did not have any friends. He lived with his parents, and his parents felt secure having Adam with them. His job at the accounting firm was steady.

Helena's health began to deteriorate soon after she turned sixty. She had narrowing heart valves and an enlarged heart. She was always tired, short of breath, and was on several medications. Adam was fearful of losing her, and Helena worried if her passing would send him to a deep end. Helena knew that her son would never be cured of his illness, but she prayed daily for a stable life for him.

Helena passed away in her sleep soon after her sixty-second birthday. Adam continued to have minor episodes but stayed out of the hospital for many years. Filip attended the AMI meetings and encouraged Adam to attend their social programs. Adam tried a few times but did not find them interesting. Filip retired at sixty-five. Adam qualified for Social Security Disability (SSDI) as a result of that as well as Medicare.

Filip made every effort to prepare Adam for his life without his parents. Adam wanted to continue living in the same house. It was a modest home, and Adam did not want any changes in his life. Filip arranged for Ryan and Peter, his nephews, and future trustees for Adam to meet regularly, and for them to understand Adam's needs. Adam had an accounting background and managed his personal income but did not want to know about his trust finances. Filip trusted Ryan and Peter completely but also felt comfortable knowing that my firm would work with them to manage the trust assets.

Filip passed away fifteen years after Helena's death following a brief illness. Adam was forty-three. He had never lived alone but was prepared. Ryan and Peter called him every day initially and then regularly. His mental illness may never be cured but he has a stable pattern of life.

A few changes have taken place since Filip passed away five years ago. Peter was transferred for work to Wisconsin and resigned from his trusteeship. Ryan is the sole trustee now and has made it a point to attend AMI meetings occasionally. It has been important for him to understand Adam's illness in order to help him. Ryan has arranged for a woman to visit Adam for a couple of hours every day. She makes his meals and keeps the house clean. Adam is still fastidious about his environment and particularly about cleanliness. Even at work, his desk and chair position cannot change. He parks at the same spot every day and gets very upset if he loses the spot. His coworkers understand him and have accepted the way he is. He takes long walks in his neighborhood, reads, and watches television. He visits his cousins occasionally, and Ryan always invites him on important holidays.

Adam had a brief hospitalization a year ago. He had been feeling depressed, agitated, and lost his appetite. He called 911 and admitted himself to the hospital and informed Ryan. He continues to take Lithium, and newer medications have also helped him. His parent's planning along with his government benefits continue to provide a comfortable life for Adam. Helena and Filip are caring for their beloved son even in passing.

INSIGHTS FROM THE KAMINSKI FAMILY

Denial and delay in acceptance of mental illness of a family member results in a crisis situation and chaos. Approaching a psychiatrist early on when the first symptoms appear may help avoid later crisis.

Mental illness may not be cured. Long-term planning may be necessary assuming that the person may not be able to work and need government benefits, especially for health insurance. Adam could only work part time and did not receive any benefits. Medicare and Medicaid were very important for his health.

The trustee of a trust for a mentally ill person has a difficult task. They may not always have the cooperation of the person for which they are caring. The trustee may need to understand the illness and find ways to work with the person with patience and compassion.

Proper funding of the special needs trust assures a quality of life for the person with a disability. Adam is able to continue to live in his own home and work part time because of his parent's foresight and proper planning.

12

Surprise Inheritance,
Complex Options

Parents or other family members of an individual with disabilities on SSI and Medicaid must communicate with relatives before bequesting or gifting assets. Leaving assets directly to the person with disabilities jeopardizes eligibility for government benefits and requires additional complex planning.

On a late evening in summer of August 2012 Max Bell received a phone call from his father Andrew. Andrew's Uncle Ronald, his father's youngest brother, had passed away at the assisted living home he lived in a northern suburb of Detroit. He was Max's great uncle but everybody called him Uncle Ron. Max and his wife Vickie were sad for Andrew's loss. They were not close with Uncle Ron but he was family and they planned to attend his funeral two days later.

Max and Vickie attended the funeral with their daughter April, seventeen, and Benjamin, their twenty-two year old son with autism. Benjamin was very curious about Uncle Ron's death and asked endless questions about why and how he died. As usual, he repeated his questions over and over until April lost her patience and snapped at him. Ben became quiet.

The Bell family members attended the funeral to pay their last respect to Uncle Ron. He was the last of Andrew's father's siblings to survive. Ron was eighty-six, the youngest of his siblings and lived in the assisted living facility for the last ten years. He was never married and rarely attended family events. Andrew and his older brother and sister called Ronald periodically and checked on him. He was always polite but did not care to maintain a relationship with anyone.

Ronald Bell lived in the same small ranch house for over forty-five years. He worked as a mechanic at a tool and die company retiring twenty-five years before he died. None of Max's cousins knew much about him. He was always invited to the family's Thanksgiving and Christmas as well as other family gatherings but he rarely attended. Ron was a loner and did not have any friends. Andrew continued visiting him periodically.

Max and his sister decided to celebrate their parent's fiftieth wedding anniversary at Max's home in September the year before. Everybody in the family agreed to attend. Andrew insisted Ronald attend and spend the night at their home. Max offered to bring Ronald from his assisted living home. This time Ron relented and agreed. More than thirty family members attended, including Max's sister and family, uncles and aunts, his cousins and their children. Andrew and his siblings had seven children and thirteen grandchildren. April was the youngest. Ben found these family gatherings difficult as he did not like the noise and the crowd. He was recently been given an IPad, quickly mastered it and loved it. He carried it everywhere and stayed occupied away from the crowd.

After dinner the elder members of the family settled in the family room and the younger ones entertained themselves in the basement with a pool table and a large television. Max checked on Ben and was amused to find him in a friendly conversation with Uncle Ron. He was showing him his IPad and Ron was very intrigued. Ben rarely sat still to have conversations with anyone and Max had never had a meaningful conversation with Ron. And yet Ron seemed to have bonded in that short time with

Ben, who was challenged by his own social skills and ability to make friends his age. Ben talked about Ron for several days after the anniversary party and wanted to meet him again.

To Max's surprise, Ron called Andrew and asked if he could spend Christmas Eve and Christmas with them. The Bell family celebrated Thanksgiving together but Christmas was always spent with immediate family. Andrew was more than happy to bring him home. Ron had never asked to be part of any family event before. Interestingly, he asked about Ben as soon as he arrived. Ben was delighted to see him like a long-lost friend. Ben loved children younger than him and got along well with elderly people. Ben promised Uncle Ron that he would visit him and Grandpa Andrew was glad to take Ben to visit Ron several times.

Ronald Bell's funeral was short and attended by his immediate family and a few people from the assisted living facility. Ben appeared confused and restless. He later told Vickie "I just found a friend and already he is gone." At the lunch following the funeral, Andrew asked the family to meet in two weeks to discuss Ronald Bell's will. The family was surprised to learn Uncle Ron had a will and wondered if he had any assets. He was an unusual man but now there was a mystery around him too.

Andrew, his two siblings and their children met at Andrew's home. Ron had given his will to Andrew during his recent visit and mentioned he had appointed Andrew the executor of his will. He indicated he requested his attorney to visit him to update his will. The will included an attached list of assets and he requested Andrew open the will only after his death. Everyone was curious and then unprepared for what the will disclosed.

Ronald Bell was not a wealthy man but he was a saver. He had a modest income but was frugal all his life, with very few outside interests. He had a lot of tools and read frequently, sold his house and most possessions when he moved to the assisted living facility. His health deteriorated in the last few months and he died of a heart attack. He had several Certificates of Deposits in a bank and a brokerage account with stocks and bonds adding up to over $600,000. The family was in shock and unprepared for the news, especially when they learned how the estate was divided.

Ronald left ten thousand dollars each to his two loyal helpers at the assisted living facility and ten thousand dollars to the church he occasionally attended before moving to the assisted living facility. From the remaining assets, two thirds were to be divided between Andrew, his sister and brother. It was Uncle Ron's wish that they keep half the amount for themselves and distribute the other half to their children equally. Then came the biggest surprise. Benjamin was given one third of his estate. Max and Vickie's jaws dropped but immediately they were very concerned whether Ben could own assets.

Vickie and Max had attended a special needs planning workshop presented at Ben's school before he turned eighteen. They learned about the importance of qualifying Ben for government benefits such as SSI and Medicaid and the qualifying rules. He could not own more than two thousand dollars under his name. They also became aware that they could not depend upon the government benefits alone for Ben's future. They would need to create a plan to leave assets for him in a trust that had specific language. This allowed the trustee to use the income and principal of the trust to supplement his government benefits but not replace them. This was called a Third Party Special Needs Trust.

Ben qualified for SSI and Medicaid when he turned eighteen. Max and Vickie also obtained limited guardianship for medical, residential and educational purposes. He began working through the transition coordination at school to determine his skills for employment. Maintaining the Medicaid eligibility for

Ben was very important for his future. Although they meant to complete their financial and legal planning on Ben's long-term future, they had not finalized plans yet.

Ben was diagnosed with autism at two and a half years old. Ben's symptoms in early childhood were of great concern to Vickie and Max. His development was delayed in most areas. He missed on most of the milestones and walked at two years age. He had a very difficult time sleeping and wore Vickie and Max out. Both Vickie and Max's parents took turns helping out at nights after Vickie returned to work when Ben was three months old. She was a dental hygienist and worked very close to home. Max was an Information Technology specialist and worked for a large engineering company. Max and Vickie expressed their concern to the pediatrician at every checkup. The pediatrician diagnosed Ben with autism following several tests.

Ben began attending the early intervention program at school soon after he was diagnosed. As he grew he attended some special education classes and some general. He was always restless and had difficulty playing with other children. He received speech therapy for many years and learned to converse in short sentences. At home, both his parents worked tirelessly on his vocabulary, reading skills and math. He worked well in some areas but had impaired development in social interaction and communication. His social behavior in his early teen years was unpredictable and sometimes embarrassing and yet he was sweet and caring.

Vickie was emotionally not prepared to have another child after Ben's diagnosis. What if the second child also had a disability? Vickie went through a period of depression during those early months of uncertainty. April's birth five years later was pure joy. She grew as expected and brought normalcy in their household.

By the time Ben was sixteen he was reading at eighth grade

level but comprehended at a lower level. He did not have any sensory issues and managed to take care of himself but could not be trusted to be alone for long periods of time. He was not social but was scared to be alone for too long. And he also had obsessive compulsive disorder. He wanted items around the house and especially in his room placed in a certain way and became upset if they were not.

Grandpa Andrew was very touched and overwhelmed by Uncle Ron's generous and surprising gesture toward his grandson. He recalled his last visit with Uncle Ron when he commented, "Ben reminds me of how I was at his age. He is a sweet boy but he will need help." The family was unaware that Uncle Ron's gift to Ben would create planning challenges.

Max and Vickie researched the consequences and options of Ben's inheritance during the time Uncle Ron's estate went through probate. They consulted with my firm as advisors along with attorneys. Ben could lose his SSI and Medicaid eligibility unless the inheritance was converted into exempt assets such as a prepaid funeral service, burial plot, an automobile, other personal use assets or even a home in his name. His parents were not ready to consider buying a home for Ben yet, he lived at home under their care and was only twenty-two.

The best option for Max and Vickie was to create a First Party Irrevocable Special Needs Trust and have the Probate Court approve the transfer of the inheritance to this trust. This type of special needs trust is usually funded with a settlement resulting from a tort action or inheritance received inadvertently by a person with disabilities. Max and Vickie learned that by transferring assets in this trust, Ben could maintain his eligibility for SSI and Medicaid. Upon his death the remaining assets of the trust must first be used to pay back any state medical agency providing benefits. Any amount remaining could be distributed to Ben's heirs.

Another option to consider was a 'Pooled Accounts Trust,"

often established by a not-for-profit entity in which the small amount of assets of many trusts are combined for investment purposes but are managed individually for distribution purposes. A master-trust document is adopted to govern the trust. A pooled trust is usually a first-party trust and funded by the assets of the person with disabilities Some pooled trusts provide for assets remaining in the pool when the special needs person dies. The assets are retained by the trust for the benefit of other beneficiaries of the master trust.

Max and Vickie gave considerable thought to the best option. They understood the reasons for the state payback provision of the First Party Special Needs Trust but were initially hesitant. It also made them realize that they needed to coordinate their own financial and legal plan with the First Party Special Needs Trust. They felt that it was important to share their planning strategies with both Max and Vickie's parents.

Uncle Ben's inheritance and Ben's future planning process forced Vickie and Max to face the reality of Ben's future. They had buried their fears and concerns deep in their hearts in the business of their day to day lives. Now they needed to think about how much funding Ben would need in addition to the government benefits. They wondered whether there were guarantee of the government benefits in the future. Where will Ben live? Will he be able to have his independence? What kind of family support will he need and have? The Bell family was close-knit but all Ben's cousins may not be available to provide support. April was considering attending a New York fashion institute to major in Fashion Design and Business Management. Her parents did not wish to hold her back from achieving her dreams. Many of Max's eleven nieces and nephews had already left the Detroit area for work or education. Vickie's only sister lived in Texas and rarely saw her two nephews.

Ben's parents were equally concerned about lack of adequate employment opportunities for those with disabilities. Fortunately, Ben still had four more years in special education until he was twenty-six per Michigan special education rules. His parents considered community college but believed Ben was not a good candidate. They worried how he would keep himself occupied after school or if he could find a job and maintain it. Both Max and Vickie's parents advised their worries were warranted, yet they should create plans to the best of their ability and adjust them as circumstances change.

For the inheritance, Max and Vickie opted for the First Party Trust. They were also careful and creative in using the inheritance with the help of proper financial planning guidance. Ben would most likely need funds in the future since his parents could provide what he currently needed. Three quarters of the funds were used to purchase a single premium Second to Die Permanent Life insurance on Andrew and Donna**. They were in their early seventies and healthy. The death benefit was almost two and a half times the premium paid. The concept of using leverage to create a tax-free death benefit seemed practical to the family. The remaining funds in the trust was kept for summer camps, trips and other miscellaneous expenses.

Max and Vickie had been saving for April's college and Ben's future as well as for their own retirement. Considering the longevity in their family, they were not sure how much of their savings would be available at their death for Ben's future. They decided to use the same concept of leveraging and insuring themselves to fund a Third Party Special Needs Trust that they created. Unlike the First Party trust, the remaining assets of this trust would be distributed to Ben's heirs. Max and Vickie also created their own living trust and coordinated it with Ben's special needs trust. Their parents were recommended by my firm to do the same. When both trusts were funded, the First Party trust with state payback provision would be used before the funds of the Third-party trust.

Vickie and Max were relieved once their finances were organized and planning completed. They realized that that was just the beginning of the future planning. Vickie and Max tried to be optimistic about their son's future but their hearts sank every time they heard about government budget cuts and lack of residential and employment opportunities for those with disabilities. They agreed to research residential facilities where Ben could be safe, independent, occupied and remain motivated. They could use savings set aside under their own names for Ben's future, some of the funds from Uncle Ron's inheritance and Ben's SSI income to pay for the right facility.

In the following months and years, Max, Vickie and Ben visited Melmark New England in Massachusetts,[7] Brookwood Community in Texas[8] and Stewart Home School in Kentucky. [9]Each one of them were well acclaimed for their educational, vocational, residential, clinical and rehabilitative services. Vickie and Max were not ready for Ben to leave yet but they knew they would consider one of them when the time was right where he could enjoy his independence, have a quality of life and be safe.

The Bell family wondered if Uncle Ron had lived on the autism spectrum as well. He lived a normal life but had some quirks and personality traits similar to Ben. His gift to Ben was a seal to their brief bonding and steps toward Ben's financial security.

---

7 Melmark New England, www.melmarkne.org
8 Stewart Home & School, www.stewarthome.com
9 Brookwood Community, www.brookwoodcommunity.org

Coordination of a plan created for a person with disabilities with other family members is important to avoid mistakes. Occasionally, loving relatives such as Ben's uncle bequest and gift assets to a child with good intentions without realizing the adverse consequences. Parents or other family members of an individual with disabilities on SSI and Medicaid must communicate with relatives. This avoids leaving assets directly to the person with disabilities and jeopardizing their eligibility for SSI and Medicaid. The best option is leaving the bequest to the Third Party Special Needs Trust created for them.

An Irrevocable First Party Special Needs Trust investment planning should be done carefully. Whether it is funded by a settlement of a tort action or inadvertently received inheritance, the funds should be planned carefully. This trust has the state payback language but it may also be the only asset the disabled person may have and it may need to last his/her life time. Investments may need to be tax efficient and growth oriented to supplement the SSI, Medicaid and other government benefits. Family members may not want to leave an inheritance to a First Party Special Needs Trust. It should be directed to a Third Party Special Needs Trust to avoid the remaining assets being subject to the state payback up to the amount spent by Medicaid for the individual.

ABLE account may be considered as an alternate to creating a First Party Special Needs Trust if the amount of inheritance or settlement is fifteen thousand dollars or less. Achieving a Better Life Experience Act of 2014, or better known as the ABLE Act, allows tax-advantaged savings accounts for individuals with disabilities and their families. The beneficiary of the account is the owner of the account and the income earned by the account is tax deferred, and the distribution from the account is income-tax free. Family, friends, as well as the individual with disabilities, is allowed to fund the account not to exceed fifteen thousand dollars per year. (For more details, please review Nuts and Bolts of Special Needs Planning at the end of this book.)

* * Guidelines for funding strategies for a First Party Special Needs Trust may vary from state to state. Rules applicable in the state of the residence of the beneficiary of the First Party Special Needs Trust should be verified prior to deciding on investment strategies.

13

Planning with Determination
and Love

*Taking action and planning for the life of a special needs
child is critical despite the emotions involved. Success of
a well-thought-out plan often depends on involvement of
as many family members as possible. Disabilities cannot
be changed, but a child's quality of life can be ensured
by a parent's planning and adjustments as circumstances
change. This includes ensuring the right care, education,
and suitable housing.*

Robin Hall was overjoyed to finally have a little brother. She
was seven, and almost all her friends at school, church, and the
neighborhood had at least one or two siblings. Robin wanted a
brother or sister since she was three years old and wished for
one on every birthday and Christmas. When her brother was
finally born, she visited him at the hospital and couldn't wait
for her mom to come home with the baby. Her parents were
delighted and relieved. Donna had a very difficult pregnancy
with Robin and was scared to have another child after having
gestational hypertension and spending the last two months
before Robin's birth in bed. But she and her husband, Keith,
wanted more children and tried for five years before nearly
giving up. They were, however, concerned. Donna was thir-

ty-seven and was considered high risk due to her experience with Robin's pregnancy and her age.

Scott was born prematurely in April 1976 and was small but appeared healthy. He remained in the hospital's intensive care unit for a few more weeks before going home. The Hall family anxiously awaited their son's arrival and were relieved to have him home. Keith and Donna's family felt complete with their beautiful children. Robin was a doting older sister and loved her little brother. Donna went back to work in September, thankful her mother was caring for Robin and now Scott.

Donna and Keith lived in Northville, a lovely suburb of Detroit. Donna felt blessed her parents lived within a few miles from her in Livonia. Her sister Nancy, two years older, lived in nearby Plymouth with her family. Donna was a middle-school English and history teacher at the Livonia Public Schools. Keith was a pharmaceutical representative. Keith's parents and older brother lived in Grand Rapids. They both loved their jobs and had close relationships with their families. Donna and Nancy were particularly close and enjoyed their friendship and sister-hood.

Living near each other meant the families could be together often. Nancy was married to Derek and had two sons, Josh and Nathan. Josh was two years older than Robin, and Nathan was a year younger. The cousins spent a lot of time together and were great friends.

The Hall family settled into a routine once Donna began working after her maternity leave. Keith saw Robin off to school every morning at the bus stop while Donna took the baby to her parent's home on her way to work. Her father picked up Robin after school and Donna brought the children home. Robin loved her time with the baby and couldn't wait for him to grow up, start talking, and running around. Donna's mom, Sophie, was the first to express some concern about Scott. Scott did not enjoy his tummy time and cried every time he was put on his belly. Although he seemed healthy in every way, something was not quite right. She did not mention anything to Donna for a while until Donna asked her if she had noticed anything different about Scott. Scott did not seem to lift his head and was content lying in the same position. The pediatrician did not seem overly concerned during the baby's initial checkups. He was gaining weight at a normal pace and looked healthy.

The following months confirmed the family's fears as Scott failed to reach other milestones such as turning on the side or trying to sit up. He walked late and began talking late as well. His responses to simple instructions were blank stares. The pediatrician verified through several tests that Scott had mild retardation, a term no longer used to describe a mental disability; now it is described as intellectual disability or cognitive impairment. But it would take time to determine to what extent his development was affected. Donna and Keith were devastated by Scott's diagnosis. Robin was eight years old and sensitive to her mother's silent tears and the somber atmosphere in the house. She knew her parents were worried about her brother but couldn't tell why. She finally asked Grandma Sophie why everybody was so sad. Sophie explained to her gently that her parents were worried about Scott not growing as fast and as well as he should. Robin worried if he was going to be like Parker, her classmate with Down Syndrome, but Scott did not look like Parker. That evening, Robin told her parents, "Don't be so sad, Mom and Dad; my brother is beautiful and I love him. He is my brother and I will always love him." Robin's loving words were heartfelt and touched Donna and Keith deeply. Their eight-year-old child was teaching them about unconditional love and reminding them to be hopeful.

Keith was a pharmaceutical representative with a fair amount of knowledge about the human body and mind. Donna was an educator and naturally curious. Together they were determined to learn every medical detail about Scott and his prognosis. They also wanted to ensure he had the opportunity to get the education he needed. There were too many unknown factors. Was there a genetic predisposition? Was it Donna's high-risk pregnancy status, the premature birth? What caused Scott to have a mental impairment? After several visits to different doctors, they could not find any definite reason or any other diagnosis except mild retardation. They slowly began to accept this new reality without knowing what might happen as Scott developed.

Grandma Sophie and Donna worked with Scott at home with basics like his alphabet, numbers, colors, and shapes. His response was slow. He had difficulty with grabbing and throwing objects. Donna extensively researched a landmark national 1975 law related to access to special education. In 1975, Congress enacted the Education for All Handicapped Children Act (EHA.) The law's goal was to ensure that children with disabilities gained access to a free and appropriate public education. This provided local and statewide support and protection to children and youth with disabilities, as well as their families. Under EHA, all public schools were granted federal funding providing equal access to education for children with physical and/or mental disabilities. Schools were required to evaluate children and create an educational plan that paralleled the academic experience of their non-disabled peers. EHA requirements also provided parents and families the necessary support systems to ensure their child received appropriate and adequate services, along with the services needed to dispute decisions made on behalf of the child.[10]

Donna educated herself with the help of her colleagues in the special education department at Livonia Public Schools about educating her son. She then approached the Northville

10 The Education for All Handicapped Children Act was a breakthrough law for special education in 1975. It was later amended to the Individual with Disabilities with Education Act, (IDEA) 2005. U.S. Department of Education.org

Schools, discussed her son's disability, had him tested again at school, and enrolled him at age four. Scott began weekly physical therapy and speech therapy. Donna and Keith visited the school regularly to ensure Scott was getting the attention he needed and to keep up with his progress. They were equally attentive to Robin's needs, both in school and with her extra activities in sports and music. Robin started middle school the year Scott started pre-school. Donna and Keith communicated well with each other about their hopes and dreams for their children and also about their anguish and worry about Scott's future. Donna shared her deep fears about his future with her sister, Nancy. Nancy was a patient listener, understood her sister's distress, and allowed her to express her feelings and be a comfort to her.

Scott continued to progress at a slower-than-normal but steady pace. He eventually learned to read up to sixth grade level and comprehend at fourth grade level. Math was very challenging for him. He was social, made friends, and smiled a lot. He spoke in short sentences but gradually added to his vocabulary. He loved the outdoors, and with years of physical therapy, his large and fine motor skills markedly improved. He began participating in Special Olympics by age twelve—in track and field and in bowling. He also attended SCAMP, a camp for special needs children in Bloomfield Hills Schools. Donna and Keith kept him busy and involved him in household chores, and Robin spent a lot of time playing games with her brother, reading books, and helping him with his homework. She was mature for her age even as a child and always very protective of her brother. Donna and Keith admired her unwavering love for Scott and her interest and involvement in his well-being.

Robin eventually graduated from high school and decided to attend Wayne State University for a degree in nursing. Biology and medical matters interested her a lot. She decided to commute from home rather than living in an apartment near the university like some of her friends. She wanted to be close to her family and stay involved in her brother's life.

Keith and Donna had other challenges as their parents aged. Keith's father passed and his mother became ill, requiring Keith to make frequent visits to Grand Rapids. He felt fortunate because his older brother, who was unmarried, worked nearby and was able to care for his mother. Donna's parents were aging as well and began requiring frequent doctor's visits. Meanwhile, Scott had good and bad days at school but managed them well. Robin and Scott also endured a car accident causing minor injuries and severe damage to their parent's car while driving home from a movie. The most difficult challenge for the family was Donna's diagnosis of breast cancer at age forty-seven. The cancer was diagnosed early, but Donna went through treatment and a lumpectomy. It left Donna vulnerable and worried about her future and her family, especially Scott.

Keith and Donna attended a workshop my firm had provided at Northville schools about long-term financial and legal planning for a special needs child. We always encourage grandparents and older siblings to attend as the entire family is often involved in the future planning of a child with disabilities. I was pleased to meet Sophie and Robin, who attended with Donna and Keith. When they arranged a meeting for a consultation, Robin insisted on attending as well. She was twenty-three, had completed her undergraduate degree in nursing, and was starting a master's program. I was very impressed with the sense of responsibility Robin felt for her brother. Donna and Keith learned extensively about the government benefits for which Scott could be eligible, the need to protect his financial future through proper funding of a special needs trust, and coordination of Scott's special needs trust with his grandparent's planning. Donna and Keith would have done everything they needed to take care of their son, but Robin pushed them gently and firmly until they completed their planning. At our recommendation, they also joined the local ARC, an advocacy organization for families with children with disabilities.

The Hall family financial planning entailed securing the financial stability of the surviving family in the event of either Keith or Donna's untimely death or disability through term insurance until Keith turned sixty-five. Their cash flow was analyzed to maximize their retirement savings contribution. Keith's employer provided a good restricted stock option that was helpful in accumulating their retirement savings. Robin was named the secondary beneficiary of both Keith and Donna's retirement plans. They also purchased a second-to-die universal-life policy for Scott's future. Nancy was named the successor trustee after Donna and Keith's passing. Robin would step in first as a co-trustee with Aunt Nancy at age thirty and then independently at thirty-five. Cousin Josh was named as a successor to Robin once he reached thirty-five. Keith and Donna created their joint revocable living trust and also a separate stand-alone revocable special needs trust for the benefit of Scott. Other documents such as pour-over wills and financial- and health-care powers of attorney were part of the documents. Robin had a power of attorney for health as well.

Keith and Donna continued researching and learning about all aspects of Scott's care as he grew into adulthood. They attended other workshops my firm and other advocacy organizations such as the Arc provided, including "Housing arrangements for the special needs individuals," "Sibling's Role as a Future Trustee," and "Creating a Letter of Intent." They implemented all they learned in the workshops as much as possible. During one of our review meetings, Donna showed the "Letter of Intent," a journal of everything they knew about Scott. Robin helped coordinate and include as much information as possible including Scott's behavior, medical matters, his fears, and things that he enjoyed doing. They continued to add to this document and shared it with Aunt Nancy and family.

After attending an informational session on housing/residential planning for the special needs individuals held by the local Arc, the Hall family began to consider future options for Scott. He was only eighteen, and they did not feel rushed, but they believed in thinking and planning ahead. Donna was deeply saddened that night, and the thought of Scott someday being alone or living in an unfamiliar surrounding tore at her heart. Robin understood her parent's predicament and emotions about Scott's future but assured them that she would be there for Scott and for his future care. Keith and Donna never doubted about Robin's commitment toward her brother, but was it fair to expect so much from her? Robin had a right to live a life of her own without feeling trapped carrying for her brother.

Robin rented an apartment in Royal Oak during the last semester of her master's program. She had also accepted a job at the Henry Ford Hospital as a surgical nurse after completing her advanced degree. The move was exciting for Robin; she had stayed at home longer than most of her friends. Scott missed her, and they spoke on the phone every day, sometimes twice. Robin and her parents were acutely aware of other life changes that may affect Scott, including if Robin began serious dating or considering marriage.

Robin met a new friend, Aaron, at a picnic. He was charming and very attentive to Robin. Aaron had finished his Master's of Business Administration in Human Resource Management and was working at a Fortune 500 automotive-supply company. Robin liked him instantly. She had not yet dated anybody seriously, instead focusing on her studies and future career. Robin and Aaron agreed to meet the following week. They both felt a mutual attraction and enjoyed talking about their common interests in sports, music, books, movies, and college experience. When Aaron asked Robin again on a date, she had a long conversation with him on the phone before they met. She explained to him about Scott, his disability, and her love for him and her commitment to stay involved in his life. Before their relationship became serious, she wanted to make certain that Aaron or any life partner she chose would always support her involvement in Scott's life. Aaron was in awe of Robin and her dedication to Scott. He would always support her. There was one problem: Aaron was from the Cincinnati, Ohio, area and was hoping to go back to that area eventually after gaining professional experience at his current job. Robin did not want to think that far in the future. She was happy to be in a relationship with Aaron.

More events took place affecting the family in the following years. Donna's father passed away after a short illness. Sophie agreed to move in with her older daughter, Nancy. Both Josh and Nathan moved away from home, although they still lived in the Detroit metropolitan area. It was a practical decision for Sophie. Robin and Aaron were married after dating for more than two years and lived in an apartment in Novi, not too far from her parents' home. Scott began working at a nursing home while still attending school. As part of the transition planning under special education, the school district helped Scott work with Michigan Rehabilitation Services, a government agency that provides specialized employment and education-related services and training to assist teens and adults with disabilities in becoming employed or retaining employment. Scott had a job coach, and he learned to work in the laundry room and also helped out in the maintenance department. Robin and Aaron made sure they spent time with Scott over the weekends. Scott also enjoyed being at their apartment and really liked being with Aaron.

Keith and Donna had given considerable thought about where Scott would live eventually. They involved Scott in their discussion. They had visited several group homes and had mixed emotions about them. Some were maintained well but most had a long waiting list. They were learning about the difficulty of finding the right kind of caregivers even if they were to buy a place for Scott. Donna and Keith were also beginning to plan for their retirement. Scott would graduate from high school at twenty-six, Donna and Keith would then be sixty-three and sixty-five. Donna wanted to retire when Keith retired at sixty-five. Three years before Scott's graduation, Donna and Keith put Scott's name on waiting lists for a few group homes. Their decision was also prompted after Aaron received an offer for his dream job at Procter and Gamble in Cincinnati. Robin's parents never expected her to be completely responsible for Scott or even live with him after they passed. But they recognized the challenge if Robin lived five hours away. Robin was excited for Aaron but also broken-hearted at the thought of leaving Michigan, her family, and her little brother Scott.

The Hall family reviewed their financial and legal planning periodically, but we met them for a detailed review in anticipation of Keith and Donna's retirement and Scott's leaving school at twenty-six. Sophie was in her mid-eighties and had moved into an assisted living facility in Plymouth. Keith's mother passed away a few years after her husband. Keith and Donna were fortunate to be eligible for pensions. They did not have any debts and saved a decent amount in their retirement plans. They were, however, concerned about long-term care expenses considering the longevity in their families. We recommended long-term-care insurance for both of them to preserve their assets and for better quality care. Even though Donna had been cancer-free for a number of years, she could not qualify for the insurance. Keith rolled over his 401(k) plan as an in-service withdrawal available for employees over the age of fifty-nine-and-a-half to manage his funds with more options and introduce risk management strategies in his portfolio. We also reviewed Scott's financial needs if he were to live in a group home or if his trust funds had to be used to purchase a home for him with care-giving expenses. The Halls were concerned about an ongoing budget crisis at their Community Mental Health and the quality of care they would be able to provide. They were also aware that although they had done their own planning and for Scott, their resources would never be able to replace what the government benefits could provide.

We educated them all along that planning for Scott was a combination of their planning and his eligible government benefits. The Halls impressed me with their love and emotions for their son, and always used their energy, time, and finances to be practical about his planning and implementing the right strategies.

Robin visited her family once every month when they first moved to Cincinnati. Aaron's parents lived there as well as his older sister. The visits became somewhat less frequent once their son Sean was born and two years later when a second son, Neil, was born. Once Keith and Donna retired, they began visiting Robin once a month to see the grandchildren. Scott loved to see his sister and Aaron, but the nephews and Uncle Scott had a very special bond. The Halls had hoped to travel, especially in winter months. They began using the respite services for Scott. He was able to go to a home with aid from Community Mental Health for up to seven days at a time for two weeks a year. This was important for Scott to adjust to moving into a home on a permanent basis. The waiting list for a group home was moving very slowly, and it concerned Donna and Keith a great deal. They wanted to have a plan for Scott ready before they had age-related disabilities or before they passed away. Scott kept his steady job and was busy during the day. His transportation was provided from the providers at Community Mental Health, who would take him to the nursing home.

The most challenging time the Hall family faced was in April 2013, when Keith had a stroke resulting in paralysis of his left side. The sudden change from being an active and healthy couple brought their comfortable and stable world crashing down. Keith came home for care after hospitalization and then a rehabilitation facility. He did not want to move to a nursing home . . . not yet. Donna always managed the responsibilities of the house and Scott. Keith handled all of their financial and medical matters. He made sure Donna could take over banking and keep a tab on their bills and medical appointments in the event he could not. Despite her familiarity with all of that, Donna was overwhelmed with Keith's illness, his caregiving, and all of her routine responsibilities. Managing Scott was not that difficult, but he needed help in many daily matters. They needed professional help for Keith. Robin took a two-week leave of absence from work to help out. She interviewed companies providing home health care and selected one for her father. They arranged for round-the-clock service . . . three eight-hour shifts. It was expensive. Robin filed the claim for the long-term care coverage for home health care. The insurance did not cover the total expenses, but Keith and Donna could use their personal assets.

Robin and Josh visited the group homes where Scott was wait-listed to see if they could help out, considering their emergency situation. There was no opening right away, but staff assured them they would review his application. Donna took charge of all of the other responsibilities once Keith needed less of her attention. Donna was also grieving the sudden loss of her life companion and her best friend due to his lessened mental capacity. Scott's presence and his innocent childlike personality were comforting for her. She missed Robin dearly. Her ability to take charge and solve problems was a huge relief for her. Robin drove from Cincinnati every weekend for a few months. Keith passed away eight months later, just before Christmas. It was a sad Christmas for the family but also an end to Keith's suffering.

A month later, Donna received a call from staff from one of the group homes with an opening for Scott. It had taken years, but Donna was not ready. She had just lost her husband and she could not imagine losing Scott so soon. Scott was independent in many ways and was trained by his parents to handle the transition to a place of his own. Robin was very sympathetic, but they could not lose the opportunity for Scott. Two months later, Scott moved to his own room in a three-bedroom ranch home within five miles from his home in Plymouth. The house had three other residents. Two of them shared a larger bedroom. Scott had a smaller room to himself and was happy. Donna, Josh, and Robin helped him on his big day. The move was more difficult for Donna than Scott. Scott continued to work at the same nursing home. Donna picked him up on weekends. Scott settled in gradually, and his easy personality helped him get along with the other residents. Not everybody went home on weekends. They all had plans with their direct-care staff for weekends such as bowling, movies, or just a trip to the mall. Scott occasionally spent weekends with his housemates and gradually visited home less and less. Donna was proud of his independence and was relieved but missed him terribly.

When Derek—the husband of Donna's sister, Nancy—passed away two years after Keith, the two sisters decided to rent a condo in Florida for two months during the winter. Scott flew in with one of his direct caregivers for the weekend. Things seemed to all fall in place. Nancy and Donna agreed to continue to visit Florida each year. Scott was happy at his home after a few months of adjustment. Donna adjusted to her new life without Keith and Scott. Robin considered moving Scott to Ohio . . . somewhere closer to her. After some research, she realized that it was not practical to uproot Scott from his job and new home. Robin was relieved that her parents' planning allowed both her mother and Scott to have a comfortable life. She is very aware that her mother will not always be there and that she will be the trustee for Scott. He will visit her in Cincinnati with a companion; Scott will accompany Robin's family on vacations. The group home has a copy of Donna's Letter of Intent with all of Scott's details including medical records. Robin visits her mother and brother once every three months. Josh picks up Scott from time to time for a Tiger's baseball game or for a hamburger. The Hall family financial and legal planning was updated after Keith's death and is monitored by my firm.

The Halls did the best they could do in planning for themselves and for Scott. Their foresight, timeliness, and willingness to be practical in making several of the planning decisions helped complex needs go smoothly. The closeness of the family members and their involvement is also remarkable. Scott functions at a much higher level than many other adults with disabilities, which has made the transitions somewhat easier. Robin had promised to love her brother always when she was a little girl. She continues to keep her promise.

INSIGHTS FROM THE HALL FAMILY

Accepting the disability of a child takes time and courage. Realistic approaches to planning help families find more options for the future care of their loved ones. The entire family's involvement in careful planning, research, and information on available resources can help in all aspects of care. The Halls involved their daughter and relatives from the start, helping them understand Scott's needs and their roles in Scott's future planning.

The success of a plan in place for an individual with disability depends upon the family's ability to adjust to changes in their lives and circumstances. Creating alternative plans and resources in coordination with available government benefits make things easier for everybody including the person with disabilities. Scott's move to a group home, his father's death, and his sister's moving to another city was managed well and carefully without creating a trauma for him.

Inspiring Advocates:

Five Profiles
on Committed Leaders

Advocates are those exceptional human beings who tirelessly lend their voices to a cause, ensuring positive change where directed. The following chapter honors the efforts of five inspiring trailblazers and families within the special needs community. As parents and professionals, their commitment to bettering the lives of those with disabilities is exemplary and humbling.

I salute these individuals for their ongoing service and dedication to the special needs population.

The Brown Family. From left, Craig, Ross, Bryan, Linda.

Linda Brown

A Son's Dream:
I Want My Own House

One day, Bryan Brown's mother Linda read him a book about making dreams. She asked her son with developmental disabilities what his dream would be if he could have anything he wanted. Bryan's disabilities prevented him from speaking clearly, and he spelled out on a special letter board communication device, "I want to move out and get my own house." Linda's heart melted. Bryan had so many challenges in his young life, she decided she would do everything possible to make his dream a reality.

Bryan was diagnosed with autism, ADHD, depression, tic disorder, and was persistently angry and defiant by the age of fifteen. When he was six, he became self-abusive and aggressive, and his issues sky-rocketed at fifteen. His puberty was very difficult, and he was in distress physically and emotionally. He could no longer tolerate the academic and social pressure of school. Bryan began a home- and community-based educational program funded by the school and supervised by Community Mental Health.

Bryan's brother, Ross, also was diagnosed with autism and later bipolar and many challenges. He fought his own battles during puberty but managed to remain in school.

Linda's decision to move Bryan into his own home eventually became her top priority. The path from the day she and her husband, Craig, decided to fulfill Bryan's dream until he moved to his own home was long, arduous, and took another three years. The lessons learned about finding housing for their special needs son became the foundation for Linda's life work. Linda had set aside her career as an attorney after her sons were diagnosed. She is now a dedicated advocate for helping families plan and find housing for their special needs children in Michigan.

Linda and Craig began their married life in Michigan but relocated to Wisconsin for nine years for Craig's work in the finance area for a Fortune 500 automotive supply company. Their first-born Ross developed normally until twenty-two months and then regressed, losing his speech and fine motor skills. He was diagnosed with autism at two-and-a-half years old. Linda was expecting their second child and was confused and worried. Ross had difficulty sleeping, adding to her anxiety and sleep deprivation. Their second son, Bryan, also showed health challenges and developmental delays and was diagnosed with autism at three-and-a-half years of age. Linda made the difficult decision to give up her lucrative law career to care for her sons' severe neurological challenges. She decided to do everything in her power to help her sons achieve the best they could. She became obsessed with determining what an autism diagnosis meant in terms of having a "normal" life for them. She hoped they might be able to attend college and have their own homes. She spoke and read to them about having their own dreams, attending college, and having a home.

Raising two severely autistic children had trying moments every day. Linda loved her sons dearly yet had moments when she wished she could walk out the door and give the exhausting job of caregiving to someone else. Craig encouraged her to become active in the Autism Society at the local and state level.

She soon became a member of a Wisconsin Taskforce for Individuals with Autism. She helped outline the educational definition and assessment of autism, and later became a member of a multi-disciplinary team trained to educate and assist school districts to work with students with autism.

The Browns returned to Michigan when the boys were seven and five years old to be close to their families. In Michigan, Linda continued to work in volunteer positions as well as a research attorney in disability law for a short time. Then Bryan's teen-aged physical and mental health crisis meant leaving school and required his parent's attention. Ross and Bryan's needs became Linda's primary concern, and she refocused on their care full time.

Ross and Bryan's autism affect them in very different ways. Their needs and preferences are opposite because of differing sensory dysfunction needs. Ross has extremely sensitive hearing and Bryan has hearing loss and vocal tics resulting in loud and long vocalizing. This is painful for Ross, and he wears noise-cancelling headphones. Bryan cannot stand bright light, and Ross likes the lights turned on.

Linda began planning for Bryan to move out soon after learning his dream at fifteen. Craig was not quite ready for Bryan to move out but agreed with Linda that Bryan's wishes were important. Linda also needed to be sure Ross knew that he did not have to move just because of his brother. He could continue living with his parents or move out with Bryan. Her planning included:

- Finding the right house, who should own it, how it should be titled and arrange financing. The location, proximity to their own house, neighborhood, and affordability were important.

- Finding a roommate. The Browns needed two roommates at first as caregiving is more cost effective when spread over the right number of special needs residents. Then Ross decided to move in with Bryan, and his parents found a home they thought would work. Ross liked the home they picked and agreed to move. Linda recognized that age, compatibility, and caregiving needs of other roommates are important considerations and found the needed third roommate through Community Mental Health.

- Preparing the home for their unique and specific needs. The home needed to be a ranch house, all one level with a basement, a back yard, and a screen porch. It had to be away from a busy street and could not be near water for safety.

- Ensuring quality caregiving staff. Ross and Bryan had very complex care issues. The staff needed to be informed of and trained on their behavior plans, sensory diets, medicine, diet restrictions, and other allergies.

Ross and Bryan both had a Children's Medicaid waiver before age eighteen due to the severity of their disabilities. Linda and Craig waited until Bryan was eighteen years old when both Ross and Bryan were approved for an Adult Habilitation Waiver. This waiver provides higher level of support services to recipients in a range of community settings for social activities, employment, and caregiving. Linda and Craig found the right house near their home with the requirements they had. They had been saving for a long time but needed to determine whether they would need a mortgage and if the boys' Supplemental Security Income (SSI) would be adequate to pay the monthly payment, property taxes, as well as the maintenance of the home. Linda and Craig were fortunate to receive a gift from her parents. Their own savings in addition to the gift helped them buy the home and make Bryan's dream become real.

I met Linda and Craig in 2007 and was impressed by their focus on housing needs. My firm did their financial planning and helped them revise earlier legal planning. Their legal plan included special needs trusts for Ross and Bryan as well as trusts for Linda and Craig. They acquired life insurance for their financial security and to fund the special needs trusts. They owned the home purchased for Ross and Bryan in an LLC with the plan of leaving it in their special needs trust.

Ross and Bryan moved into their home in 2008 at the ages of twenty and eighteen. This was no ordinary accomplishment for Linda and Craig. Most parents find it difficult to think about their child moving out of their home and from under their care. Too often a move follows a parent's illness or death, creating a disruption in a child's life and emotional set back. Linda felt strongly about starting to use her experience, knowledge, and educating the families about the process, options, and planning required to find a future home for their loved ones. More importantly, she believed parents also need a gentle nudge to think proactively and help transition their special needs child while they are alive to help them cope with this major change in their lives.

"It's about their quality of life after we're gone," she said. "No one will ever take care of them as well as we do. That's the scariest part, having to let go, not having control. Having to trust others you may not even know. Craig and I are always looking for ways to minimize the potential downside."

The planning process to help her sons move was long and complex. Linda now shares lessons she learned from her experience and advice with other parents.

1. Make a plan but be ready to change it. "There are so many moving pieces, you may have to change a few of the first options you chose to make it work. They usually work better anyway," Linda said.

2. It's important to build the expectation in your son or daughter that they will have their own place, someday, as an adult. "It is important in their progression into adulthood, but also because parents will not always be there," Linda said. "I didn't want to have them be so dependent on us that when we are gone they will be lost."

3. Treat your children like the adults you want them to be. "When we treated Ross and Bryan like the adults they were, they acted like adults. We tried to do that within our home, but they needed their own home to feel it," Linda said. "When Bryan stayed overnight at one of our home helpers, he did all kinds of things he wouldn't do for us. He made his bed, put his dishes in the sink, took three showers (getting one shower a week was a battle!) It was obvious that keeping him with us was not in either his or our best interest."

4. Respect their right to decide if and when they need to see you once they move out. "Everyone is different. When they are ill or something is not right, they want us there to help, but if things are good, they may say, 'You can stay home, Mom.' I miss them, but I'm happy that they are building their own life," Linda said. "That is not to say that we don't insist on at least a short visit if we haven't seen them in a while!"

5. Think about the things that are important to their everyday comfort, security, and well-being and try to build those things into the new living arrangement. "For us it was helping to build a relationship with at least some of their staff ahead of the move so they could 'read' our nonverbal sons, knew their dietary restrictions, and their likes/dislikes."

Linda worked closely with the Community Mental Health experts to set up housing for Bryan and Ross. The Community Mental Health (CMH) of a resident's county plays a major role in financing the benefits of a special needs person including housing and caregiving through their providers. The funding to develop the housing was three-pronged. First were government benefits including SSI, Adult Home Help Care, and Medicaid. Second was Medicaid funding for staffing preapproved and budgeted through a developed person-centered plan, or a Prepaid Inpatient Health Plan (PIHP.) The third was Linda and Craig's personal funds.

Linda set up housing for her sons by herself but consulted the Community Housing Network (CHN) to make certain she was on the right path and was not missing important considerations. CHN opened their doors in 2001 with funding and a contract from Oakland County Community Mental Health Authority to create a Housing Resource Center. CHN coordinated affordable housing development and provided property management for special needs children and their families. CHN also developed affordable housing and provides properties for families.

Linda recognized that the knowledge she gained was invaluable and thought of starting a nonprofit entity to help families navigate the system. Her career path, however, worked out slightly differently. Linda was invited to be a panel member on a presentation on different housing options for adults with disabilities by Macomb Oakland Regional Center, a human services agency coordinating long-term supports for individuals with physical and intellectual disabilities and the elderly in Southeast Michigan. Community Housing Network experts presented the overall picture, and Linda presented personally on how a family can buy a home. Her passion and expertise evident in the presentation caught the attention of CHN president Mark Craig. He learned Linda was interested in educating parents and asked her to join the organization.

Linda was intrigued. She could no longer go back to a traditional legal job. She had to be available for Ross and Bryan in case they needed her. She enjoyed working with people and families like her and not writing briefs and making court appearances. Her interest in law was driven by her desire to help people, help them find justice, and to personally feel intellectually challenged. Her experience in court appearance did not always accomplish that.

Linda took a part-time position as a housing resource consultant for the Community Housing Network in 2009. She ran a variety of programs over eight years, often concurrently. During that time, she also returned to serve on the board of Autism Society Oakland County in Transition and Adult Services. Lisa Kowalski, the then president, was trying to create an educational program for families with special needs children on transitioning to adults. As parents aged, they needed information on housing and a long-term plan for their adult children. Following Linda and Craig's success in creating a home for Ross and Bryan, members of the Autism Society Board approached the Community Housing Network. They asked Linda to develop a program for planning housing to help other families of adults with autism and other developmental disabilities.

A program called Getting My Own Address (GMOA) was already in existence but had little funding and was struggling. With a grant from the Autism Society to Community Housing Network and help from Linda, a book was written on community living for adults with autism in Oakland County in four overview presentations. Linda and Lisa had co-authored the book, "GMOA for Individuals with Autism Spectrum Disorder and Other Developmental Disabilities," in 2011. It was revised and retitled "Getting My Own Address: Achieving Housing for People with Disabilities" in 2015. "Getting My Own Address" became a viable service that could be used to accomplish the organization's mission.

Linda and Lisa put a major effort in creating a two-hour presentation with Craig's help under the title, "Getting My Own Address." Her presentation to be given on behalf of Community Housing Network was based on their experience and explained all steps on finding suitable housing for a person with special needs. She emphasized finding a proper home in a safe environment with proper caregiving staff as one of the most important requirements in planning for a special needs person. It is also the most difficult task for families to accomplish. Mental preparation of the parents and the child as well as working through the maze of the government rules and availability of funding for both the different types of homes and care-giving staff is often arduous.

Linda's presentation included:

- Making housing goals using principles around a person-centered planning process and a self-determination principle that include each person's individual needs and ability to determine their own goals.

- Creating a housing budget, including private and public funding sources.

- Deciding what direct care and other supports are needed.

- Options for affordable housing through renting or buying.

- Finding a roommate to share housing costs and companionship.

Linda began sharing her presentation in 2011 to support groups, parent groups, intermediary school districts, other educational service organizations, non-profits, community mental health providers, special needs estate and financial planners, and others. Linda's personal story of her family's own experience, journey, and their trials and tribulations connected with her audiences. She spoke with compassion and urged the family members to plan early. The program started in Oakland County but grew with Linda's reputation, and she received requests in other counties and cities within Michigan and a few national organizations.

Community Housing Network does not find homes for the families. The experts provide education and guide them through options including leading them to the sources that can help them. Linda has played the role of educating families as well as holding their hands while they go through the process and through the transition. Linda feels proud she has motivated parents to find ways of placing their children with disabilities in proper homes. Some have done it successfully and some not so well. Caregiving or roommates can often be reasons for unsuccessful attempts, she said. Many parents do not feel ready even after listening to Linda's presentation a few times. Linda is satisfied that she has planted a seed in their minds. She believes in time they will be ready.

CHN administrators had to make a difficult decision in 2017. They were unable to continue the "Getting My Own Address" resources provided for the last several years. The Medicaid program locally and nationally experienced a severe budget crisis, limiting the resources available to provide direct care support for in homes for special needs individuals. The "Getting My Own Address" program was put on hold temporarily until guaranteed funding was available for independent housing.

Linda was disappointed but remains vigilant in continuing her goal. She has taken a break from doing presentations yet remains a strong advocate for those with special needs and is continuing to find other ways to stay involved with the community. Her experience as a mother, an advocate, housing resource specialist, and as an attorney is vast and valuable. She would like to work toward a better partnership between the private and public sector and have more secure staffing for the homes with better wages. She hopes the schools will be more involved under their transition planning for special needs children and provide education and awareness to parents on housing and caregiving matters. She believes parents also need to approach their government officials for better solutions for their children's future.

"Many parents fear the very things that are currently happening, lack of funding to develop good, supportive, safe, sustainable living arrangements," she said. "With low wages comes high turnover; unfilled positions lead to understaffing; overtime goes up and caregivers are exhausted."

Linda and Craig have battled many daily challenges in raising Ross and Bryan. Although the family no longer lives together, they work closely with their dedicated direct care staff and are very much part of their lives. Both Ross and Bryan have ongoing health issues and other complexities that Linda and Craig have to manage. As busy as she is, Linda thinks constantly about all the adult children with disabilities that need help. Linda became an advocate because of her children's needs but it is her big heart that has made her a loving and caring, sympathetic advocate.

"It's scary, that's why we're working so hard, harder than ever," she said. "Don't wait for someone else to do it; it's too critical."

From left, Larry, Greg and Mary Collette, Special Dreams Farm, St. Clair Township, Michigan.

Special Dreams Farm, St. Clair Township, Michigan.

The Collettes

An Unwavering Mission: The Right Job for Their Son

Gregory Collette's restlessness and anxiety worked against his many attempts to learn job skills in high school. He worked hard at a beer distribution company throwing the returned empty beer bottles through a chute. He kept breaking the bottles and jamming the machines. As in most of his jobs, Greg could not sit for long and had difficulty with his fine motor skills. He did not last long.

Gregory has autism and got his jobs through programs helping transition special needs students after high school, including employment, social, and recreational activities. He entered the transitional planning services once he began his post-secondary program in high school. Government agencies associated with the program work with school districts to train and help students prepare for the real world. Greg got his job at the beer distributorship through the Michigan Rehabilitation Services and Creative Employment Opportunity (CEO.)

Mary, Greg's mother, was very frustrated with Greg's work experience with different employers and his issues finding suitable employment. Mary and her husband, Larry, knew their son well. The standard jobs available for special need adults in janitorial work, grocery stores as baggers/stockers, or in fast food restaurants were not appropriate for Greg's personality or ability.

Greg needed a job coach one-on-one and for longer periods of time. Mary learned about a horse farm where he could work if he had a coach. One of the job coaches agreed to work with Greg at the farm. Greg was strong, could lift and push heavy equipment, and loved working outdoors. Mary was relieved to see how much he enjoyed working outside with animals and in the barnyard. Unfortunately, the job was offered for a short time. Mary and Larry agreed they had to look for better options than what was offered by the school district, Michigan Rehabilitation Services and other government agencies for their son.

Michigan is the only state in the country offering special education until age twenty-six; most others do so until age twenty-one or twenty-two. The additional four or five years are extremely valuable for the students in gaining work experience and other skills for life after age twenty-six. Many workshops and employment programs for adult children with special needs are offered through various government agencies. Although Larry and Mary could not find suitable programs for Greg through the programs, they needed official approval and a job coach if the parents found a job appropriate for him.

Larry came across a possible opportunity through the Huron-Clinton Metroparks, a regional park system of thirteen parks in Metro Detroit. Larry was working in the park system as a pipefitter for a large construction company and discussed Greg's employment dilemma with his supervisor. They decided to ask if Greg could be trained to work in the park. The outlook seemed promising, but unfortunately Larry and Mary were denied when they approached the local Metro Park Management office on Larry's possible employment in the park.

The Collettes never learned the reason. But the experience reinforced the need to work around long procedures and requirements often associated with government agencies and resources for those with special needs.

Gregory was the youngest of Larry and Mary's three children born in 1978. They were in denial when Greg was first diagnosed with autism at age three. Their concerns about his delay in speech and walking, aloofness, and lack of interest in playing with toys or other children led them to seek medical advice early on. The doctor recommended patience, but Mary, a part-time licensed nurse, was concerned. She knew Greg was different from Keith and Holly, her two other children seven and five years older than Greg. Both parents were confused about what autism meant and were troubled. They wondered if they could be genetically responsible for their son's disability.

Mary tried to keep life as normal as possible for Keith and Holly, but Greg's obsessions and his continuous hand flapping and rocking were embarrassing for them. The family had ups and downs focusing around Greg and his needs. Greg's behavior controlled the house, and the entire family felt devastated. Mary worked closely with Greg's school and teachers on his academic programs and extracurricular activities. By the time Greg was eighteen and began transition planning at school, he was tall, energetic, and able to read and comprehend at seventh/eighth grade level. He was non-verbal but he was quite good on his spelling communication board.

"We knew from work he did around the house with us that he was very capable," Larry said. "He just needed guidance and opportunity."

Mary communicated regularly with one of Greg's teachers, Dolores Jones, and expressed her concerns and frustration about not finding the right job for her son. Dolores was an exceptional teacher and took deep interest in her students' personal lives even after they left school. She concurred that Greg was not the only special needs student who had difficulty adjusting in typical workshops or similar job environments. As a result, many students were forced to stay home after leaving school. Mary learned about a residential farm called Bittersweet Farm in Ohio that worked with adults with autism and mentioned it to Dolores. She encouraged them to visit.

Larry, Mary, and Dolores visited the Bittersweet Farm the summer after Greg completed school. What they saw and found opened their eyes to possibilities for their son and others with autism. The Bittersweet Farm was the first of its kind in the United States started by a dedicated and activist teacher named Bettye Ruth Kay in the mid-1970s.[11] She modeled the farm after Somerset Court, a farmstead community in England for adults with disabilities. Her research in finding appropriate vocational programs for her students convinced her that multiple activities in a bucolic setting were ideal for those with autism.

Mary and Larry learned a farm has varied and distraction-free opportunities that are immediately meaningful for the students. Bittersweet Farm offers activities in agriculture, horticulture, fencing, and landscaping, animal feeding and care. The services are designed to provide a secure and safe environment in which special needs students can grow and develop to their fullest potential. Activities are therapeutic and help provide students with a sense of security.

The executive director of the Bittersweet Farm program spent nearly an entire day with Larry and Mary. He explained the philosophy about employing meaning and motivation, aerobic activity, partnership and planning, structure and support. This helps provide a holistic and healthy environment in which the potential of each participant is determined and developed. Every interaction is a lesson in reciprocal communication, relationship building, and mutual cooperation between staff and participants.

Larry was very moved by his experience at the Bittersweet Farm. He could visualize how Greg could be helped in a place

---

11 www.Bittersweetfarms.org

like this. Larry and Mary were tired of trying the tedious and repetitious jobs Greg struggled with in workshops. A farm could also be an answer to many other young adults with autism or other disabilities who could not adjust to regular work environments.

Larry and Mary were determined to change whatever they needed to offer new hope for their son. While driving home, they discussed their unwavering mission to find him a meaningful job and decided to start their own farm in Michigan with Delores' full support. They decided to begin the leg work on starting the farm before asking their Community Mental Health officials. Neither parent had farming background or experience. They made several more visits to the Bittersweet Farm in the following months to gather necessary information for their own work and received help and encouragement from the staff. They were also cautioned that the Community Mental Health in every state works differently and they might not get the support from the Community Mental Health from their county as much as Bittersweet Farm did.

Mary and Larry began by holding meetings with other parents with children with autism to talk about their plan. They approached the Transition Planning Committee at the school to discuss the idea. Dolores talked to other parents in school as well. The concept resonated with many parents as they had similar experiences with lack of programs and training once their children left school. They also created a name, and Special Dreams Farm (SDF) had its first business meeting in November 2004. A slate of officers and a board of directors of committed experts and parents were created. They were fortunate to have advice from attorney John Burns, an experienced corporate attorney who helped establish Special Dreams farm as a non-profit entity. The first year was dedicated to establishing the business end of the new venture, including the mission statements, by-laws, bank accounts, insurance, brochures, and strategies. The board decided all participants would be called farmers, and Special Dreams Farm would serve farmers of all developmental disabilities.[12]

Their first real work as a farm began in 2006 with a one-season agreement to start their program on a private farm in nearby Ira Township. It was a learning experience for the board as well as the student farmers. The farmers learned to plant flowers and vegetables, harvested what they planted, and enjoyed their new jobs. The board members learned about the abilities of the farmers, their scheduling, and what was expected of them.

The following year, Special Dreams Farm was invited to a new farm in Wolcott Farm in Ray Township. Wolcott is a learning farm owned and operated by the Huron-Clinton Metropolitan Authority (Metro Parks.) The ten SDF farmers were allotted space for a large garden, and the staff at Wolcott taught them how to care for the smaller animals. They were very patient and encouraging to the farmers. The farmers were proud of their accomplishment, loved the outdoors, working with their hands and seeing the results of their hard work.

Larry and Mary were very pleased with what they had started. Yet there was much work ahead and many challenges. They could not keep hoping they would obtain farms owned by others to work on each year.

"We learned a lot from our first experience on the farm," Larry said. "We knew that somehow we needed to get our own property."

The board made an important decision in 2008 to buy a farm. Financing was a critical issue as costs were higher than they earned through fundraising so far. The board had been holding spaghetti dinners, sending out appeal letters for donations and raising funds through various activities, and needed even more. Larry looked into hosting a Detroit River Cruise on a first-class

---

12 www.Specialdreamsfarms.org

yacht. Larry's employers, the W.J. O'Neill Construction Company, and construction colleagues were very generous donating money for the cruise. The fundraiser was successful and raised thirty-five-thousand dollars. Larry and Mary put a down payment on a thirty-one-acre farm on Fred W. Moore Highway in St. Clair Township.

The farm was a pre-1900 farmhouse with a barn and outbuildings on the property, a classic Michigan dairy farm. The farm had been unoccupied for about four years and required renovations to make it safe and comfortable for the farmers. The property was transformed in the first year with the donation of time and materials from the Detroit-area construction industry, along with the hard-working board of directors and friends. During that time, a limited program for farmers was offered with board members supervising activities.

Larry and Mary completed all planning necessary to protect Greg while they worked diligently on their hopes for him on the farm. I met them early on at a workshop and helped them with their planning. Greg has a special needs trust, and life insurance on his parents to fund it. Larry and Mary have their own financial and legal planning in place. Keith and Holly are successor trustees of Greg's special needs trust and will ensure Greg has a comfortable and secure home and a place to go to work every morning.

Marry and Larry remember an important visit with Greg's former employment coordinators at Creative Employment Opportunity after the farm began operating. They liked the farm and loved the concept. Mary also asked if they were interested in sending any special needs workers looking to work at the farm. They wanted to generate interest in other providers and workers in addition to helping around the farm. CEO staff drove several young workers in their van to work at the farm. Special Dreams Farm staff treated them well and provided snacks and beverages. Most of the workers resided in group homes.

Although they were making progress, Larry and Mary recognized they needed to be an approved employer and provider with their Community Mental Health offices. Typically, the Community Mental Health office reimburses the employer per person per day a certain amount. However, the farm did not receive any compensation from the Community Mental Health or CEO for providing work for the workers. CEO stopped participating when the Collettes approached staff to request having workers on a regular basis with a financial agreement. An employer has to be approved by the agency to be compensated for every special needs worker as an employee.

The Collettes learned many parents were glad to send their special needs children to work at Special Dreams Farms. Yet they had obstacles to overcome and accomplish that. Many parents could not provide needed transportation to drop the farmers off in the morning and pick them up in the afternoon. The student farmers also needed job coaches for training and supervision. The job coaches were approved and funded by Community Mental Health, another reason Special Dreams Farm needed to be an approved provider/employer. Larry diligently began the application process while both he and Mary continued talking to more families and recruiting more student farmers.

While working on approval, Special Dreams Farm began operating as a farm with several special needs adults working as farmers. Their families dropped the farmers at 9:30 a.m. and picked them up at 1:30 p.m. The farm operated five days a week, fifty-one weeks a year. Each farmer paid fifteen dollars a day to the farm from their own SSI/SSDI income. The families worked independently with Community Mental Health to have a job coach. Larry approached the CMH of St. Clair County in 2011 and applied to be a provider so other special needs adults could work at their farm. The organization's staff said they loved the concept and could see why the farm would be an ideal work place for many young adults with disabilities. Larry and Mary were very encouraged by their willingness to consider the farm as a provider. Unfortunately, within a few months of starting the process, the Collettes were notified Special Dreams Farm could not be considered as a provider due to a large deficit in their operating budget.

Larry was deeply disappointed with another setback but determined to continue the mission. He retired from his contractor job the year before and began putting his maximum effort, time, and energy toward the growth and recognition Special Dreams Farm needed. Larry and Mary were bolstered by two families who were their supporters and board members from the very beginning. Marian and Jim Helton had a daughter with Down syndrome, Kelly. And Jeanne Vance had a cognitively-impaired daughter, Jill. Both Kelly and Jill were student farmers. Together they worked hard to add more farmers. They invited people from the media, advocacy organizations such as Autism Alliance, Autism Society, and others to visit their farm. They raised funds through golf outings, bowling, and other charity events. Their efforts also helped create an awareness of the need of those with special needs and job training challenges. The news media published articles about the farm, and the positive press helped, but it was not enough. Larry and the board were very aware of the need for Special Dreams Farm to be approved by Community Mental Health. The finances were their major challenge.

Still determined, the board hired a consultant and approached the Community Mental Health of Macomb County where Larry and Mary lived. The executive director was not aware of the farm even though the office support coordinator worked routinely with Mary and Greg. The executive director visited the farm with his key people a couple of weeks later and was very impressed. He assured them he would work on approval and thought at least fifty farmers could participate. He, however, had a few conditions to ensure standards. He wanted SDF to obtain a Commission on Accreditation of Rehabilitation Facilities (CARF,) a very expensive and time-consuming process. Reluctantly, Larry began to work on the CARF only to be advised by another consultant that it was not necessary for a small operation like theirs. Larry met the executive director again. This time he was reassured the project could continue, beginning with ten to twelve farmers a day and offer transportation.

Delighted, Larry put the documents together, had several more meetings with the deputy director, and the CMH staff continued visiting he farm. Unfortunately, based upon Medicaid rules, the Community Mental Health officials dictated conditions that were cost-prohibitive for SDF. The office wanted Special Dreams Farm staff to provide transportation to the farmers. They also required farmers without disabilities to be paid by SDF to work with the special needs farmers.

Larry and Mary continued planning all they could and still remain frustrated by governmental obstacles, rules, and regulations. Yet they have never wavered from their mission to help their son and others. The farm operates with eight to ten farmers a day. In the summer of 2017, that number grew to thirty-five. The Collettes hope for a miracle to keep their farm growing and remain profitable for the future.

"Most of our support comes from people or companies that do not benefit from our services," Larry said. "They are sold on the concept or very impressed that we have pulled this private program off without government support."

The family has worked hard to offer a range of programs for the farmers. Mary developed a sewing and cooking program and regularly volunteers. She also organized a therapeutic horseback riding program. Jobs at the farm are based on meaningful

work, life skills, and prior experience. All the farmers participate and rotate in work that entails sewing, animal care, green-
house work, gardening, landscaping work, carpentry, wood
splitting, housekeeping, including working on clothes washers
and dryers, art class, and therapeutic horseback riding.

The farmers get their assignments for the day as soon as
they arrive. The animals of the farm including the chickens and
cats are cared for first. The farmers work in teams and sometimes individually. The farmers are given tasks based on what
they like and can handle but also are challenged to learn new
areas and improve their skills.

The farm sells eggs, vegetables, and flowers and grows
tomatoes, cucumbers, zucchini, melons, onions, peppers, and
garlic and continues to add more vegetables yearly. The green-
house provides work training for growing flowers between
February through Easter and Mother's Day. The farmers also
make crafts in winter months for sale and sell split fire wood
split year around. The farm's budget is small but is successfully
meeting its financial obligations.

The farmers receive personal attention daily with the Special Dreams Farm program director in charge of the operations.
The program director has many responsibilities including creating the daily schedule for each farmer, keeping track of the
tuition paid by the farmers, paying other bills, and answering
inquiries about the farm. The program director is the ambas-
sador of the farm, innovative, and works unsupervised.

Larry and Mary continue their mission to have Special
Dreams become part of a bigger picture, just as the Bittersweet
Farm motivated them as a new model of hope. Larry is trying
new approaches such as inviting the Michigan Rehabilitation
Services program for teens and adults with disabilities to
expose students to farming while still attending school. Larry
is confident that the farm will get the financial help, add more
farmers, and continue to make a positive impact on many lives.

The Collettes were encouraged when Oakland University completed a research project on the Special Dreams Farms business model and hailed the farm as an ideal adult skill-building program.

Larry is concerned who will carry the mission after him. His children Keith and Holly are involved in the farm and deeply care about what their parents have started. But they are also involved in managing their own careers and families. They may not be able to be involved in the same capacity as Larry. Larry is hopeful he will find another parent to lead the farm who is as concerned about his child's training as he and Mary were for Greg.

"My greatest fear is the farm will fail because there is no one to take my place," he said.

Larry and Mary also dream about finding residential arrangements for their farmers nearby. They have talked with a developer to make appropriate living arrangements for Greg and other farmers. It will be another long process working with Community Mental Health for direct- care services and staffing to provide care and supervision for the residents. This will provide permanency in taking care of their son and many other special needs adults.

"It was always our dream to have residences on our property. All our parents want that," Larry said.

Mary and Larry are tenacious and never stop dreaming and working toward their mission of creating a safe and interesting workplace for their son and other special needs adults. They collaborated and supported each other and continue to do so. Their positive energy and determination to make their goal a reality is exemplary. Their legacy will continue to make a difference in many lives.

Dr. Susan Youngs

A Life's Mission:
Helping Special Needs Children

Susan Youngs had a God-inspired dream and a mission in her heart as a fifth-year resident in a combined pediatric and physical medicine rehabilitation program in the late 1990s. She yearned to help families with special needs children as they struggled to find resources. She wanted to provide care for special needs children differently in ways that helped families holistically.

Like many fortunate experiences in Susan's life, she was asked an important question during a community pediatrics rotation at the Oakwood Hospital & Medical Center in Dearborn, Michigan. Dr. Jeffrey DeVries, Oakwood's Director of Children Health Services, asked Susan what she wanted to do when she finished her residency. Susan told him of her passion for helping special needs children. Dr. DeVries shared the interesting recent results of a community survey with local pediatricians who unanimously agreed a professional liaison was needed to coordinate care for special needs children. Susan couldn't have asked for more to make her decision. Six months later, in July of 1998, Dr. Susan Youngs started in the basement of the hospital what is now The Beaumont Center for Excep-

Dr. Susan Youngs, Beaumont Center for Exceptional Families, Dearborn, Michigan.

tional Families with one telephone, determination, and her passion.

On more than one occasion, Susan prayed and was led to choose a path making a difference in people's lives and to serve. During her third year of medical school at the University of Michigan, as part of a special program, she was one of the thirty students on rotation at Henry Ford Hospital. These students were specifically interested in mission work or working with indigent families in the United States or internationally. Several of them were part of the Christian Medical Society. One day, during her rotation with pediatrician Dr. Mary Ann Schuur at the developmental disability clinic, Susan had an overwhelming spiritual experience while working with special needs children. That day she knew what she was created to do and realized that she had a mission; her Jesus was putting her at the right places to lead her to the right path. Overwhelmed by her emotions, she called her mother that evening, sobbing uncontrollably. She declared she knew what she wanted to do when she grew up. She wanted to be the next Dr. Mary Ann Schuur for children with disabilities.

The year 1998 was significant in Susan's life. She completed her five-year combined residency program in June from the University of Michigan and was married in July. She started the Center for Exceptional Families at the same time with her faith and a determination to make a difference in the lives of children with disabilities and their families. It was a courageous move, yet she was confident that if Jesus wanted it done, that he would make it happen This was the first time a practice was being established solely for children with special needs providing comprehensive benefits. She needed support, finance and patience. Her three initial companions in this unknown frontier were Michelle, a social worker, Trish, a nurse coordinator, and a front desk receptionist.

Beaumont Center for Exceptional families (CEF) has grown to a renowned institution for helping special needs children and families with Susan as its founder, leader, and director. Susan founded CEF as more than a medical practice and on the principal that the professionals are more than experts imparting medical solutions. She acknowledges that she and her team are not perfect and do not pretend to have all the answers in caring for a child with special needs. They strive to find as many solutions as possible, including parenting and taking care of children with disabilities together. They are truly authentic and staying true to that authenticity is the most important criteria in the way CEF is managed and run.[13]

Susan was always a very bright student and well-rounded. She grew up in a Christian Lutheran family with two sisters in Brighton, Michigan. She was involved in sports, choir, and student council. Life was good for her. Every summer she attended the Christian Lutheran camp. At fifteen, Susan experienced a life-changing moment at the summer camp. She experienced an overwhelming presence of love and the existence of Jesus. She yearned to know him more. A friend's mother from catechism prayed with her to receive Jesus. and life changed for her from there forward. She believed very early on that her life was more than just about herself; it was also for those who needed to know his love more. She was not sure where this desire to help others would lead her. She was confident that her walk with Jesus and prayers would provide her with the answers and open doors for her.

Attending college was a given in Susan's family. Her real goal was to get married and be a stay-at-home Christian mom, yet college education was an important back-up plan in case she also needed to be a provider. She was always good in math and science, which led her to engineering school at Valparaiso

---

13 Beaumont Center for Exceptional Families, About CEF, Autism Care and Support, Services, www.beaumont.org

University in Indiana. She soon realized that thermodynamics was not for her and switched to biology. She paused between her first and second year to perform with the "Up with People" performing arts group, another phase of her life that molded her for the unknown future she was destined to live. She was one of one-hundred-fifty students traveling worldwide. Susan lived with fifty-six host families during the year and was involved in dance, music, cultural exchange, and community service.

During that year, she did community service for Toronto Ontario Crippled Children Center and learned about Prosthetics and Orthotics, another experience adding to her foundation for the future. She later studied prosthetics and orthotics in Dallas for a short time, and then completed her undergraduate studies in General Studies at the University of Missouri focusing on biology, psychology and physical rehabilitation. Psychology also fascinated her and prepared for her involvement in working with children with disabilities. She met many female medical students while in Missouri and felt called to join medical school while still nurturing hopes of getting married and having children.

Susan was accepted at various medical schools, one even with a full scholarship, but chose to enter University of Michigan. Her parents were delighted to have her back close to home. Susan was concerned about student loans and the long journey into the medicine world but also believed in God's grace. "When you walk in his way, he blesses you." She connected with the Troy Kensington Community Church and became immersed in the church's singles group. These were single people who loved and were dedicated to Jesus. She traveled from Ann Arbor to Troy regularly to attend the church and meet her group of friends. She also met her future husband, David, through the church.

Susan's internship between her first and second year at medical school was another stepping stone leading to her career path. Three months of working and researching in Physical Medicine and Rehabilitation under Dr. Ed Hurvitz made Susan wonder if she should consider PMR as her choice of specialty. Susan enjoyed several aspects of medicine including surgery and gynecology, but pediatrics and PMR stayed close to her heart. Susan chose to have "away" rotations in several countries while in her fourth year of medical school such as Africa, Dominican Republic. Working with children, sometimes in primitive facilities, evoked strong emotions in her and she knew she was being exposed to these situations for a purpose. The vulnerability of the children, especially the special needs children, and positive results of proper rehabilitation made her determine that she wanted to specialize in pediatrics as well as Physical Medicine and Rehabilitation.

In her fourth year, she had to apply for her residency. She was dating David but they had not made future plans. Susan was beginning to apply for five-year Pediatrics and PMR residencies in other states but wanted to stay at University of Michigan, remain close to her church and David, except that there was no combined residency program. Susan approached University of Michigan staff with another colleague with similar interests and urged them to start the combined Ped-PMR residency program at University of Michigan. They agreed, and Susan began her training in Pediatrics and Physical and Medical Rehabilitation. She continued international touring in India for her residency.

Susan's training and passion led her to start the Center for Exceptional Families in 1998, and it grew one patient at a time, one family at a time. She realized quickly that the number of special needs families needing help was dramatic. Her first five patients were children with autism. More than fifty percent of CEF patients today are on the autism spectrum. The patients come from all races, ethnicities, faiths and financial status.

Susan states that disabilities are a great equalizer. No parent asks to deliver a child with special needs. Parents have the same common questions: Will my child be able to walk, talk, live independently, and be emancipated? The CEF was created to help families lovingly find their answers in a judgement-free setting.

The center has evolved over the years and has a very clear mission:

> "Through the Center for Exceptional Families
> medical home model of comprehensive and innovative
> rehabilitation care, children with special needs and
> their families will be supported throughout their
> unique life journey.
>
> "They will evolve and grow in strength to advocate
> for health, education, independence and community
> inclusion. They will learn to negotiate the joys and
> realities of living with differing abilities, and they will
> emerge as young adults and families able to pursue their
> own dreams."

CEF has become a medical and rehabilitative facility that treats all developmental disabilities, disorders, and diagnoses. The children range from mildly developmentally delayed to multiple-impaired patients with fragile health conditions. The children seeking help at CEF have cerebral palsy, muscular dystrophy, autism, intellectual disabilities, or genetic syndromes. They also can have conditions related to other illnesses, accidents, or traumatic births and PANDAS, autoimmune disorders which can follow strep in children. The center now has pediatric specialists in physical, occupational, speech, and feeding and swallowing therapies at CEF. They help the children work to gain independence and skills that allow them to participate in the world around them. The center is unique in that the medical team and rehabilitation teams work together and collaborate on care under one roof.

The center is also unique in that it supports the whole family, among Susan's top priorities. A range of support groups are available for mothers, fathers, and other caregivers. This includes groups for parents of children with autism as well as educational groups on special education, community resources, financial topics, and parenting. For siblings of patients with disabilities, "sibshops" are offered, a recreational-based support/ wellness program for siblings. Fitness, nutrition, and recreational events are also offered for the whole family to attend together. Additionally, summer camps are hosted with play and social skills groups, and affordable private-pay options for families without insurance benefits.

In living its mission and operating a welcoming learning environment for families and professionals, CEF serves as a model for future medical professionals, educators, and families. The inclusive opportunities offered help children and families gain confidence to demand inclusion in their communities. The center provides leadership and mentoring to help teens and young adults with disabilities pursue their dreams.

CEF provides exceptional medicine; the expertise in coordinating care for children with special needs and guiding families through the overwhelming number of specialists, programs, agencies, and school issues that they face is truly one of a kind. In addition, the multidisciplinary medical clinics for children requiring spasticity management, autism diagnostics, and follow-up and management of chronic health conditions provide the families a "One Stop Shop' approach.

In almost twenty years, CEF has grown beyond Dr. Youngs' expectation and dreams. It has been a wonderful Jesus-ordained journey starting in the basement office at Oakwood Hospital. The center began a ground-breaking collaboration with the

University of Michigan Early Childhood Education Center and moved to a shared space on Rotunda Drive in Dearborn, Michigan, in 2008. Susan is especially proud of the autism center that was recently added in 2017 with state-of-the-art technology to help children with autism from ages one to eighteen, from diagnosis and including PT, OT, Speech, Social Skills training and ABA.

She remains concerned about the increased number of children with autism. When she first began in 1998, the statistics estimated one in five hundred children affected with autism. The current estimate of one in fifty-nine children with autism requires research and solutions. From Dr. Young's perspective, this is one of the greatest and pediatric emergencies of her lifetime and research should be the number one priority.

Susan talks passionately about the families of her patients. She admires their authenticity, perseverance, commitment, and sheer determination to do what they have to for their children. They are very aware that it is a challenging journey. There are great moments of happiness and moments of incredible fears. Sometimes they consider what it would be like to give up, but they don't have an option. She knows they are often sleep-deprived and desperate to find solutions to day-to-day problems. She believes strongly the key is to ensure the families have the right tool and learn all that is available to them. Normally a pediatrician will be a sympathetic listener to parents' issues with a child and will refer the parents to a specialist. That may not be enough, even specialists lack the specific tools that will really change a life. Behavior of special needs children is often a huge problem for parents, she said. The CEF's ability to manage all under their roof is a great relief to the families.

With increased populations of children with disabilities and a limited number of physicians with specializations in working with them, the Center for Exceptional families is a gift to the community started with one person's God-created dream. Susan's passion, commitment and love stems from the Holy Spirit that lives in her and also her love for children. She is a dedicated wife and mother of her three children, Maggie, Annee, and Jack. She is deeply devoted to her patients and their families. More people like her, and the resources the center provides, are needed nationwide. This requires funding and dedicated professionals with a heart and commitment.

Susan holds an annual summer barbeque in her backyard with many of her older (sixteen and above) patients and their families. They all proudly talk about their accomplishments and many have managed to attend college. Most just share their personal journeys; both the highs and the lows. Her summer picnics are a celebration of lives and people pursuing their own dreams.

Dr. Susan Youngs, founder and medical director of the Beaumont Center for Exceptional Families, is grateful to her fellow physicians and also to her nurse practitioners, the physical therapists, occupational therapists, speech-language pathologists, social workers, dieticians, nurses, medical and administrative assistants, BCBA's, Behavior Technicians, and thousands of volunteers, donors, and an incredible Advisory Board. In addition, she also is proud to have mental health practitioners, neuropsychologist, orthotists, and seating specialists as part of their team.

"I am so blessed to work alongside and with amazing, committed, authentically loving colleagues! I tell the medical students that rotate with me that I hope that they will someday love their jobs as much as we do at the center," she said.

Her one-day rotation at Dr. Mary Ann Schuur's developmental disability clinic changed her life. She hopes more medical students have similar experiences when they rotate at the center. The future needs more Susan Youngs.

Janice Fialka

Being Included:
Doing the Right Thing Matters

When Janice Fialka speaks in her calm and confident voice, people stop and listen. She has the unique ability to reach her audience, readers, and people in the community deeply through her sensitive, intentional messages related to children with disabilities. Over the years, Janice has created a special place in the hearts of thousands of families with children with disabilities. She has also reached professionals as a strong advocate and author on issues related to disabilities, family-professional partnerships, inclusion, raising a child with disabilities, sibling issues, and post-secondary education.

Born and raised in Flint, Michigan, Janice grew up in a loving family where riches that come from kindness and community were emphasized more than material possessions. Compassion and service were instilled in her very early on. Janice's mother was a nurse to a primary physician working with children with disabilities. Her mother taught Janice crucial lessons on working with people with disabilities and the importance of support for families. She remembers how her mother always saw the gifts in each child and made sure she told parents what she noticed about their child.

The Fialka-Feldmans. From left, Janice, Rich, Micah and Emma.

Janice was involved in the peace movement and women's movement while attending Central Michigan University for a degree in sociology in the early 1970s. In 1983, she received her Master's in Social Work at Wayne State University.

"My involvement in the women's movement and at my consciousness-raising groups taught me that 'the personal is political,' that discrimination we faced as women was not just an individual issue but was rooted in the larger society issues and constraints," she said.

"I learned that I was not alone in my struggles as a woman; that these injustices came from the larger political world. I began to see the importance and necessity to advocate with others for our rights as women and to assume responsibility for achieving our rights. Later, these lessons were fundamental to how I understood my experience as a mother of a child with a disability. The discrimination he experienced was not a personal issue but based on a long history of injustice and discrimination against people with disabilities. I knew the necessity of connecting with other parents and advocates."

Janice began her career in social work overseeing and operating three teen health centers focused on adolescent sexuality and family planning, two in Detroit and one in Taylor, Michigan. Janice then helped write the first curriculum on sex education for Detroit Public Schools with another woman. She continued to work in the field of adolescent health for twelve years, opening the first community-based teen health center in Taylor in 1987.

Janice met and married Rich Feldman, an activist, author, and employee at a Ford Motor Company truck plant. Their son, Micah, was born in September 1984. Rich and Janice's life took a different direction after Micah's birth. Micah was born with a developmental disability that shifted Janice's career focus. She was challenged and deeply worried by a colicky baby who couldn't nurse due to low muscle tone. In the following months and years, Janice experienced moments of guilt and shame as professionals diagnosed Micah with labels such as Failure to Thrive, Developmentally Delayed, and neurologically impaired.

"I thought, 'Why me? What is my identity? Why could I not give birth to a typical child?" she said.

Calling on her lessons that she learned in the woman's movement, Janice reached out to other mothers and professionals for help and guidance. Like most parents, Janice and Rich wanted to do everything for their child and build on his strength and intervene when needed so he had a fighting chance. Micah began his education in a beautiful neighborhood preschool run by a friend. It had a garden, chickens, and unique teaching methods. When learning about civil rights heroine Rosa Parks, the children replayed sitting down on a bus and took turns re-enacting Rosa's interaction with a police officer who arrested her for doing so. Micah was introduced to an enriching environment with his family's social justice values from the start.

Janice's journey in raising Micah had many memorable events, each leading her to a path that defines her today. One night when Micah was about four years old, Janice was unable to sleep. Earlier that day, she learned that Micah's developmental delays were significant and permanent. A private conference on Micah's challenges was attended by Micah's neurologist, occupational and speech therapists, other medical staff, Janice, and Rich. It was a difficult session, and although the medical team tried its best to tell Rich and Janice about Micah delicately, to Janice they sounded clinical and lacking in empathy. Rich and Janice felt devastated. That night as her tears flowed, Janice transferred her thoughts and feelings on a yellow writing pad. She wrote a poem, "Advice to Professionals Who Must Conference Cases." The emotional poem described her desire to have well-meaning professionals go beyond giving a clinical report and empathize with a mother who is scared and grieving.

"I wanted to hear, through their words and gestures, that

they understood that this news was hard to bear. I wanted them to pause from their reports and just BE with me and my scattered feelings of being stunned, scared, vulnerable, and uncertain. I wanted my feelings acknowledged, responded to, validated, or just heard," Janice wrote.

Janice's poem was published nationwide through various media and resonated with other parents wrestling with diagnoses given to their children with delays and disabilities. They related to her sensitive and honest appeal. Professionals were also drawn to the poem as it helped them understand what many parents wanted when being given "life-changing news" of labels. This was the first of many writings that Janice would publish.

She later wrote a book comprised of poems and essays about her experiences with Micah, "*It Matters: Lessons from My Son.*"[14] In two of her poems, she tells the stories of strong mothers who fought hard to ensure that their children received what they needed from the professionals and in school.

Their second child, Emma, was born when Micah was about four. Emma was beautiful, and to her parent's relief seemed "typical." Micah was delighted to have a playmate and a younger sibling. Emma grew up with her brother, and they were in the same school for one year when Micah was in fifth grade and Emma was in first grade. Over time, she noticed his developmental differences, his stuttering, and his inability to read. In second grade, she asked about what she was noticing.

"Emma asked me, 'Why does Micah go ah-ah-ah?' (referring to his stuttering.) Why can't he read?" Janice wrote.

Janice wondered when Emma might notice and wanted to respond in a supportive and helpful way. With profound wisdom, she answered, "You know how your grandma uses a cane? Well,

14 Fialka, Janice, It Matters, Lessons From My Son, Inclusion Press, 2004

Micah needs support like your grandma uses a cane, so he has extra people to help him with his reading." She added, "You know how we met Dr. Daly? He is a speech doctor and he is going to help Micah with his stuttering." Emma was satisfied. There was no labeling her brother, just a very simple explanation.

An incident that took place when Micah was in first grade created a foundation for Janice and Rich to build their goals for Micah. The school had a special room, the "Opportunity Room," which was a self-contained classroom for the students with disabilities. The children entered the class through a separate door. One day Micah declared to his parents, "I want to go in the same door as all my other friends." This was an eye-opener for his parents. Micah always let his parents know what he wanted, and his parents always listened. This happened during the mid-eighties, when there was a lot of support for full inclusion for those with disabilities.

Full inclusion at school and in the community for Micah became Janice and Rich's goal. They recognized that being able to integrate with others side by side in and out of the classroom was a much-needed skill. Inclusion with other students helps develop a sense of belonging in the classroom. Janice believed that her experience in the woman's movement was transformative for her and for Micah. This was not just a special education issue but a social justice issue. Over time Janice and Rich learned that Micah had a right to be included with needed supports in all ways as his own person. As Janice attended more workshops on inclusion, she began hearing about positive results in classrooms when students with disabilities were included in regular classrooms. Some of the most difficult kids who were mean to others and difficult began demonstrating kindness and improved behavior. All students benefited from learning side by side with peers with and without disabilities. Rich concluded the first goal of an Individualized Education

Plan (IEP) should be to change the community or the school to be inclusive of all children. Janice also believed that the timing was right, because schools were emphasizing training and consultation on effectively and intentionally including students with disabilities in general education.

Micah was about eight or nine when Janice heard Norm Kunc, an international speaker and activist on disabilities, speak at a conference. Janice and Rich watched Norm's four-minute video "Credo for Support."[15] Kunc emphasizes how individuals with disabilities prefer being treated. The video struck Janice in thinking about disabilities from a very different perspective. As Janice and Rich attended parent-to-parent conferences, they met many people who reinforced that Micah belonged in a world with everyone else. It helped them understand what Micah should expect and experience. They were learning to expect more, not accept less.

Janice was beginning to feel the demands of juggling her work at the teen centers, supporting Micah and being his advocate. In 1987, an addition on early intervention to the Individuals with Disabilities Education Act (IDEA) was launching. A new Early Intervention State Grant program to serve infants and toddlers from birth through the age of two was launching. The program become Part H of the Education of the Handicapped Act. To kick off the new law, Janice was approached by the Washtenaw Intermediate School District to be the keynote speaker of the conference on Early Intervention, referred to in Michigan as Early On. Her experience as a social worker working with young adolescents, an advocate, and a parent of a child with disabilities helped her prepare for the address. Janice and Rich believed that the parents and professionals of children with disabilities are partners similar to being in a dance. To prepare for the keynote, Janice and Rich identified what they wanted from professionals who were working with Micah and

15 Norman Kunc, A Credo for Support, People First, YouTube, 2016

their family. They identified ten ways that professionals could make an important difference in a parent-professional relationship. The ten ways were based on their experiences, insights, wishes, and all they were learning. This began the core of Janice's talk, and she called it "The Dance of Partnership: Why do my feet hurt?" She later added a tag line to the title: "Strengthening the Family Professional Partnership."[16]

Janice's keynote speech dealt with sensitive issues well interspersed with anecdotes, humor, and positivity. Her suggestions to the professionals included not to be intimidated by a parent's anger and negative feelings, but to allow the parents to emote. She talked about the importance of listening and being a witness to the range of feelings a family might experience; she encouraged professionals not to "rush to solutions and not to focus on fixing the child." She urged parents to focus on the dreams and strengths of the child.

"The world of parents with children with disabilities can be lonely. Break the silence of their lonely world and gently lead them to the sounds of compassion and respectful curiosity," she wrote. "Help them prepare for the mood swings and challenges of birthdays and holidays. Parents change forever once their child is diagnosed to be different. Professionals can help them gradually build the bridges back to their old world. Help the parents to know their own child. They are not familiar with the complexities of the disabilities and their child's world. Bring information/literature to the parents that help them understand their child's disability. Recognize every small milestone/ achievement of the child with the parents. They are not small for them. Keep them focused by pointing out the successes and celebrate them. Parents will have moments of despair. Give them the space to be in the dark. Give them the feeling of hope so that they can face the next birthday party or be ready for their next appointment or can use the word 'disability.'"

16 Fialka, Janice, Dance of Partnership, 1987, Dance of Partnership.com

Janice's gift of reaching her audience emotionally and intellectually shone through. She spoke with conviction and intention with kindness and compassion. She began to receive requests for workshops for parents as well as professionals at numerous national, state, and local conferences throughout the United States and Canada. She also spoke at schools, human service organizations, and parent advocacy groups. Janice touched people with her true stories. She was honest and cautioned the parents that raising children with disabilities is not easy. It is important to find the meaning and to celebrate the gifts of the child.

"You will have the worry, you will be afraid, you will have the frustration, but you will have the joy and love for your child and you will not be alone," she said.

People often drove for hours to listen to Janice and related deeply to her presentations. Parents told her they were motivated, rediscovered the energy to keep going, and felt uplifted after her workshops. She continued to write about the relationship between parents and professionals including inclusion, parent-professional partnerships, raising a child with disabilities, and sibling rivalry. Janice was sensitive to the issues siblings faced from watching her daughter Emma with Micah and understanding her curiosity about her brother, her embarrassments, and her challenges. Her real-life experiences helped her address those issues in her presentations on siblings of those with disabilities.

The success of her talks led Janice to team up with Karen Mikus, a psychologist from Ann Arbor, Michigan. They received a grant from the Kellogg Foundation and developed a full-day training for professionals based on her keynote talk. The training was immediately successful with great demand. Janice became too busy to balance her work with her personal life and family so decided to take a sabbatical from her work at the teen center, although she remained a consultant. A subsequent grant from Kellogg also allowed Janice and Karen to print a small book under a title: "Do you Hear What I Hear? Parents and Professionals Working Together for Children with Special Needs" that sold 7,000 copies. Eventually, Corwin Press published the booklet under the title, "Parents and Professionals Patterning for Children with Disabilities: A Dance that Matters." The original book was expanded by Karen and Rich's sister-in-law, Arlene K. Feldman, an education consultant and retired special education director in Montgomery, New York. Based on Janice's original idea, the authors used a dance metaphor to capture the complexities of building strong partnerships between professionals and parents of children with disabilities.

A new door opened for Janice in the early 1990s when she was asked to co-teach a graduate school social work class at Wayne State University. The university started a new model inviting community faculty such as a parent to teach a class dealing with early intervention. It was a novel idea of preparing the students from a parent's experience to work in the field and see how collaborative relationships work. Janice taught at Wayne State for several years and received additional grants to continue teaching other related topics. It helped her continue growing, building new relationships, and connecting with members of the community related to those with disabilities.

Meanwhile at home, Rich and Janice continued encouraging Micah to express what he wanted, carefully listened to him, and inspired him to follow his goals. Janice believes that there is another ingredient to the formula of a parent and child working together with professionals. They engaged those they met in the community of those concerned with disabilities and families to be part of their circle and called the group the Circle of Friends and Circle of Support. The concept originated in Toronto and was started by two trail blazers, Judith Snow and Marsha Forrest, advocates for inclusion. Circle meetings bring together the people who know and care about a person to support him or her in planning, decision making, and thinking about their lives. The circle of friends and support may take on roles to enable the person to meet their objectives of various life planning. The circle group may meet at regular intervals with the person in a relaxed setting at a convenient time so they can plan together. A circle meeting often includes a facilitator.

Janice and Richard approached the school social worker when Micah was in the third grade and suggested they create a "Circle of Friends" with Micah's classmates. He was willing to try it. He talked to all the students about the importance of friendship and helping each other. The following week, when Micah was not in the class, the teacher talked about how Micah might need some support and help to be included in school activities. He explained that they were starting a circle of friends that would meet weekly with Micah to have fun and help think about ways he could be included during lunch, recess and in other school activities. He asked for those interested. Most of the students volunteered, about eight were selected, and they began to meet regularly. The circle resembled a school club where students meet to do projects, hang out during recess, and brainstorm ways to resolve concerns. They learned how best to work with each other, and the circle created a strong foundation for Micah. He learned to approach people when he needed help. He later created his circle of friends and support wherever he went.

Micah's parents wanted Micah to benefit from real inclusion, not just in classrooms but also outside. Janice and Rich wondered how to keep him occupied after school and maintain his health. His peer mentor called JJ, a junior and the captain of the high school cross-country running team, suggested that Micah join the team. Janice and Rich thought it was a great idea. Micah was less enthused. Running was not his thing, yet Micah liked JJ and agreed to give it a try for a couple of weeks. The coach of the team set a goal for Micah to start practicing for a one-mile run. He made extra efforts to include him in the practices and considered his safety. He had no knowledge of inclusion, but he understood what it meant from his heart. That fall, Micah ran a mile in eleven minutes and thirty-two seconds to the cheers of his family and friends, a strong showing for anyone with physical challenges. Janice and Rich watched their son with pride and tears of joy. Micah's determination to meet the goal set by his coach, and the coach's encouragement and willingness to include him right from the beginning, set a stage for Micah to continue to set new goals. To this day, Micah jogs and exercises on a regular basis.

Janice and Rich supported and taught both Micah and Emma to have dreams and be interdependent. Micah was determined to meet his challenges and was eager to enter college when he finished high school at age nineteen. He wanted to be with his friends, attend football games, and keep learning. Janice worried about his dream of inclusion and of always going in the same door as his friends. She wondered whether his dream of attending college with other students could be achieved. Students with intellectual disabilities—formerly referred to as mental retardation— did not attend college at the time Micah was in high school. However, Micah was insistent that he enter this door, the college door. With the strong support of a few forward-thinking educators, Janice and the team created a fully inclusive college program on a college campus. In 2003, Micah and several other students with intellectual disabilities attended regular classes at Oakland University through a Transition Program sponsored by his school district in collaboration with the university.

Attending Oakland University meant walking up to the bus stop from his home, crossing a major street, and taking two buses twice every day irrespective of the weather. Prior to attending college, Micah was not comfortable crossing a busy thoroughfare of Coolidge Road and 11 Mile Road. When he realized that he could not attend college without crossing the dreaded road and taking the bus, he found a cool, young student, a poet from Detroit, who took the bus every day to help him. He learned to cross the street from her and mastered it in three days. He continued to expand his circle of friends and support everywhere. He attended classes, actively participated in student organizations and extracurricular activities, volunteered in the Student Activities Center and the childcare center, and was an "OU" student. Four years later, in 2007, the university initiated a new program called "Options," which allowed Micah and other students to continue learning as students at the university.

When Emma decided to attend Mount Holyoke College in Massachusetts, the family helped her move to the dormitory. Micah was getting tired of traveling for two hours each day to attend his classes. He wondered why he couldn't live at the dorms at Oakland University. He thought he was missing out on an important part of college life. But university staff said he couldn't live on campus, because he was in a special program and not a matriculated student. His parents and friends made several efforts to negotiate with the university, many students supported Micah, and they spoke out on the broader issue of discrimination and the university's discriminatory actions. The family discussed options with Micah and what he could do. Micah was a peace-loving non-confrontational young man but knew to ask for what he believed was his right. His foundation was based on his parents' strong belief of social justice. He met with Michigan Protection and Advocacy Service, Inc., and decided to file a lawsuit against the university for discrimination. It was not an easy decision for Micah, and yet his intentions were very clear.

"If I give up, most things will not change," he emailed a friend using his voice-to-text technology.

The lawsuit took eighteen months of meetings, depositions,

and two hearings in federal court. Micah's lawyer argued his case based on Section 504 of the Rehabilitation Act of 1973. As amended, it is a civil rights law that prohibits discrimination on the basis of disability. This law applies to public elementary and secondary schools, among other entities Six months later, in December 2009, a U.S. District Court judge in Michigan ruled that Oakland University had discriminated against Fialka-Feldman and should be allowed to move into the dorm

"The judge's decision is a wonderful victory for Micah's dream to live in the dorm and a victory for so many other students and folks with cognitive disabilities," Rich said. 'Now it's their right to be fully included in the college dormitory experience."

Micah had a rewarding and rich college experience. He studied public speaking, created Power Point presentations on group dynamics, studied the differences between the ways males and females greeted each other in the sociology class, learned to use more hand gestures when speaking, studied social movements, and traveled to Israel. He participated at a student leadership retreat, wrote papers, gathered two pages of facts he discovered with support of a peer, and taught students how to use the voice-to-text software program to communicate. The growth he achieved, the friendships and social networks he created, and enhanced skills to navigate are immeasurable.

Micah made important contributions to his campus and several others across the nation. Most importantly, he learned to be his own advocate and have the power of persistence. He learned about community and to ask for help. Emma, too, has grown to be a strong advocate for disability justice. She considers herself not just the sibling of a brother with an intellectual disability. She is a classroom teacher learning about how to make inclusion work, a goal her family worked toward for years. She chose to be a teacher because she wanted other siblings to see that their brother or sister is valued in school. She is an advocate for inclusion because she wants siblings like her to know that their brother or sister has friends, real friends. She wants to be a teacher of more children like Micah, perhaps with even more significant disabilities, and let them know that it is okay to have a disability. She wants to help build support systems to allow them to take risks in order to be safe. She wants to encourage and support parents to understand the importance of allowing children to take risks and make mistakes.

Micah has become a better problem solver, more confident, and in some ways safer because of his risk-taking and trying new things. His community has grown both in size and connection. Janice and Rich's philosophy in raising Micah is carrying forward to the next generation through Emma's work.

Micah was invited to Syracuse University in August 2011 to speak at two conferences that were sponsored by the School of Education. Micah was excited. The Syracuse University community and culture is progressive, inclusive, and values diversity. Micah felt welcome in that environment. As he said to Janice, "Mom, they get me here." He decided he wanted to move to Syracuse, four-hundred-twelve miles from their Michigan home. As always, Micah pursued his ideas. He approached one of the conference organizers and a professor to discuss what it would take for him to work at the university. With support of a friend, he wrote a letter to the Dean of Education, Doug Biklen, indicating his interest in working on campus. Many conversations followed convincing the university how both could benefit from Micah. More phone calls and Skype calls continued. Micah also learned about a possible job opportunity at Syracuse University and applied. His persistent efforts paid off, and Micah received the job. He moved to Syracuse six months later.

He began working in the School of Education as a graduate assistant in January 2012. He is a teaching assistant in the School of Education with a doctoral student. He has learned to create his circle of friends and support. He has worked with a program called Peer-to-Peer, which links college students with other college students with disabilities. He also helps with another disability rights groups. Micah continues to receive government benefits to supplement his needs not covered by his income. He posted a housing flyer on Facebook and found an apartment within walking distance from his work and then a roommate. Micah is part of the New York State's Person-Centered Planning Program and has a Start-Up Broker as well as a Medicaid Service Coordinator. With their help, Micah has learned to shop, cook, manage his finances, and also participate in recreational programs such as horseback riding and therapeutic skiing. All along he asked his parent's advice and others from his Circle of Friends and Circle of Support as needed. Micah lives a rich and meaningful life and is happy.

Micah's intellectual disability challenged his parents to bring changes in the system that support the growth and interdependence of their son. Micah learned from activists with disabilities to see disabilities not as a deficiency but as a difference, as a part of his identity. His parents raised him with the principles and dreams of great expectations and the belief that every individual has the right and responsibility to find his or her passion and make life's journey a path to discovery and meaning. Janice believes that Micah in turn has taught them that the only way to navigate life is to have high expectations, build a circle of support, build a community, and ask for help. Rich and Janice did that. From the initial years of worrying "Can I survive the struggle of raising him?" they now feel blessed with a deep purpose of being in the world.

Micah has allowed Janice to strengthen her voice and support other families with her stories. Her third book, *What Matters: Reflections on Disability, Community and Love* (Inclusion Press, 2016), chronicles Micah and his community's groundbreaking journey from early diagnoses with intellectual disabilities to full inclusion in K-12 schools, college, work, living, and life. The book includes essays, poems, and interviews with Micah, his sister, friends, and colleagues.[17] Janice, Rich, and Emma have traveled with Micah in his remarkable path. Technology has played a very important role in his ability to learn and communicate. He connects with people easily and maintains friendships. People Micah meets are drawn to his friendly and caring spirit. Many families have said to Micah, "You give me hope." Most parents worry about their children's future whether or not they have disabilities. Rich and Janice are no different. Janice worries if people will underestimate his abilities and not challenge him. She knows she and Rich will not always be there for Micah.

"I hope Micah's Circle of Friends and Support including his sister continue to be in Micah's life as they are now and help him live a meaningful life." Janice said.

In 2018, a new documentary, *Intelligent Lives,* was released. Micah is one of the adults with intellectual disabilities featured in the film.[18] Micah's story and the practical guidance and wisdom of Janice and Rich continued to be told through the film and conversations. In the film, Emma poignantly talks about her relationship with Micah. Her words capture the spirit of Janice and the entire Fialka-Feldman family: "You just never know what is possible."

Janice and Rich have had a beautiful partnership in their common goals in raising their children, especially Micah. In raising Micah, Janice discovered her own strength and emerged as a strong advocate not only of her son but of the entire community of those with disabilities.

---

17 Fialka, Janice. What Matters: Reflections on Disability, Community and Love, Inclusion Press, July 2016. Excerpts reprinted by permission.
18 Intelligent Lives, Institute on Disability, University of New Hampshire, iod.unh, edu,, 2018

From left, Ben, Alexandra, Jeff, Christina, Michelle and Brian.

Jeffrey and Michelle Proulx

Seeing the Beauty of Every Child

Jeffrey was about ten when his Cub Scout pack spent a day at a special classroom for children with moderate to severe disabilities, a rare setting in the late 1960s. The scouts helped the students in the room, and Jeff began thinking of having a job working with people with disabilities when he grew up. A seed was planted, and he began to believe that he could understand disabilities and the needs of these children and enjoy the usefulness of working with them.

Years later in high school, a visiting occupational therapist demonstrated how he worked with children with disabilities to help them with motor skill development and life skills. Jeffrey was fascinated and intrigued. He also wondered if he could take care of them at his own home. He began hoping that someday he would have children of his own, but he would also adopt children with significant challenges. He believed even at that early stage he could deal and meet those challenges as a calling. He knew he could learn from his children, and they could learn from him.

Jeffrey loved music and he loved helping people. During his freshman year of music school at Eastern Michigan University, he began volunteering at a nursing home close to the campus. He ran a sing-along called the Happy Hour with soft drinks and chips and sang songs like When Irish Eyes are Smiling, You Are My Sunshine and Daisy Belle. It gave him the experience of playing in front of people and entertaining the seniors at the same time. The residents loved Jeff and looked forward to his visits.

A year later, Jeffrey wanted to move on and start singing in a restaurant but did not have the heart to disappoint the nursing home residents. On the first day of college in his sophomore year, he attended an introductory meeting at the Music Therapy Club for all the students, including fifteen music therapy students. When Jeff asked the group if someone could take over the happy-hour singing for the nursing home, one person volunteered. Her name was Michelle; that first introduction was the beginning of a great friendship and commitment of two people who were unaware how similar each other's passion and goals were in helping others.

For the next two years of music school, Jeff and Michelle's lives criss-crossed, and they worked in close proximity. They practiced in adjoining piano rooms and often shopped for groceries together. They became close friends leading to a more meaningful romantic relationship. They married in July 1990 after graduating as music therapists in December 1989.

Both Michelle and Jeff began working as music therapists; Michelle for Detroit Public Schools and Jeff for the State of Michigan at a residential school for boys. He later changed to Detroit Public Schools as well. Michelle used music therapy for the physically disabled children as an exercise, improvement in coordination, and participation in an activity from which they were previously barred. With music therapy, Jeff found his students with emotional impairment learned to stay more focused, follow directions better, and express their feelings without the necessity of words. Jeff's nurturing personality helped bring out the best in some of the most difficult and unruly students through music at the residential school. He trained them in drums and other instruments to start a marching band that played in parades and at Special Olympics. It was life changing for many students who were never before appreciated for their talents, had difficult home lives, and were now in detention. Jeff brought joy and pride in their lives through music.

Jeff and Michelle were passionate about their work and found it very rewarding. They shared compassion and empathy for their students with various disabilities and worked diligently to bring joy to their lives. The therapy was extremely beneficial to the children with disabilities.

"Music is a fundamental element of life, and nearly everyone finds some sort of identity with music as they grow and develop," he said. "Music is a universal experience that supersedes, defines, and unifies cultures, generations, ages, genders, and milestones. No one needs to necessarily learn an instrument to participate in music, dance, singing, or artistic and creative experiences. This is why music is so powerful."

Michelle unfortunately had rheumatoid arthritis, which was worsening, and had to make changes in her career. She began experiencing difficulty in playing instruments. Michelle continued her education while working and eventually received a specialist's degree in school psychology. She left music therapy to be a school psychologist and continued working with the Detroit Public Schools. As a school psychologist, she examined children with behavioral and emotional problems in school, helping determine why they were not learning to their potential. She also helped them obtain needed services including physical therapy, occupational therapy, speech therapy, or even specialized instruction that would meet their needs more effectively.

Jeff continued to practice music therapy but also continued his education and received a Master's Degree in Special Education. The combination of music and special education helped him work with very needy students that were also behind academically.

"I thought it might be possible to be a teacher and also bring music to them daily, along with reading, writing, and math." Jeff said.

Jeff and Michelle discussed having children once they completed their secondary degrees. They both loved children and couldn't wait to start their family. They had similar goals to parent two children of their own and then adopt two or three children with disabilities. They had the training to work with children with disabilities as special education teachers. They were anxious to have children they could love and nurture even at home.

Michelle and Jeff's attempts to have children were unsuccessful. Jeff had urological tests and was told it would be difficult for him to conceive a child.

"I think this was hard for each of us at first to accept," Jeff said "The doctor's statement ended up being the most emasculating experience of my life. I never looked into the abyss of emptiness as I did on that sad, rainy afternoon. Suddenly forced to look inward, I was finding myself unworthy."

There is a process, however, where one learns to accept things as they come, accept each other, and stand courageous. Michelle, equally saddened but loving and supportive to her husband, took this in stride. Jeff and Michelle agreed to move their plan up for adoption of children with disabilities. They never wavered from their decision. The time had come.

"I think we wanted a child with special needs because we believed we had talent for it, that we were built for it emotionally, and that we would learn a lot about what love is as we came to need them as much as they needed us," Michelle said. "We probably had enough experience by the time we adopted our first child to know that disabled children were a lot like regular children, and that parents of disabled kids had lots of joy and many triumphs to be proud of just like any other parents."

Michelle and Jeff signed with Lutheran Adoption Services

to receive a foster care license and become potential adoptive parents. After the final day of their training, they were asked to stay after to talk.

"They said 'We think we have a match for you,'" Jeffrey said. "Those were the most beautiful words we had heard."

Christina, the baby, was a ward of the state and on the Michigan Adoption Resource Exchange (MARE). Within two months of obtaining their foster license, on December 26, 1996, Michelle and Jeff adopted Christina, their daughter, as their first child in their loving home.

Christina was born developmentally on track, then physically abused by her birth parents when she was only forty-two days old. She was shaken, raped, and beaten. Virtually every bone in her body was broken, including a skull fracture. Christina spent a year in the hospital in a body cast, and was not predicted to survive. She eventually left the hospital with serious physical and emotional challenges. When Michelle and Jeff adopted Christina just before her second birthday, she was having up to three-hundred seizures a day, had a feeding tube, and could not hold her head up. They were told she would never walk or progress. Christina was placed on a special diet at age four, suffered her last seizure, and began to walk. Her frontal lobe damage created a life of emotional struggles, and the lack of the ability to communicate verbally made this even more difficult

Adopting a child with such severe disabilities was not an easy decision nor an easy task. Not everybody they knew welcomed the decision. Several people questioned their decision about adopting a child with disabilities, including medical people as well as some of their friends. Jeff and Michelle remained committed and caring.

Jeff and Michelle learned a lot about the laws and rules related to adoption as they proceeded to adopt Christina in December 1996. The process was not difficult. They paid a nominal fee of about two-hundred dollars for the training necessary to qualify. There were no other expenses unlike a regular adoption. Michelle and Jeff discovered that children with special needs go through a process whether they have disabilities, have been abused, and are not safe with their family. They first go into foster care through the state agency Department of Health and Human Services (DHHS). The foster parent's role was often seen as temporary, then. Now slightly more than half of children who enter foster care are reunified with their birth parents.[19] Foster parents are frequently asked to support these efforts. If DHHS does not have foster placements, the child is then placed with private foster agencies. Adoptions take place from foster agencies when children are not returned to the biological parents. Today hundreds of children with special needs are waiting for permanent homes. Parents willing to adopt children with special needs may find fewer restrictions than those adopting healthy infants.[20]

Christina was already a ward of the state in 1996, which made it easier to adopt her. Jeff and Michele fell in love with Christina as soon as they held her in their arms. Christina was fragile, and her care was difficult. They took turns obtaining parental leave for three months each. The summer holidays gave them the added time to stabilize their new life. Christina also started fulltime special education at age three. Christina was eligible for an adoption subsidy, a monthly income in addition to the medical assistance program. Her severe disabilities meant she also qualified for diapers, wipes, medical supplies, and medical equipment.

As Christina grew, Jeff and Michelle became anxious to have more children. They made plans to have more foster children followed by adoption and made an important decision. With the caregiving their children would require, they both could not

19   Childwelfare.gov, Who are the children waiting for families, U.S. Department of Health and Human Services
20   American Baby, Adopting a Child with Special Needs, Parents.com, 2018

work. Jeffrey decided to take a leave of absence from work as long as it was necessary. They lived modestly and knew they could manage with Michelle's salary and the adoption subsidy.

They soon became foster parents to a boy and a girl from different parents, Brian and Alexandra, before adopting them. They were only four months apart and needed to be cared along with Christina's ongoing needs. Brian struggled since the day he was born prematurely. He had Down Syndrome and was always in distress. The doctor diagnosed him as a colicky baby. and assured them that he would outgrow it but he never did. At age three he was diagnosed with reflux and given medication. He was underweight and cried frequently with persistent diarrhea and stomach aches. He was not able to be potty-trained due to his stomach issues.

Alexandra was born premature at twenty-six weeks and weighed one pound, ten ounces. Both her parents had mental disabilities. She was born with drugs in her system and came to Jeff and Michelle with oxygen and an apnea monitor. For the first year of her life, she slept about twenty-three hours a day.

Michelle and Jeff never hesitated before agreeing to foster Brian and Allie. Their new foster children had challenging medical conditions and needed a lot of attention, hands-on care, and love. Michelle and Jeff were ready and hopeful to provide it.

Brian and Allie were adopted two years later. Jeffrey's days were spent taking Christina, Allie, and Brian to therapies including physical, occupational and speech, special education services, and managing the household. If he was not driving or at an appointment somewhere, he said he was likely standing at the kitchen sink with dishpan hands.

Life was extremely demanding for Michelle and Jeff. Although they would have loved to have more children, they were exhausted and knew adopting more would take away time to care for the three others. However, a surprise was waiting when they returned home from a vacation in 2006. Their foster agency had been searching for Christina's new parents since her birth mother had another infant. They asked if Jeff and Michelle would foster Christina's baby brother. They hesitated for only a minute or two, and then decided they would.

Ben was a heaven-sent baby, and Jeff and Michelle felt truly blessed to have him. He had no physical or mental health issues, was Christina's half-brother, and they thought he was an extremely easy baby while they were stretched with the care of the other three children. Christina was eleven and having a lot of behavior issues; Allie was four and was still having difficulties with her emotions, since she struggled to express herself verbally. Brian was four and still in diapers with tummy aches every day. Ben was always happy, slept through the night, and was a joy. This was also a blessing when Michelle had three major back surgeries in November and December 2006, when Ben was six months. Ben's easy temperament often felt odd as Michelle and Jeff had not dealt with a typical child. He brought sunshine into their lives.

Michelle and Jeff's path has taken courage, determination and unwavering love to open their hearts and home to their very special children. It is also a miracle that two very remarkable individuals with such noble intent and giving hearts found each other to make a difference in children who had no chance. Here are some of their thoughts and philosophies about adoption, children with disabilities, and their lives as parents and educators.

Jeffrey and Michelle Proulx

LEARNING ABOUT THEMSELVES AS PARENTS OF SPECIAL NEEDS CHILDREN

"We learned a lot. It WAS different from being a teacher. When you're a teacher, you work to help children, but when you're a parent, you have a stake in their well-being and their development. When you're a parent, you make plans for their future, you worry about them, and it's on you as the parents to provide all the necessary things they will need to learn and grow. Their education, future residence, and well-being are all parents' responsibilities

It is a fact that special needs children bring additional stress in the lives of the parents. Also, there are disabilities that fit certain people's temperament better than others. For example, children with cystic fibrosis require lots of hands-on percussion, exercises, and treatments. If you are not a physical parent who is touchy-feely by nature, this could prove difficult for you. Or if you have a child with autism, but as the parents you tend to be strict, inflexible, or controlling—that child might add a lot of stress to your lives.

Parents of special-needs children also have unique joys. When a child reaches a milestone that no one believed was possible, or when they demonstrate love toward you or give you some sort of glimpse into their soul, their inner self—that can put you over the moon. Instead of graduation, your child might transition into vocational skills; instead of little league, there is Special Olympics. It is the same joy.

We think that when one adopts a disabled child, there is no "Welcome to Holland" surprise experience that parents who give birth to a biological child might have. Parents of disabled biological children often go through feelings of guilt that adoptive parents usually don't have to deal with. Biological parents always wonder what they could have done differently to prevent the disability from appearing. Maybe they took a drink before

253

they knew they were pregnant, or they gave their toddler immu-
nizations and immediately noticed changes in their ability to
communicate and grow, or perhaps they are carriers of some
recessive gene that didn't show up until now. It's easy to feel
the weight of that disability that could have been prevented
somehow. Guilt is common with parenting, but biological parents often get an extra dose.

There is also something to be said for recognizing the beauty
of everyone regardless of their physical or mental state. One
does not have to be an excellent student or athlete or model
to deserve love. Maybe it's a mystery why people love who they
do and there's magic in that mystery. Why does someone like
a song or why do they think that a dish is delicious? And why
is a particular child absolutely perfect just the way he or she
is? One can feel the love because they see what is beautiful
and what is good. That's when one knows that Life is Good! No
birth defects are seen as damaged goods. Their physical body
may be disabled but that spirit, the child within, is whole and
human and healthy. So you see that child and you hope that
if you are lucky enough to call them yours you will never take
them for granted or fail to be grateful for the things that make
them unique and special. You won't be perfect, but that urge
to love and love deeply and powerfully will motivate you to be
all you can be. Then in that instant and forevermore, that child
stops being disabled and becomes once again: a child."

CONTINUING THEIR JOURNEY AS SPECIAL EDUCATION TEACHERS AND PARENTS OF CHILDREN WITH DISABILITIES:

"Having children with special needs of our own help us every
day in our jobs. We have the perspective of the parents, and
the patience from living every day with the challenges children
bring. We definitely try to be the best parents we can be, but we

are also very tired. As each year goes by, we feel the fatigue of age. While our friends are empty-nesters, we have twenty-four-hour care and full-time jobs to keep up with. Some days are hard, but in the end we wouldn't have it any other way. "

SUMMARIZING THEIR EXPERIENCE AS ADOPTIVE PARENTS AND A WORD OF ADVICE TO OTHER PARENTS:

"We feel we have had rich life experiences since adopting that first time. If you are considering adopting a special-needs child, and it makes sense to you, then you should go ahead and do it. Many, medical people especially, tried to caution us when we decided to adopt Christina. The secretary at my school counterbalanced that by telling me, "Love can change a lot. I am glad that you are eager to do this." But we also believe in being realistic. It is and always has been the dreamers and the artists that have changed the world. When love is not able to do more, our belief is that it stems from us not being able to understand love deeply enough. You love and you grow, accept your shortcomings and strive to become more than you were."

MICHELLE, JEFF AND THEIR CHILDREN TODAY

Christina. Christina is twenty-three and has overcome a lot of her initial challenges. She fought a lot of her emotional struggles and finally at sixteen her behavioral struggles eased and a constant smile appeared on her face. Unfortunately, Christina has been diagnosed with thyroid cancer and may only have a few short years of life. Michelle and Jeff are heartbroken but celebrate each day as a special day with her. They are happy that Christina finally loves school.

Brian. Brian was diagnosed with Celiac disease at eight and finally found relief from his gastro-intestinal issues. He is six-teen and is diagnosed with Oppositional Defiant Disorder and Obsessive-Compulsive Disorder. He can be very challenging behaviorally, but always apologizes by singing a song on his guitar. Brian has liked to run away and explore since the age of four. He snuck out of the neighborhood at school, home, even on a family trip to Disneyworld. He continues sneaking away now. He is very independent and wants to explore on his own. He talks of having his own house and his own bulldog. Despite his challenges with oppositional disorders, Brian is mostly loving, sweet, and makes everybody laugh and smile. Ben and Brian are best of friends.

Alexandra. Allie is sixteen. Allie's birth issues left her with a language impairment, Attention Deficit Disorder and a learn-ing disability. Allie has also developed a social anxiety disorder. She was very jealous of Christina when she was little but has matured and is kind and loving to her sister. She babysits all of her siblings every day after school. Allie is smart, giving, always laughing, and has a way with animals. She loves to spend time with Michelle and wants to rescue and work with animals.

Ben. Ben is twelve and has been a special gift to Michelle and Jeff. Ben started identifying letters at age three without instruc-tion. He is curious like Jeffrey and can carry on adult conver-sations with others. He is a good athlete and very competitive. School is easy for him, which makes Allie mad, and his love of sports and friends are his first priority before excelling academ-ically. Ben is social and makes friends wherever he goes. He is sensitive and will defend others with disabilities. Ben accepts his siblings as they are. He looks up to Allie and watches out for Brian when they aren't rough-housing, breaking things and putting each other in headlocks as brothers do.

Jeffrey went back to work when Ben turned six and is a special education teacher at Mount Morris Consolidated Schools. Michele is the Director of Special Education at Lapeer County Intermediate School District. She struggles with her rheumatoid arthritis and would like to retire early. Jeff and Michelle feel the pressure of being behind in their retirement planning but are working hard to catch up. They have taken the necessary steps to do both their financial planning and created legal documents including special needs trusts for their three older children. Christina receives SSI and Medicaid and Brian will qualify at age eighteen. They both purchased substantial life insurance soon after adopting Christina. Jeff added additional coverage after adopting Brian and Allie, but Michelle could no longer qualify due to her rheumatoid arthritis.

The Proulx family is a unique and an exceptional family. Michelle and Jeff have used their skills to balance their work and family life. Michelle is organized and the planner in the family. She has a good understanding of financial matters and has taken care of the family finances and future planning. Her role as a special education administrator has also helped navigate her children's school career. This has been important as she can communicate better with the teachers during their IEP (Individualized Education Program) meetings.

Jeffrey is a talented musician and plays drums, guitar, banjo, bass, piano, trumpet and flute. He is compassionate and naturally nurturing. He is responsible for the children's medical matters and manages the home responsibilities.

Michelle and Jeff have accepted that they do not have the luxury to go out as a family for fun very often. They do not have much time alone. They take turns accompanying the children to events. On rare occasions they enjoy music and sports events. They have made a lot of sacrifices, but they would not change anything about their life. They have dreams for their future and are beginning to think about options. They are considering retiring in New Mexico, maybe buying a farm for rescue animals and starting a group home called Brian's House. Brian's House would provide a permanent home to their children and others with disabilities.

Jeff and Michelle have been inspired and motivated by this beautiful poem by Edna Massionilla, who raised a daughter with Down syndrome. Edna was a musician, songwriter and chaplain for the Hospital for the Disabled in Delaware.

HEAVEN'S VERY SPECIAL CHILD

A meeting was held quite far from Earth

It was time again for another birth.

Said the Angels to the Lord above –

"This special child will need much love.

His progress may be very slow

Accomplishment he may not show.

And he'll require extra care

From the folks he meets down there.

He may not run or laugh or play

His thoughts may seem quite far away

So many times, he will be labeled different,

helpless and disabled.

So, let's be careful where he's sent.

We want his life to be content.

Please, Lord, find the parents who

Will do a special job for you.

They will not realize right away

The leading role they are asked to play.

But with this child sent from above

Comes stronger faith, and richer love.

And soon they'll know the privilege given

In caring for their special gift from heaven.

Their precious charge, so meek and mild

Is heaven's very special child."

15

Nuts and Bolts of Special Needs Planning

It can take many years for parents to start thinking about future planning for their child with a disability. The initial years are struggles between diagnoses, prognoses, treatments, education, finances, denial, confusion, and finally acceptance of the reality of a special-needs child. Usually when the child enters the teen years or approaches high school, parents begin to worry about the financial planning process and future strategies.

Planning for family members with special needs can be overwhelming, especially when many decisions must be made that have lifelong consequences. The best way to proceed is with a team approach of professionals specialized and experienced in planning for those with special needs. Planning is usually done in phases depending upon the age of the special-needs child and the parents.

Professionals can include a financial planner, estate planning attorney with elder-law and special-needs background, an accountant familiar with tax filing of a special needs trust, social workers, housing specialists, and advocacy specialists. Some professionals may not be needed until the parents begin transitioning their child into independent living and planning for their own retirement.

The following pages describe the planning components necessary for special-needs planning. Providing lifelong care for a child with a disability is a partnership between parents' own planning and government programs available for those with special needs. Parents' planning entails both legal and financial considerations. Each segment of the planning process requires thorough understanding of the law, government benefits, the disability of the child, and the financial planning necessary for the parents and other members of the family. The description provided is basic information only. Readers including professionals seeking more in-depth information on special-needs planning may refer to a suggested reading at the end of this chapter.

BASIC PLANNING CONSIDERATIONS

Planning for the future of a child with a disability begins with devising a financial plan for the parents. This entails an inventory of assets and liabilities and an estimate of the size of their future estate through savings and growth. Parents' planning includes several important components, including their retirement income needs, long-term care needs, and financial security of a surviving spouse in the event of the untimely death of the primary wage earner. Planning for the education expenses of the other children of the family should also be considered. And review is required for all insurance and investment options to fund the specific needs of the child.

In addition to standard planning considerations, professionals and parents must carefully analyze the special-needs requirements of the special-needs child.

The following questions can serve as a starting point for discussions between planners and parents of a child with a disability:

1. What is the age of the child and the nature of the disability?

2. What is the estimated life expectancy of the child?

3. Where will the child reside after the parents retire and after the parents pass away?

4. Does the nature of the disability require the child to live in a group home or a place where special care can more adequately be provided?

5. What is his or her earning potential and ability to survive without ongoing care and supervision?

6. What are the major expenses today, and how will they change in the future?

7. How will the future needs of the other children and the retirement plans of the parents be affected?

8. How can the child be ensured to remain eligible for government benefits?

9. Are there other family members who may help provide care and supervision today and once the parents have passed away?

Planning should also assume the worst-case scenario. Parents can assume a child will have a normal life expectancy and not be able to look out for himself or herself in the future. The child will be better off if the proper precautionary plans are in place even if the situation does not turn out as dire.

Anticipating retirement needs of the parents and size of the estate are challenging, especially as average life expectancies grow. Yet it is vitally important to do so when the future of a child with a disability is at stake. Assets that may be left for the child should be identified early to ensure that assets will grow for financial support in the future.

GOVERNMENT ASSISTANCE PROGRAMS

For most families, providing funding for lifelong care of a special needs child is cost prohibitive. Government benefits available for a person with a disability are crucial for the financial security and quality of care. These benefits should be addressed at the beginning of the planning process.

SSI AND MEDICAID

Supplemental Security Income (SSI), consists of federal funds managed and operated by the Social Security Administration and a small portion paid by the state government in some states including California, Delaware, District of Columbia, Hawaii, Iowa, Michigan, Montana, Nevada, New Jersey, Pennsylvania, Rhode Island and Vermont. The SSI benefits are entirely needs-based, or welfare. Children with disabilities become eligible after their eighteenth birthday unless their parents' assets and incomes are below certain levels. In such cases, they can be eligible at any age. SSI consists of a monthly income and is accompanied by Medicaid. This income varies depending upon where the child lives. It can be reduced if the child lives in a home funded by the state or federal government, such as a group home.

In general, Medicaid is a needs-based government benefit program that benefits the elderly, blind, disabled, and poor. It represents a partnership between state and federal governments that have their own eligibility standards. Medicaid is automatic if a person is eligible for SSI benefits. Medicaid provides for various medical benefits, including medication and other key long-term mental health services, benefits such as group homes, workshops, job training programs, respite, and transportation that the disabled individuals need. Since it is difficult to obtain health insurance for a person with a disability, Medicaid is often considered the most important government benefit.

SSI and Medicaid benefits are needs based programs. All recipients must meet eligibility requirements for assets and income. For years, rules have required that unmarried individuals cannot have more than $2,000 in cash or other countable assets. For employed individuals, the compensation level must be below a certain dollar amount. The recipient can own a burial plot, prepaid funeral services, and life insurance with low limits. Personal residence, cars, and other personal items such as a computer, video games, and iPads are considered exempt assets for SSI and Medicaid purposes.

MEDICAID WAIVER

It is a lesser-known program for those with severe disabilities. Many people who qualify for waiver services are not always aware that they exist. Families struggle alone to provide care, creating economic, physical, and emotional strain. States do not educate people about these programs, and it is often only through crisis that people realize help is available.

The 1915(c) waiver is known as the "home and community-based services waiver" (HCBS) because it allows states to treat certain Medicaid populations in home or other community-based settings rather than in institutional or long-term care facilities such as hospitals or nursing homes.

The waiting period to get onto a waiver program can be many years, and it varies by state. Unfortunately, waiver eligibility does not transfer from state to state.

States can offer a variety of unlimited services under an HCBS Waiver program. Programs can provide a combination of standard medical services and non-medical services. Standard services include but are not limited to case management (i.e. supports and service coordination), homemaker, home health aide, personal care, adult day health services, habilitation (both day and residential,) and respite care. States can also propose "other" types of services that may assist in diverting and/or transitioning individuals from institutional settings into their homes and community.

SSDI AND MEDICARE

Upon the retirement, death, or disability of their parents, individuals previously receiving SSI often begin receiving Social Security Survivor or Disability Insurance (SSDI). These are non-needs-based benefits, and survivor benefits are funded by the federal government through FICA taxes. Payments are based on the Social Security taxes the parents have paid into the system. The child's disability must be diagnosed before age twenty-two. The benefits may not have asset requirements for eligibility. However, Medicare alone will not be sufficient, and Medicaid is an extremely important benefit to maintain.

The individual with a disability may still need to stay at or below the asset level required by SSI to continue receiving Medicaid. Children with disabilities may also be eligible for other government benefits programs such as food stamps, veteran's benefits, and housing assistance with the U.S. Department of Housing and Urban Development (HUD.)

If parents ignore eligibility requirements and/or inadvertently provide additional income and assets to their children with disabilities, the government benefits will be lost. Even well-to-do parents should not disregard these requirements. All children can benefit from government-funded training workshops and opportunities to work and interact with others.

Although the government benefits are extremely important,

they are subject to changes due to budget constraints. The rising population of adult children with disabilities and the elder population requiring long-term care have strained funding available for Medicaid. Planning for special-needs children requires regular review to stay current.

IMPLEMENTING THE PLAN

In a traditional and comprehensive financial planning program, planners and parents discuss all financial planning matters as well as estate planning strategies. During their lifetimes, most parents complete their wills, trusts, and other legal documents that describe how their assets will pass to their heirs. Parents of children with disabilities are best served by leaving the inheritance in a special-needs trust, also known as a discretionary or supplemental trust. There are two basic types of special-needs trusts: a third-party trust and a first-party (also known as a self-settled) trust.

Third-party trusts. The trust is established by the third party such as parents or other family members for the benefit of a child with a disability. It is funded with the assets of the third party. These trusts are used because the children have limited assets to remain eligible for government benefits. The language of the trust is important to ensure that future government benefits are not lost or reduced. The wording emphasizes that the trustee will use his/her discretion and use income and or principal of the trust to "enhance the quality of the life" of the child with a disability.

It also specifies that the principal and income will only supplement the government benefits, not replace them. It can provide items such as travel, job training, therapy, and medical expenses not covered by Medicaid, plus hire an advocate to assist in the care of the child. Upon the death of the special-needs child, the remaining assets in the trust are distributed to the named people, usually siblings of the person with disabilities or their heirs.

A third-party special-needs trust can be created "testamentary," where the special-needs trust is a part of the parents' trust and becomes effective after the death of the parents. But it is practical to create a stand-alone revocable trust. Some states require the special-needs trust to be irrevocable, and irrevocable trusts cannot be changed once they are created. Care should be taken to have flexibility in the irrevocable trusts to avoid creating a new trust to make changes or be processed through the probate court. The process is coordinated with the parents and other family members' legal documents. These are generally funded upon the demise of the parents.

First-party trust or a self-settled trust. This is usually funded with the assets of the person with a disability. It must be established and funded by a parent, grandparent or the guardian of the person with a disability, or by the court for a person with a disability under the age of 65. The trust is usually irrevocable, and the special-needs person is the only beneficiary of the trust. The trust is usually funded with a settlement resulting from a tort action or inheritance received by a person with a disability received inadvertently. Upon the death of the person with a disability, the remaining assets of the trust must first be used to pay back any state medical agency providing benefits. Any amount remaining can be distributed to the heirs of the person with a disability.

"Pooled income" is another alternative, often established by a not-for-profit entity in which the small amount of assets of many trusts are combined for investment purposes but are managed individually for distribution purposes. A master-trust document is adopted to govern the trust. A pooled trust can be a self-settled trust or a third-party trust, depending on whether the assets used to fund the trust belong to the special-needs person or to a third party. Some pooled trusts provide that assets remain in the pool when the special-needs person dies. The assets are retained by the trust for the benefit of other beneficiaries of the master trust.

OTHER IMPORTANT CONSIDERATIONS

Letter of intent: This is one of the most important non-legal documents that details all the appropriate needs and care instructions required by the special-needs child. The legal documents such as the special-needs trust and powers of attorney are necessary to ensure that the child's affairs are handled in the most effective and efficient manner. The letter of intent communicates crucial information to all parties who may assume some responsibilities for the child, both during the parents' lives and following their deaths.

The letter of intent should list names and contact details of family members, medical professionals, and legal representatives. It should provide the details of the mental and physical disabilities that affect the child's well-being, as well as descriptive history of the child's family life and past and current living arrangements. It should include a section about jobs held, assets owned (if any), and government benefits received. The parents should also provide relevant personal information such as likes and dislikes, entertainment choices, dietary needs, other medical issues, and even religious affiliations. Legal information such as guardianship, appointment of trustees, existence of wills, power of attorneys, and other important documents should be included.

By creating the letter of intent and updating it periodically, parents can help ensure that their child with disability will be able to maintain the same quality of life to which he or she is accustomed. A letter of intent gives the parents peace of mind in knowing they have done everything they could to provide for their children even after they have both passed away.

Guardianship/conservatorship: A guardian is a court-appointed individual responsible for making financial, health care, and other personal decisions for a person who has been deemed mentally incapacitated by the appropriate court. Since there is no federal statute related to this issue, state laws determine when someone can be declared incompetent and in need of a guardian. All fifty states and the District of Columbia allow the court to appoint a guardian for an individual with limited mental capacity. Guardianship is a court appointment and requires periodic renewals.

A conservator or a guardian of the estate is an individual appointed by the court to make financial decisions on behalf of someone who is unable to manage his or her financial assets. Conservatorship will not become an issue for children with disabilities if their parents are planning for them through a special-needs trust.

Anyone older than the age of majority is considered legally competent unless a court of appropriate jurisdiction has determined otherwise. Often, individuals with disabilities are capable of holding jobs and caring for themselves to some degree. Most parents are sensitive about becoming guardians of an adult child, because it represents taking away all rights. Some parents opt for partial or limited guardianship for education, residential, or health-care decisions only.

Medical Power of Attorney may also be considered as an alternative to guardianship for health where applicable.

ABLE Act: Achieving a Better Life Experience Act of 2014, or better known as the ABLE Act, allows tax-advantaged savings accounts for individuals with disabilities and their families. The beneficiary of the account is the owner of the account and the income earned by the account is tax deferred, and the distribution from the account is income-tax free. Family, friends, as well as the individual with a disability, is allowed to fund the account not to exceed fifteen thousand dollars per year.

The amount may be adjusted periodically to account for inflation. Under current tax law, $15,000 is the maximum amount that individuals can make as a gift to someone else and not report the gift to the IRS (gift tax exclusion.) The total limit over time that could be made to an ABLE account will be subject to the individual state and their limit for education-related 529 savings accounts. Many states have set this limit at more than three hundred thousand dollars per plan. However, for individuals with disabilities who are recipients of SSI, the ABLE Act sets some further limitations.

The SSI benefits are suspended if the ABLE account exceeds one hundred thousand dollars in value; benefits will be reinstated once the account falls below the threshold. It is important to note that while the beneficiary's eligibility for the SSI cash benefit is suspended, there is no effect on the ability to receive or be eligible to receive medical assistance through Medicaid. Also, upon the death of the beneficiary, the state in which the beneficiary lived will have the first claim on the remaining assets in the account for an amount up to the amount spent since the time the individual ABLE account opened.

The ABLE account can be only used to pay for qualified expenses. These may include education, housing, transportation, employment training and support, assistive technology, personal support services, health care expenses, financial management and administrative services, and other expenses that help improve health, independence, and/or quality of life.

A new law, part of the major tax cut legislation of 2017, permits limited transfers from 529 College Savings accounts into ABLE accounts. The total amount that can be contributed to any beneficiary's ABLE account in 2018 is fifteen thousand dollars. A twenty-nine percent account transfer eats into that limit. Much greater annual contributions are permitted for 529 accounts, and they are not limited to individuals whose disability appears before age 26 (as are ABLE accounts.)

ABLE accounts may not be considered as a planning tool for the long term for a person with a disability due to its limitation. Parents may still consider creating the special-needs trust but also research the benefits of an ABLE account if applicable.

References:

Rajput, Minoti H. CFP ChSNC. Planning for families of children with disabilities. Journal for Financial Planning, August 2001

Social Security Administration, www.ssa.gov, 2011

Suggested Reading on Special-Needs Planning:

Nadworny John CFP and Cynthia Haddad, CFP, The Special Needs Planning Guide: How to Prepare for Every stage of Your Child's Life, Paul H. Brooks, Publisher, 2007

Wright, Hal, The Complete Guide to Creating a Special Needs Life Plan, Jessica Kingsley Publishers, 2013.

Roscher, Webber Barton, Providing for Adult Children with Disabilities in a Traditional Estate Plan, Probate and Property Magazine, Volume 27, 2013.

Stevens, Bart, The ABC's of Special Needs Planning Made Easy, Stevens Groups LLC, November 1, 2002

Acknowledgements

In sharing these stories of compassion, persistence, and hope, I have been inspired and supported by countless people to whom I owe my deepest gratitude:

My niece, Supriya. You were diagnosed with autism in 1977 at three years of age. You opened my eyes to the world of autism and served as my earliest inspiration to help those with special needs.

My husband, a true partner and rock, Hemant. I could not have pursued this book without your endless support in all my dreams and ventures.

My daughters, Keya and Shaili. You are my constant sources of encouragement and pride. You have taught me what selfless love is.

My parents, Sudhir and Devi Rani Dasgupta, who gave me the courage to walk the road less traveled.

My colleagues, for your unending support.

Phyllis Kramer, a compassionate special needs planner and inimitable educator. I am forever indebted to you for your wisdom and guidance in helping me embark on my journey into special needs planning.

The community of special education teachers, professionals, and volunteers for your tireless efforts and commitment to enriching the lives of people with disabilities.

The attorneys whose legal expertise and cooperation have

given me the confidence to plan for hundreds of families with special needs children. I am grateful for your partnerships.

Organizations including Community Opportunity Center, New Horizon Rehabilitation Services, FAR Therapeutic Arts and Recreation, Friendship Circle, Special Dreams Farm, and countless others who dedicate their services to the special needs population. It has been an honor to work closely with you and see firsthand the impact you have on the families you serve.

The team at Mission Point Press for your invaluable expertise in creating and publishing this work. A special thank you goes to Jennifer Carroll, my guiding editor, writer, and gentle coach. Your thoughtful advice and handholding at each step gave voice to my story, allowing me to share my journey in helping special needs families and be the storyteller I wanted to be.

Lastly, I thank the parents of children with disabilities. I salute you for your unconditional love and for never giving up in pursuing your hopes and dreams for your children.

Index

ABLE Act, 173, 269-270

Adoption, special needs, 245-257

ADHD, 81, 193

Adult caregiving options, 50

Alliance for Mental Illness, Dearborn, 32, 35, 40

American Disabilities Act (ADA,) 3

Applied Behavior Analysis (ABA,) 95, 101

Arc Service of Macomb, Inc., 26, 133-134, 142

Arc of Oakland County, 181-182

Autism, 2, 5, 27, 56-57, 63, 76-79, 81, 82, 83, 89, 91,100-101,
    164, 168, 172, 193-195, 200, 207, 209, 213, 220-225, 253

Autism Clinic, University of Michigan, 63

Autistic Impaired Program (AI,) 94

Autism Spectrum Disorder (ASD,) 101, 200

Beaumont Center for Human Development, 81

Beaumont Center for Exceptional Families, 217-18, 220-26

Beaumont Hospital Neuro-Education Center, 44-45

Bipolar, 32, 78, 83-84, 89, 148, 157, 193

Bittersweet Farm, 208-209, 215

Brain and Behavior Research Foundation, 33, 40

Brown, Craig and Linda, 193-204

Circle of Support, 236, 242

Cognitive Impairment, 3, 20, 23, 25, 89, 177

Collette, Larry and Mary, 205-216

Community Living Services (CLS,) 88, 89

Community Mental Health, 14, 16-17, 26, 28, 42, 51, 54, 78, 86-87, 89, 92, 120, 122, 143-144, 185, 193, 196, 199, 201, 209, 212-214, 216

Conservatorship, 269

Down syndrome, 3, 9-10, 15, 17, 177, 213, 251, 258

Educable Mentally Impaired, 44

Fialka, Janice, 227-243

First Party Irrevocable Special Needs Trust, (D (4) (A,) 107, 129, 169, 173, 267

Gateway, 86, 88

Greenspan, Dr. Stanley, DIR/Floortime therapy, 57, 76

Guardianship, 74, 88, 92, 167, 268- 269

Group Homes, 28, 50, 54, 88-89, 183-184, 186, 211, 263

Havenwyck Psychiatric Hospital, 82

Housing options, 28, 42, 50, 54, 199

Immigration and Nationality Act of 1965, 58

Individual Disabilities Education Act (IDEA,) 3, 178, 233

Institute for the Study of Mental Retardation and Related Disabilities, University of Michigan, 44-45

Job training, 6, 14, 213, 263, 266

Kadima, 35-36, 41

Kramer, Phyllis, 2, 273

Letter of Intent, 18, 59, 136, 181, 188, 268

Life Insurance, 11-12, 22-23, 25, 33, 74, 102, 103, 106, 119, 125-126, 144, 160, 171, 197, 211, 257, 264

Living Trusts, irrevocable, 28, 126, 128, 267

Living Trusts, revocable, 23, 28, 128, 130, 160, 181, 188 , 267

Macrocephaly, 45

Mandy, David and Jane, 19-27

Medicaid, 3, 6, 14, 23, 25, 31, 49, 51-52, 90, 103, 107-108, 117-118, 124, 126-127, 143, 159-160, 163-164, 167, 169, 173, 196, 199, 202, 214, 242, 257, 263-265, 266, 270

Medicare, 3, 14, 52, 143, 161, 163, 265

Mental Health Alliance, 35

Michigan Special Education, 75, 84, 171

Nigro, Dr. Michael, 20

On My Own, 72

Pooled Income Trust, 267

Proulx, Jeffrey and Michelle, 245-259

Residential treatment, 86

Reynolds, Russ and Betty, 42-53

Rose Hill Center, 86-90

Salaty, Dr. Larry, 21

SCAMP camp, 179

Schizophrenia, 2-3, 30, 32

Shuler, Carl and Noreen, 131-147

Special Dreams Farm, 204, 209-216, 274, 277

Special education, 5-6, 7, 13, 21, 43-45, 47-49, 61, 72, 74-75, 77, 81, 83-84, 102, 168, 171, 178, 183, 206, 224, 232, 236, 247-248, 250-251, 254, 257, 273

Special needs trusts, 22, 23, 25, 28, 49, 197, 257, 266

Special needs trustees, 10, 18, 26, 28, 32, 41, 74, 102, 106, 131, 135, 147, 160-162, 211, 269

Special Olympics, 22, 48, 50, 179, 247, 253

Social Security, 3, 11-12, 14, 23, 38, 127, 132-133, 143, 161, 263-265, 271

Social Security Disability Insurance, (SSDI,) 3, 14, 25, 51, 161, 212, 265

Successor Trustees, 32, 74, 147, 160, 211

Supplemental Security Income (SSI,) 3, 25, 31, 49, 90, 117, 160-161, 164, 167, 169, 172-173, 196, 199, 212, 257, 263-265, 270

Supported Independence Programs, 50, 54

Supportive Alternative Living, Milford, 50, 52

Third Party Trust, 171, 266-267

Trainable Mentally Impaired, 45, 47

Visions Unlimited, Farmington School District, 47

Youngs, Dr. Susan, 217-226

Michael A. Jonas Photography

MINOTI RAJPUT, a Certified Financial Planner and Chartered Special Needs Consultant, has served as the founding president of Secure Planning Strategies for nearly three decades. She has dedicated her practice to helping families of special needs children. Rajput recognizes the importance of a financial advisor understanding what families go through when caring for a child with a disability, especially when it determines the level of planning needed.

Rajput, born and raised in India, studied finance and worked in banking before her arrival to the United States in 1980, helping small business owners with financial planning. In 1989 she formed her firm offering comprehensive wealth planning with a subspecialty of life planning with financial and legal guidance to families of special needs children. For the past 29 years her firm has counseled 1,500+ families of children with special needs. Her thriving practice based in Michigan, also services affluent retirees and pre-retirees, small business owners, and women in transition. Her firm, Secure Planning Strategies, represents nearly 300 clients with $330 million in assets under management.

Her specialties include the following:

- **Families with Special Needs Children**: Rajput is a nationally recognized expert in planning for families with special needs family members. She is dedicated to finding the right ways for these families to plan and provide lifelong care for their loved ones.

- **Comprehensive Wealth Management Planning for Retirees**: Planning for post-work life is a combination of financial and life planning. A longer life expectancy and an ever-changing economic environment requires creative solutions and ongoing counselling. Planning needs to begin years prior to retirement and focus on comprehensive planning beyond investments

- **Wealth Management for Women**: As a pioneering woman in the financial planning industry, Minoti understands the importance of empowering women to achieve financial security and feel confident handling their finances.

- **Exit Strategy Planning**: Many successful business owners find the transfer of ownership issue to be overwhelming. The SBA notes the primary cause of failure as lack of planning. Minoti has nearly 30 years of experience in helping business owners develop an exit strategy based on an individual's goals and time frame.

- She served as the president of the Oakland County Financial and Estate Planning Council. In 2005 she made the Michigan Governor's Honor Roll for her outstanding community service to the special needs population. She also has held voluntary board and advisory positions with organizations serving the special needs community, including new Horizons Rehabilitation Services, FAR Conservatory, Special Dreams Farm, and Community Opportunity Center.

She has served as the president of the Oakland County Financial and Estate Planning Council. In 2005 she made the Michigan Governor's Honor Roll for her outstanding community service to the special needs population. She also has held voluntary board and advisory positions with organizations serving the special needs community, including New Horizons Rehabilitation Services, FAR Therapeutic Arts and Recreation, Special Dreams Farm, and Community Opportunity Center.

Rajput frequently speaks before groups about women and finance; planning for special needs children; retirement planning for Baby Boomers and business planning and business exit strategizing.

A member of The Financial Planning Association and Academy of Special Needs Planners, she earned her MBA from Gujarat University in India. Rajput and her husband have two daughters and reside in West Bloomfield, Michigan. For more information, please consult: www.spsfinancial.com.

98085041R00162

Made in the USA
Lexington, KY
04 September 2018